MISCELLANEOUS ACTS

Annotated by

BUTTERWORTHS LEGAL EDITORIAL STAFF

LONDON
BUTTERWORTHS
1981

ENGLAND:
Butterworth & Co. (Publishers) Ltd.
London: 88 Kingsway, London WC2B 6AB

AUSTRALIA:
Butterworths Pty. Ltd.
Sydney: 586 Pacific Highway, Chatswood, NSW 2067
Also at Melbourne, Brisbane, Adelaide and Perth

CANADA:
Butterworth & Co. (Canada) Ltd.
Toronto: 2265 Midland Avenue, Scarborough, M1P 4SI

NEW ZEALAND:
Butterworths of New Zealand Ltd.
Wellington: 31 – 35 Cumberland Place, Wellington

SOUTH AFRICA:
Butterworth & Co. (South Africa) (Pty.) Ltd.
Durban: 152 – 154 Gale Street, Durban

USA:
Butterworth & Co. (Publishers) Inc.
Boston: 10 Tower Office Park, Woburn, Mass. 01801

ISBN 0 406 54801 3

Printed in Great Britain by Butler & Tanner Ltd,
Frome and London

PUBLISHERS' ANNOUNCEMENT

This volume contains six Acts passed in 1980.

The Protection of Trading Interests Act 1980 provides protection for persons in the United Kingdom from certain measures taken under the laws of overseas countries when those measures apply to things done outside such countries and their effect would be to damage the trading interests of the United Kingdom or would be otherwise prejudicial to its sovereignty or security.

The National Heritage Act 1980 establishes a National Heritage Memorial Fund to assist in the preservation, maintenance and acquisition of property of importance to the national heritage. It also amends the law relating to the acceptance of property in satisfaction of capital transfer tax and estate duty liability.

The Betting, Gaming and Lotteries (Amendment) Act 1980 amends the Betting, Gaming and Lotteries Act 1963, s. 7 and the 1977 Amendment Act, s. 2, in accordance with recommendations made in the Final Report of the Royal Commission on Gambling (Cmnd. 7200).

The Licensed Premises (Exclusion of Certain Persons) Act 1980 empowers the courts to make exclusion orders prohibiting those convicted of offences in licensed premises, during which violence was used or threatened, from entering those or any other specified licensed premises.

The Industry Act 1980 makes many changes to the National Enterprise Board and the Welsh Development Agency, and amends provisions relating to regional development grants.

The Transport Act 1980 makes wide changes in the law. Inter alia, new provisions governing passenger service vehicles are introduced, the undertaking of the National Freight Corporation is transferred, and the pension arrangements under which British Rail and the National Freight Corporation receive government support are amended. A host of amendments are made to previous transport legislation.

January 1981   BUTTERWORTH & CO (PUBLISHERS) LTD.

CONTENTS

THE PROTECTION OF TRADING INTERESTS ACT 1980

(1980 c. 11)

PRELIMINARY NOTE

This Act, which came into force on receiving the Royal Assent on 20th March 1980, provides protection for persons in the United Kingdom from certain measures taken under the laws of overseas countries when those measures apply to things done outside such countries and their effect would be to damage the trading interests of the United Kingdom, or would be otherwise prejudicial to the sovereignty or security of the United Kingdom. The Act also provides for the non-enforcement of certain foreign judgments and enables recovery to be made of foreign awards of multiple damages. The Act repeals the Shipping Contracts and Commercial Documents Act 1964 (s. 8 (5), *post*.)

S. 1, *post*, provides a number of means by which the Secretary of State for Trade may counter measures which are taken or proposed to be taken by or under the law of overseas countries for regulating or controlling international trade, and which are or would be damaging to the trading interests of the United Kingdom. First, he may make orders specifying the measures concerned. Second, he may make further orders requiring persons in the United Kingdom who carry on business there to notify him of any requirements or prohibitions imposed or threatened to be imposed on them under such measures. Third, he may prohibit compliance with such measures. International trade is widely defined to include any business activity.

S. 2, *post*, provides that where a person in the United Kingdom has been or may be required to produce to a court, tribunal or authority of an overseas country commercial documents outside that country or to furnish commercial information the Secretary of State may give directions prohibiting compliance with that requirement. The section specifies the circumstances in which a direction may be given, which are broadly comparable to the circumstances in which a United Kingdom court would refuse a request made by an overseas court for evidence under the Evidence (Proceedings in other Jurisdictions) Act 1975.

S. 3, *post*, provides penalties for failure to comply with requirements imposed under ss. 1 and 2, *post*. It provides for a maximum fine of £1,000 on summary conviction and for an unlimited fine on conviction on indictment.

S. 4, *post*, provides that in proceedings under the Evidence (Proceedings in Other Jurisdictions) Act 1975, United Kingdom courts shall not comply with a request made by a court of an overseas country when the Secretary of State has given a certificate that the request infringes United Kingdom jurisdiction or is otherwise prejudicial to United Kingdom sovereignty.

S. 5, *post*, provides that judgments for multiple damages given in civil proceedings by courts of overseas countries shall not be enforceable in the United Kingdom. It further provides that judgments given in overseas countries based on competition laws which have been specified by an order made by the Secretary of State shall not be enforceable in the United Kingdom.

S. 6, *post*, enables United Kingdom citizens, United Kingdom corporations and other persons carrying on business in the United Kingdom to recover back sums paid under foreign judgments for multiple damages in excess of the compensation for the loss of the person in whose favour the judgment was given. It also permits courts in the United Kingdom to entertain such proceedings even if the defendant to them is not within the United Kingdom.

S. 7, *post*, enables Orders in Council to be made providing for the enforcement in the United Kingdom of judgments given under laws of overseas countries corresponding to s. 6, *post*. [1]

ARRANGEMENT OF SECTIONS

An Act to provide protection from requirements, prohibitions and judgments imposed or given under the laws of countries outside the United Kingdom and affecting the trading or other interests of persons in the United Kingdom

[20th March 1980]

NORTHERN IRELAND
   This Act applies; see s. 8 (7), *post*.

1. Overseas measures affecting United Kingdom trading interests

(1) If it appears to the Secretary of State—

   (*a*) that measures have been or are proposed to be taken by or under the law of any overseas country for regulating or controlling international trade; and

   (*b*) that those measures, in so far as they apply or would apply to things done or to be done outside the territorial jurisdiction of that country by persons carrying on business in the United Kingdom, are damaging or threaten to damage the trading interests of the United Kingdom,

the Secretary of State may by order direct that this section shall apply to those measures either generally or in their application to such cases as may be specified in the order.

(2) The Secretary of State may by order make provision for requiring, or enabling the Secretary of State to require, a person in the United Kingdom who carries on business there to give notice to the Secretary of State of any requirement or prohibition imposed or threatened to be imposed on that person pursuant to any measures in so far as this section applies to them by virtue of an order under subsection (1) above.

(3) The Secretary of State may give to any person in the United Kingdom who carries on business there such directions for prohibiting compliance with any such requirement or prohibition as aforesaid as he considers appropriate for avoiding damage to the trading interests of the United Kingdom.

(4) The power of the Secretary of State to make orders under subsection (1) or (2) above shall be exercisable by statutory instrument subject to annulment in pursuance of a resolution of either House of Parliament.

(5) Directions under subsection (3) above may be either general or special and may prohibit compliance with any requirement or prohibition either absolutely or in such cases or subject to such conditions as to consent or otherwise as may be specified in the directions; and general directions under that subsection shall be published in such manner as appears to the Secretary of State to be appropriate.

(6) In this section "trade" includes any activity carried on in the course of a business of any description and "trading interests" shall be construed accordingly.

[2]

SUB-S. (1): APPEARS
For a discussion as to the effect of the use of this and similar expressions such as "in the opinion" and "satisfied", on the power of the courts to review administrative action, see 1 Halsbury's Laws (4th Edn.), para. 22.

SECRETARY OF STATE
I.e., one of Her Majesty's Principal Secretaries of State; see the Interpretation Act 1978, s. 5, Sch. 1, A.L.S. Vol. 258. The Secretary of State here concerned is the Secretary of State for Trade.

LAW OF ANY OVERSEAS COUNTRY
For the meaning of this expression in the case of a federal state, see s. 8 (3), *post*.

PERSONS
The expression "person" includes a body of persons corporate or unincorporate; see the Interpretation Act 1978, s. 5, Sch. 1.

CARRYING ON BUSINESS
The words "carry on business" denote something of a permanent character, not merely an isolated transaction and a business is carried on only where there is some degree of management or control; see *Brown* v. *London North Western Rail. Co.* (1863), 32 L.J.Q.B. 318; [1863 – 73] All E.R. Rep. 487; *Graham* v. *Lewis* (1888), 22 Q.B.D. 1, C.A.; and *Cain* v. *Butler*, [1916] 1 K.B. 759, at p. 762; but contrast *Cornelius* v. *Phillips*, [1918] A.C. 199; [1916 – 17] All E.R. Rep. 685, H.L. See also *Kirkwood* v. *Gadd*, [1910] A.C. 422, at p. 423; [1908 – 10] All E.R. Rep. 768, H.L., at p. 771; *Newman* v. *Oughton*, [1911] 1 K.B. 792 and *Transport and General Credit Corporation, Ltd.* v. *Morgan*, [1939] Ch. 531; [1939] 2 All E.R. 17; and *Re Brauch (a debtor), Ex parte Britannic Securities and Investments, Ltd.*, [1978] 1 All E.R. 1004, C.A. See also the note "Business" to s. 2, *post*.

UNITED KINGDOM
I.e., Great Britain and Northern Ireland; see the Interpretation Act 1978, s. 5, Sch. 1. "Great Britain" means England, Scotland and Wales by virtue of the Union with Scotland Act 1706, preamble, Art. 1, as read with the Interpretation Act 1978, s. 22 (1), Sch. 2, para. 5 (*a*). Neither the Channel Islands nor the Isle of Man is within the United Kingdom, but note, as to the possible extension of this Act thereto, s. 8 (8), *post*.

SUB-S. (2): CARRIES ON BUSINESS
See the note "Carrying on business" to sub-s. (1) above.

SUB-S. (4): STATUTORY INSTRUMENT; SUBJECT TO ANNULMENT
For provisions as to statutory instruments generally, see the Statutory Instruments Act 1946, A.L.S. Vol. 36, and as to statutory instruments which are subject to annulment, see ss. 5 (1) and 7 (1) of that Act.

SUB-S. (6): IN THE COURSE OF A BUSINESS
Something is done "in the course of" a business if it is done as part of its activities; cf. *Charles R. Davidson & Co.* v. *M'Robb (or Officer)*, [1918] A.C. 304, at p. 321, *per* Lord Dunedin. See also

London Borough of Havering v. *Stevenson*, [1970] 3 All E.R. 609, and *Wycombe Marsh Garages, Ltd.* v. *Fowler*, [1972] 3 All E.R. 248. On the meaning of "business", see the note to s. 2, *post*.

OFFENCES
For offences in connection with sub-ss. (2) and (3) above, see s. 3, *post*.

DEFINITION
For "overseas country", see s. 8 (2), *post*. Note as to "trade" and "trading interests", sub-s. (6) above.

ORDERS UNDER THIS SECTION
At the time of going to press no order had been made under sub-s. (1) or (2) of this section.

2. Documents and information required by overseas courts and authorities

(1) If it appears to the Secretary of State—

    (*a*) that a requirement has been or may be imposed on a person or persons in the United Kingdom to produce to any court, tribunal or authority of an overseas country any commercial document which is not within the territorial jurisdiction of that country or to furnish any commercial information to any such court, tribunal or authority; or

    (*b*) that any such authority has imposed or may impose a requirement on a person or persons in the United Kingdom to publish any such document or information,

the Secretary of State may, if it appears to him that the requirement is inadmissible by virtue of subsection (2) or (3) below, give directions for prohibiting compliance with the requirement.

(2) A requirement such as is mentioned in subsection (1) (*a*) or (*b*) above is inadmissible—

    (*a*) if it infringes the jurisdiction of the United Kingdom or is otherwise prejudicial to the sovereignty of the United Kingdom; or

    (*b*) if compliance with the requirement would be prejudicial to the security of the United Kingdom or to the relations of the government of the United Kingdom with the government of any other country.

(3) A requirement such as is mentioned in subsection (1) (*a*) above is also inadmissible—

    (*a*) if it is made otherwise than for the purposes of civil or criminal proceedings which have been instituted in the overseas country; or

    (*b*) if it requires a person to state what documents relevant to any such proceedings are or have been in his possession, custody or power or to produce for the purposes of any such proceedings any documents other than particular documents specified in the requirement.

(4) Directions under subsection (1) above may be either general or special and may prohibit compliance with any requirement either absolutely or in such cases or subject to such conditions as to consent or otherwise as may be specified in the directions; and general directions under that subsection shall be published in such manner as appears to the Secretary of State to be appropriate.

(5) For the purposes of this section the making of a request or demand shall be treated as the imposition of a requirement if it is made in circumstances in which a requirement to the same effect could be or could have been imposed; and

    (*a*) any request or demand for the supply of a document or information which, pursuant to the requirement of any court, tribunal or authority of an overseas country, is addressed to a person in the United Kingdom; or

(*b*) any requirement imposed by such a court, tribunal or authority to produce or furnish any document or information to a person specified in the requirement,

shall be treated as a requirement to produce or furnish that document or information to that court, tribunal or authority.

(6) In this section "commercial document" and "commercial information" mean respectively a document or information relating to a business of any description and "document" includes any record or device by means of which material is recorded or stored. **[3]**

SUB-S. (1): APPEARS; SECRETARY OF STATE; UNITED KINGDOM
See the notes to s. 1, *ante.*

PERSON
See the Note "Persons" to s. 1, *ante.*

COURT, TRIBUNAL OR AUTHORITY OF AN OVERSEAS COUNTRY
For the meaning of this expression as it relates to a federal state, see s. 8 (3) *post.*

SUB-S. (6): BUSINESS
It has been said that "the word 'business' . . . means almost anything which is an occupation, as distinguished from a pleasure — anything which is an occupation or duty which requires attention is a business" (*Rolls* v. *Miller* (1884), 27 Ch. D, 71, C.A., *per* Lindley, L.J., at p. 88) and it has also been said that neither the making of a profit nor any commercial activity is essential (*Real-Brook Ltd.* v. *Minister of Housing and Local Government*, [1967] 2 Q.B. 65; [1967] 1 All E.R. 262). In other cases, however, it has been pointed out that there is a difference between "business" in this very broad sense and "business" meaning a regularly conducted commercial enterprise; see *Inland Revenue Comrs.* v. *Marine Steam Turbine Co., Ltd.*, [1920] 1 K.B. 193, at pp. 202–204; *Re A Debtor (No. 3 of 1926)*, [1927] 1 Ch. 97, at p. 106; [1926] All E.R. Rep. 337, C.A., at p. 341; *Lord Advocate* v. *Glasgow Corpn.*, 1958 S.L.T. 2, at p. 8; *Abernethie* v. *A.M. & J. Kleiman, Ltd.*, [1970] 1 Q.B. 10; [1969] 2 All E.R. 790, C.A.; *and Customs and Excise Commissioners* v. *Royal Exchange Theatre Trust* [1979] 3 All E.R. 797. It is thought that here the word has the narrower meaning of a regularly conducted commercial enterprise.

It has been held that a single transaction can be a "business" for the purposes of the Partnership Act 1890, s. 45 (*Re Abenheim, Ex parte Abenheim* (1913), 109 L.T. 219). For other purposes, however, a distinction is drawn between isolated transactions and the carrying on of a business; see *Re Griffin, Ex parte Board of Trade* (1890), 60 L.J.Q.B. 235, at p. 237; *Linstead* v. *Simpson*, 1972 S.C. (J.) 101, at pp. 104, 105; and cf. *Cornelius* v. *Phillips*, [1918] A.C. 199; [1916–17] All E.R. Rep. 685. Again, it is thought that the narrower view may well be preferable for the purpose of this Act.

It is clear that a business does not cease to be merely because it makes a loss (*Re Ogilby, Ogilby*, v. *Wentworth-Stanley*, [1942] Ch. 288), and even activities intended permanently to be carried on at a loss have been held to be a business (*Rolls* v. *Miller, supra: South-West Suburban Water Co.* v. *St. Marylebone Guardians*, [1904] 2 K.B. 174, at p. 180).

The expression "business" is clearly wide enough to include a profession; see *Re Williams' Will Trusts, Chartered Bank of India, Australia and China* v. *Williams*, [1953] Ch. 138; [1953] 1 All E.R. 563, and *R.* v. *Breeze*, [1973] 2 All E.R. 1141, C.A.; and contrast *Stuchbery* v. *General Accident, Fire and Life Assurance Corpn., Ltd.*, [1949] 2 K.B. 256; [1949] 1 All E.R. 1026, C.A.

On the meaning of "business" generally, see 38 Halsbury's Laws (3rd Edn.), pp. 10, 11 and I Words and Phrases (2nd Edn.), pp. 199 *et seq.*

OFFENCE
For the offence of knowingly contravening any direction given under sub-s. (1) above, see s. 3, *post.*

DEFINITIONS
For "overseas country", see s. 8 (2), *post.* Note as to "imposition of a requirement", sub-s. (5) above, and as to "commercial document", "commercial information" and "document", see sub-s. (6) above.

3. Offences under ss. 1 and 2

(1) Subject to subsection (2) below, any person who without reasonable excuse fails to comply with any requirement imposed under subsection (2) of section 1 above or knowingly contravenes any directions given under subsection (3) of that section or section 2 (1) above shall be guilty of an offence and liable —

(*a*) on conviction on indictment, to a fine;

(*b*) on summary conviction, to a fine not exceeding the statutory maximum.

(2) A person who is neither a citizen of the United Kingdom and Colonies nor a body corporate incorporated in the United Kingdom shall not be guilty of an offence under subsection (1) above by reason of anything done or omitted outside the United Kingdom in contravention of directions under section 1 (3) or 2 (1) above.

(3) No proceedings for an offence under subsection (1) above shall be instituted in England, Wales or Northern Ireland except by the Secretary of State or with the consent of the Attorney General or, as the case may be, the Attorney General for Northern Ireland.

(4) Proceedings against any person for an offence under this section may be taken before the appropriate court in the United Kingdom having jurisdiction in the place where that person is for the time being.

(5) In subsection (1) above "the statutory maximum" means —

(*a*) in England and Wales and Northern Ireland, the prescribed sum within the meaning of section 28 of the Criminal Law Act 1977 (at the passing of this Act £1,000);

(*b*) (*applies to Scotland*);

and for the purposes of the application of this subsection in Northern Ireland the provisions of the said Act of 1977 relating to the sum mentioned in paragraph (*a*) shall extend to Northern Ireland.   **[4]**

SUB-S. (1): PERSON

See the note "Persons" to s. 1, *ante*.

REASONABLE EXCUSE

What is a reasonable excuse is largely a question of fact; cf. *Leck* v. *Epsom Rural District Council*, [1922] 1 K.B. 383; [1922] All E.R. Rep. 784. Yet it is clear that ignorance of the statutory provisions provides no reasonable excuse (cf. *Aldridge* v. *Warwickshire Coal Co.*, *Ltd.* (1925). 133 L.T. 439, C.A.), nor does a mistaken view of the effect of those provisions (*R.* v. *Reid (Philip)*, [1973] 3 All E.R. 1020, C.A.). *Quaere* whether reliance on the advice of an expert can amount to a reasonable excuse; see *Saddleworth Urban District Council* v. *Aggregate and Sand, Ltd.* (1970), 69 L.G.R. 103.

Once evidence of a reasonable excuse emerges, it is for the prosecution to eliminate the existence of that defence to the satisfaction of the court; see *R.* v. *Clarke*, [1969] 2 All E.R. 1008, C.A.

KNOWINGLY

Knowledge is an essential ingredient of the offence and must be proved by the prosecution; see, in particular, *Gaumont British Distributors, Ltd.* v. *Henry*, [1939] 2 K.B. 711; [1939] 2 All E.R. 808.

Knowledge includes the state of mind of a person who shuts his eyes to the obvious; see *James & Sons, Ltd.* v. *Smee*, [1955] 1 Q.B. 78, at p. 91; [1954] 3 All E.R. 273 at p. 278, *per* Parker, J. Moreover, there is authority for saying that where a person deliberately refrains from making inquiries the results of which he might not care to have, this constitutes in law actual knowledge of the facts in question; see *Knox* v. *Boyd*, 1941 J.C. 82, at p. 86, and *Taylor's Central Garages (Exeter), Ltd.* v. *Roper* (1951), 115 J.P. 445, at pp. 449, 450, *per* Devlin, J.; and see also, in particular, *Mallon* v. *Allon*, [1964] 1 Q.B. 385; [1963] 3 All E.R. 843, at p. 394 and p. 847, respectively. Yet mere neglect to ascertain what could have been found out by making reasonable inquiries is not tantamount to knowledge; *Taylor's Central Garages (Exeter) Ltd.* v. *Roper, ubi supra, per* Devlin, J.; and cf. *London Computator, Ltd.* v. *Seymour*, [1944] 2 All E.R. 11; but see also *Mallon* v. *Allon, ubi supra.*

As to when the knowledge of an employee or agent may be imputed to his employer or principal, see 11 Halsbury's Laws (4th Edn.), para. 54.

CONVICTION ON INDICTMENT

All proceedings on indictment are to be brought before the Crown Court; see the Courts Act 1971, s. 6 (1), A.L.S. Vol. 200.

FINE

There is no specific limit to the amount of the fine which may be imposed on conviction on indictment, but the fine should be within the offender's capacity to pay; see, in particular, *R.* v. *Churchill (No. 2)*, [1967] 1 Q.B. 190; [1966] 2 All E.R. 215, C.C.A. (reversed on other grounds *sub nom. Churchill* v. *Walton*, [1967] 2 A.C. 224; [1967] 1 All E.R. 497, H.L.); and see also the Bill of Rights (1688), s. 1.

SUMMARY CONVICTION

Summary jurisdiction and procedure are mainly governed by the Magistrates' Courts Act 1952, the Magistrates' Courts Act 1957, A.L.S. Vol. 104, and certain provisions of the Criminal Justice Act 1967, A.L.S. Vol. 163, and of the Criminal Law Act 1977, A.L.S. Vol. 249. Procedural provisions are also contained in rules made under the Justices of the Peace Act 1949, s. 15, A.L.S. Vol. 64.

SUB-S. (2): CITIZEN OF THE UNITED KINGDOM AND COLONIES

As to citizenship of the United Kingdom and Colonies, see the British Nationality Act 1948, Part II, in conjunction with, in particular, the Commonwealth Immigrants Act 1962, s. 12 (2) A.L.S. Vol. 134, 173, and the Immigration Act 1971, s. 2 (5). Sch. 1, A.L.S. Vol. 201.

BODY CORPORATE

For the general law relating to corporations, see 9 Halsbury's Laws (4th Edn.), paras. 1201 *et seq.*

UNITED KINGDOM

See the note to s. 1, *ante.*

SUB-S. (3): ENGLAND; WALES

For meanings, see the Interpretation Act 1978, s. 5, Sch. 1, A.L.S. Vol. 258.

SECRETARY OF STATE

See the note to s. 1, *ante.*

CONSENT OF THE ATTORNEY GENERAL

Consent should be proved before the summons is issued, and the point that consent is lacking cannot be taken for the first time after the case for the prosecution has been closed; see *Prince* v. *Humphries*, [1958] 2 Q.B. 353; [1958] 2 All E.R. 725.

In certain cases the functions of the Attorney General may be discharged by the Solicitor General; see the Law Officers Act 1944, s. 1. As to arrest, remand, etc., where the consent of the Attorney General has not yet been given, see the Prosecution of Offences Act 1979, s. 1, and as to evidence of such consent; see s. 7 of that Act.

ATTORNEY GENERAL FOR NORTHERN IRELAND

By the Northern Ireland Constitution Act 1973, s. 10 (1), the Attorney General for England and Wales is *ex officio* Attorney General for Northern Ireland also; and by s. 10 (2), (3) of that Act, the functions of the Attorney General for Northern Ireland may be discharged by the Solicitor General for England and Wales in certain cases.

SUB-S. (5): PASSING OF THIS ACT

This Act was passed, *i.e.*, received the Royal Assent, on 20th March 1980.

CRIMINAL LAW ACT 1977, S. 28

A.L.S. Vol. 249.

4. Restriction of Evidence (Proceedings in Other Jurisdictions) Act 1975.

A court in the United Kingdom shall not make an order under section 2 of the Evidence (Proceedings in Other Jurisdictions) Act 1975 for giving effect to a request issued by or on behalf of a court or tribunal of an overseas country if it is shown that the request infringes the jurisdiction of the United Kingdom or is otherwise prejudicial to the sovereignty of the United Kingdom; and a certificate signed by or on behalf of the Secretary of State to the effect that it infringes that jurisdiction or is so prejudicial shall be conclusive evidence of that fact.

UNITED KINGDOM; SECRETARY OF STATE
   See the notes to s. 1, *ante*.

COURT OR TRIBUNAL OF AN OVERSEAS COUNTRY
   For the meaning of "overseas country", see s. 8 (2), *post*; and for the meaning of this expression as it relates to a federal state, see s. 8 (3), *post*.

EVIDENCE (PROCEEDINGS IN OTHER JURISDICTIONS) ACT 1975, S. 2
   A.L.S. Vol. 236.

5. Restriction on enforcement of certain overseas judgments

(1) A judgment to which this section applies shall not be registered under Part II of the Administration of Justice Act 1920 or Part I of the Foreign Judgments (Reciprocal Enforcement) Act 1933 and no court in the United Kingdom shall entertain proceedings at common law for the recovery of any sum payable under such a judgment.

(2) This section applies to any judgment given by a court of an overseas country, being —

   (*a*) a judgment for multiple damages within the meaning of subsection (3) below;

   (*b*) a judgment based on a provision or rule of law specified or described in an order under subsection (4) below and given after the coming into force of the order; or

   (*c*) a judgment on a claim for contribution in respect of damages awarded by a judgment falling within paragraph (*a*) or (*b*) above.

(3) In subsection (2) (*a*) above a judgment for multiple damages means a judgment for an amount arrived at by doubling, trebling or otherwise multiplying a sum assessed as compensation for the loss or damage sustained by the person in whose favour the judgment is given.

(4) The Secretary of State may for the purposes of subsection (2) (*b*) above make an order in respect of any provision or rule of law which appears to him to be concerned with the prohibition or regulation of agreements, arrangements or practices designed to restrain, distort or restrict competition in the carrying on of business of any description or to be otherwise concerned with the promotion of such competition as aforesaid.

(5) The power of the Secretary of State to make orders under subsection (4) above shall be exercisable by statutory instrument subject to annulment in pursuance of a resolution of either House of Parliament.

(6) Subsection (2) (*a*) above applies to a judgment given before the date of the passing of this Act as well as to a judgment given on or after that date but this section does not affect any judgment which has been registered before that date under the provisions mentioned in subsection (1) above or in respect of which such proceedings as are there mentioned have been finally determined before that date.   **[6]**

SUB-S. (1): UNITED KINGDOM
   See the note to s. 1, *ante*.

SUB-S. (2): COURT OF AN OVERSEAS COUNTRY
For the meaning of the expression as it relates to a federal state, see s. 8 (3), *post.*

JUDGMENT FOR MULTIPLE DAMAGE
For the recovery of awards of multiple damages where a court of an overseas country has given a judgment for multiple damages, see s. 6, *post.*

SUB-S. (3): PERSON
See the note "Persons" to s. 1, *ante.*

SUB-S. (4): SECRETARY OF STATE; APPEARS
See the notes to s. 1, *ante.*

CARRYING ON OF BUSINESS
See note "Carrying on Business" to s. 1, *ante.*

SUB-S. (5): STATUTORY INSTRUMENT; SUBJECT TO ANNULMENT
See the note to s. 1, *ante.*

SUB-S. (6): PASSING OF THIS ACT
See the note to s. 3, *ante.*

DEFINITIONS
For "overseas country", see s. 8 (2), *post*; as to "claim for contribution", see s. 8 (4), *post.* Note as to "judgment for multiple damages", sub-s. (3) above.

ADMINISTRATION OF JUSTICE ACT 1920, PART II
See 6, Halsbury's Statutes (3rd edn.), pp. 353 *et seq.*

FOREIGN JUDGMENT (RECIPROCAL ENFORCEMENT) ACT 1933, PART I
See 6, Halsbury's Statutes (3rd edn.), pp. 365 *et seq.*

ORDERS UNDER THIS SECTION
At the time of going to press no order had been made under sub-s. (4) above.

6. Recovery of awards of multiple damages

(1) This section applies where a court of an overseas country has given a judgment for multiple damages within the meaning of section 5 (3) above against —

    (*a*) a citizen of the United Kingdom and Colonies; or

    (*b*) a body corporate incorporated in the United Kingdom or in a territory outside the United Kingdom for whose international relations Her Majesty's Government in the United Kingdom are responsible; or

    (*c*) a person carrying on business in the United Kingdom,

(in this section referred to as a "qualifying defendant") and an amount on account of the damages has been paid by the qualifying defendant either to the party in whose favour the judgment was given or to another party who is entitled as against the qualifying defendant to contribution in respect of the damages.

(2) Subject to subsections (3) and (4) below, the qualifying defendant shall be entitled to recover from the party in whose favour the judgment was given so much of the amount referred to in subsection (1) above as exceeds the part attributable to compensation; and that part shall be taken to be such part of the amount as bears to the whole of it the same proportion as the sum assessed by the court that gave the judgment as compensation for the loss or damage sustained by that party bears to the whole of the damages awarded to that party.

(3) Subsection (2) above does not apply where the qualifying defendant is an individual who was ordinarily resident in the overseas country at the time when the proceedings in which the judgment was given were instituted or a body corporate which had its principal place of business there at that time.

(4) Subsection (2) above does not apply where the qualifying defendant carried on business in the overseas country and the proceedings in which the judgment was given were concerned with activities exclusively carried on in that country.

(5) A court in the United Kingdom may entertain proceedings on a claim under this section notwithstanding that the person against whom the proceedings are brought is not within the jurisdiction of the court.

(6) The reference in subsection (1) above to an amount paid by the qualifying defendant includes a reference to an amount obtained by execution against his property or against the property of a company which (directly or indirectly) is wholly owned by him; and references in that subsection and subsection (2) above to the party in whose favour the judgment was given or to a party entitled to contribution include references to any person in whom the rights of any such party have become vested by succession or assignment or otherwise.

(7) This section shall, with the necessary modifications, apply also in relation to any order which is made by a tribunal or authority of an overseas country and would, if that tribunal or authority were a court, be a judgment for multiple damages within the meaning of section 5 (3) above.

(8) This section does not apply to any judgment given or order made before the passing of this Act.   [7]

SUB-S. (1): COURT OF AN OVERSEAS COUNTRY
For the meaning of this expression as it relates to a federal state, see s. 8 (3), *post.*

CITIZEN OF THE UNITED KINGDOM AND COLONIES; BODY CORPORATE
See the notes to s. 3, *ante.*

UNITED KINGDOM; CARRYING ON BUSINESS
See the notes to s. 1, *ante.*

PERSON
See the note "Persons" to s. 1, *ante.*

SUB-S. (3): INDIVIDUAL
This word is used instead of the word "person" in order, presumably, to exclude bodies of persons corporate or unincorporate; cf. the Interpretation Act 1978, s. 5, Sch. 1, A.L.S. Vol. 258, and *Whitney* v. *Inland Revenue Comrs.,* [1926] A.C. 37, at p. 43, *per* Viscount Cave, L.C.

ORDINARILY RESIDENT
"Ordinarily" means here according to the way in which one's life is usually ordered; see *Levene* v. *Inland Revenue Comrs.,* [1928] A.C. 217, at p. 232, [1928] All E.R. Rep. 746, H.L., at p. 754, *per* Lord Warington of Clyffe. "I think the converse of 'ordinarily' is 'extraordinarily and that part of the regular order of a man's life, adopted voluntarily and for settled purposes, is not 'extraordinary' "; see *Inland Revenue Comrs.* v. *Lysaght,* [1929] A.C. 234, at p. 243; [1928] All E.R. Rep 575, p. 580, *per* Viscount Sumner. A temporary sojourn may become ordinary residence owing to circumstances beyond the control of the person concerned; see *Re Mackenzie,* [1941] Ch. 69: [1940] 4 All E.R. 310; and cf. *Re Bright, Ex parte Bright* (1903), 51 W.R. 342, C.A.; *R.* v. *Denman, Ex parte Staal* (1917), 86 L.J.K.B. 1328; and *Pitter* v. *Richardson* (1918), 87 L.J.K.B. 59. However, ordinary residence can be changed in a day; see, in particular, *Macrae* v. *Macrae,* [1949] p. 397; [1949] 2 All E.R. 34, C.A. See also *Hopkins* v. *Hopkins,* [1951] p. 116; [1950] 2 All E.R. 1035; *Lowry* v. *Lowry,* [1952] p. 252; [1952] 2 All E.R. 61; *Stransky* v. *Stransky,* [1954] p. 428; [1954] 2 All E.R. 356; *Lewis* v. *Lewis,* [1956] 1 All E.R. 375; *R.* v. *Edgehill,* [1963] 1 Q.B. 593; [1963] 1 All E.R. 181, C.C.A.; and *Re Brauch (a debtor), Ex parte Britannic Securities & Investments, Ltd.,* [1978] 1 All E.R. 1004, C.A.

  A person resides where in common parlance he lives, and a temporary absence is immaterial providing there is an intention to return and a house or lodging to which to return; see *R.* v. *St. Leonard's Shoreditch (Inhabitants) (1865),* L.R. 1 Q.B. 21, and *R.* v. *Glossop Union* (1866), L.R. 1 Q.B. 227. The word "reside" implies a degree of permanence (*Levene* v. *Inland Revenue Comrs.,* [1928] A.C. 217, at pp. 222, 223; [1928] All E.R. Rep. 745, H.L., *Fox* v. *Stirk* [1970] 2 Q.B. 463, at p. 477; [1970] 3 All E.R. 7, C.A., at p. 13; *Brokelmann* v. *Barr,* [1971] 3 All E.R. 29), but a person may be resident in more than one place at the same time (*Levene* v. *Inland Revenue Comrs., ubi supra; Langford Property Co., Ltd.* v. *Tureman,* [1949] 1 K.B. 29; *sub nom. Langford Property Co., Ltd.* v. *Athanassoglou*, [1948] 2 All E.R. 722, C.A.); *Herbert* v. *Bryne*, [1964] 1 All E.R. 882, C.A.; and contrast *Beck* v. *Scholz*, [1953] 1 Q.B. 570; [1953] 1 All E.R. 814, C.A.).

PRINCIPAL PLACE OF BUSINESS
As to what is a "place of business", see *Lord Advocate* v. *Huron and Erie Loan and Savings Co.*, 1911 S.C. 612. The question as to what is a principal place of business is one of fact; see *Da Beers Consolidated Mines, Ltd.* v. *Howe*, [1906] A.C. 445; *Re Hilton, Gibbes* v. *Hale-Hinton*, [1909] 2 Ch. 548; and *Egyptian Delta Land and Investment Co., Ltd.* v. *Todd*, [1929] A.C. 1. Cf. also the decisions on the meaning of the expression "principal office" in *Garton* v. *Great Western Rail. Co.* (1858), E.B. & E. 837, *Palmer* v. *Caledonian Rail. Co.*, [1892] 1 Q.B. 923, and *Clokey* v. *London and North Western Rail. Co.*, [1905] 2 I.R. 251.

SUB-S. (4): CARRIED ON BUSINESS
See the note "Carrying on business" to s. 1, *ante*.

SUB-S. (8): PASSING OF THIS ACT
See the note to s. 3, *ante*.

ENFORCEMENT OF OVERSEAS JUDGMENTS
As to the enforcement in the United Kingdom of overseas judgments given under provisions corresponding to this section, see s. 7, *post*.

DEFINITIONS
For "overseas country", see s. 8 (2), *post*; as to "entitled to contribution", see s. 8 (3), *post*. Note as to "qualifying defendant", sub-s. (1) above, and as to "an amount paid by the qualifying defendant", sub-s. (6) above.

7. Enforcement of overseas judgment under provision corresponding to s. 6

(1) If it appears to Her Majesty that the law of an overseas country provides or will provide for the enforcement in that country of judgments given under section 6 above, Her Majesty may by Order in Council provide for the enforcement in the United Kingdom of judgments given under any provision of the law of that country corresponding to that section.

(2) An Order under this section may apply, with or without modification, any of the provisions of the Foreign Judgments (Reciprocal Enforcement) Act 1933.

[8]

DEFINITIONS
For "overseas country", see s. 8 (2), *post*; as to "law of an overseas country", see s. 8 (3), *post*.

FOREIGN JUDGMENTS (RECIPROCAL ENFORCEMENT) ACT 1933
See 6, Halsbury's Statutes (3rd edn.), p. 365.

ORDERS IN COUNCIL UNDER THIS SECTION
At the time of going to press no Order in Council had been made under this section.
The power to make Orders in Council is exercisable by statutory instrument; see the Statutory Instruments Act 1946, s. 1 (1), A.L.S. Vol. 36.

8. Short title, interpretation, repeals and extent

(1) This Act may be cited as the Protection of Trading Interests Act 1980.

(2) In this Act "overseas country" means any country or territory outside the United Kingdom other than one for whose international relations Her Majesty's Government in the United Kingdom are responsible.

(3) References in this Act to the law or a court, tribunal or authority of an overseas country include, in the case of a federal state, references to the law or a court, tribunal or authority of any constituent part of that country.

(4) References in this Act to a claim for, or to entitlement to, contribution are

references to a claim or entitlement based on an enactment or rule of law.

(5) The Shipping Contracts and Commercial Documents Act 1964 (which is superseded by this Act) is hereby repealed, together with paragraph 18 of Schedule 2 and paragraph 24 of Schedule 3 to the Criminal Law Act 1977 (which contain amendments of that Act).

(6) Subsection (5) above shall not affect the operation of the said Act of 1964 in relation to any directions given under that Act before the passing of this Act.

(7) This Act extends to Northern Ireland.

(8) Her Majesty may by Order in Council direct that this Act shall extend with such exceptions, adaptations and modifications, if any, as may be specified in the Order to any territory outside the United Kingdom, being a territory for the international relations of which Her Majesty's Government in the United Kingdom are responsible. [9]

UNITED KINGDOM
   See the note to s. 1, *ante.*

PASSING OF THIS ACT
   See the note to s. 3, *ante.*

SHIPPING CONTRACTS AND COMMERCIAL DOCUMENTS ACT 1964
   A.L.S. Vol. 148.

CRIMINAL LAW ACT 1977, SCH. 2, PARA. 18, SCH. 3, PARA. 24
   A.L.S. Vol. 249.

ORDERS IN COUNCIL UNDER THIS SECTION
   At the time of going to press no Order in Council had been made under sub-s. (8) above.
       The power to make Orders in Council is exercisable by statutory instrument; see the Statutory Instruments Act 1946, s. 1 (1) A.L.S. Vol. 36.

THE NATIONAL HERITAGE ACT 1980

(1980 c. 17)

PRELIMINARY NOTE

This Act, which came into force on receiving the Royal Assent on 31st March 1980, establishes a National Heritage Memorial Fund to assist in the preservation, maintenance and acquisition of property of importance to the national heritage (Part I (ss. 1–7), *post*); amends the law concerning the acceptance of property in satisfaction of capital transfer tax and estate duty (*inter alia*) conferring on the Secretary of State and the Chancellor of the Duchy of Lancaster certain functions formerly exercised by the Treasury) (Part II (ss. 8–15), *post*); and empowers those Ministers in specified cases and circumstances to compensate certain institutions and persons if objects lent by them are lost or damaged (s. 16, *post*).

Part I (ss. 1–7 and Sch. 1) relates to the National Heritage Memorial Fund. S. 1, *post*, provides for the establishment of the National Heritage Memorial Fund in succession to the National Land Fund established by the Finance Act 1946, s. 48, Vol. 12, p. 633 and for it to be administered by a body corporate comprising Trustees appointed by the Prime Minister. The Trustees are to include persons connected with each part of the United Kingdom. Provision as to the status, tenure of office, expenses, staff and proceedings of the Trustees is made in Sch. 1, *post*.

S. 2, *post*, provides for the Secretary of State and the Chancellor of the Duchy of Lancaster ("the Ministers") to make an annual payment into the Fund within a month of the beginning of each financial year and for receipts of the Trustees to be paid into the Fund.

S. 3, *post*, empowers the Trustees to make grants or loans out of the Fund to the recipients mentioned in sub-s. (6) for the purpose of assisting them in acquiring, maintaining or preserving property of importance to the national heritage.

S. 4, *post*, empowers the Trustees to spend money in connection with the acquisition, maintenance or preservation of such property otherwise than by making grants and loans. But where they themselves acquire property under the section they may not retain it except where, and for such period as, one of the Ministers allows.

S. 5, *post*, permits the Trustees to accept gifts of money or other property. There is a similar restriction on the retention by the Trustees of property given to them.

S. 6, *post*, empowers the Trustees to invest such part of the Fund as is not required to meet current expenditure. The investment of money deriving from payments made by the Ministers is subject to Treasury control. The Trustee Investments Act 1961, A.L.S. Vol. 127, is applied to the investment of money deriving from private gifts.

S. 7, *post*, provides for the laying before Parliament both of annual reports by the Trustees and of their accounts (which are to be subject to scrutiny by the Comptroller and Auditor General).

Part II (ss. 8–15) relates to the acceptance of property in satisfaction of tax. S. 8, *post*, provides that the Ministers may reimburse the Commissioners of Inland

Revenue for the tax foregone in respect of property accepted in satisfaction of capital transfer tax under the Finance Act 1975, Sch. 4, para. 17, A.L.S. Vol. 227 (reimbursement was formerly a Treasury function). The section provides similarly in outstanding estate duty cases.

S. 9, *post*, gives the Ministers control over the disposal of property which has been accepted in satisfaction of tax. They are required to lay before Parliament an annual statement giving particulars of disposals.

S. 10, *post*, provides that receipts and expenses in respect of property accepted by the Commissioners shall be paid to, or made by, the Ministers.

S. 11, *post*, exempts from stamp duty conveyances or transfers of property in pursuance of s.9, *post*.

S. 12, *post*, transfers from the Treasury to the Ministers certain functions under the enactments relating to the acceptance of property by the Commissioners; it also makes their acceptance of property subject to the agreement of the Ministers.

S. 13, *post*, extends the enactments relating to the acceptance of property in satisfaction of capital transfer tax or estate duty to any interest on the tax or duty.

S. 14, *post*, enables Ministerial functions arising from ss. 8 – 12 to be transferred to the National Heritage Memorial Fund Trustees by Order in Council which has been approved in draft by both Houses of Parliament.

S. 15, *post*, provides for the abolition of the National Land Fund established under the Finance Act 1946, s. 48, A.L.S. Vol. 37.

Part III (ss. 16 – 18 and Sch. 2) contains miscellaneous and supplementary provisions. S. 16, *post*, makes provision whereunder either of the Ministers may indemnify any institution or body mentioned in sub-s. (2) where an object is lent to another such institution or body on terms approved by him and the Treasury under sub-ss. (3) and (4) and the object is lost or damaged while on loan. Comparable powers are conferred on appropriate Northern Ireland government departments where loans are made by institutions or bodies established or resident in Northern Ireland.

S. 17, *post*, provides for Ministerial payments and receipts to be made out of moneys provided by Parliament and paid into the Consolidated Fund and s. 18 (5) and Sch. 2, *post*, make consequential repeals. **[10]**

ARRANGEMENT OF SECTIONS

PART I

THE NATIONAL HERITAGE MEMORIAL FUND

PART II

PROPERTY ACCEPTED IN SATISFACTION OF TAX

An Act to establish a National Heritage Memorial Fund for providing financial assistance for the acquisition, maintenance and preservation of land, buildings and objects of outstanding historic and other interest; to make new provision in relation to the arrangements for accepting property in satisfaction of capital transfer tax and estate duty; to provide for payments out of public funds in respect of the loss of or damage to objects loaned to or displayed in local museums and other institutions; and for purposes connected with those matters. [31st March 1980]

NORTHERN IRELAND
This Act applies; see s. 18 (6), *post*.

PART I

THE NATIONAL HERITAGE MEMORIAL FUND

1. Establishment of National Heritage Memorial Fund

(1) There shall be a fund known as the National Heritage Memorial Fund, to be a memorial to those who have died for the United Kingdom, established in succession to the National Land Fund, which shall be applicable for the purposes specified in this Part of this Act.

(2) The Fund shall be vested in and administered by a body corporate known as the Trustees of the National Heritage Memorial Fund and consisting of a chairman and not more than ten other members appointed by the Prime Minister.

(3) The persons appointed under this section shall include persons who have knowledge, experience or interests relevant to the purposes for which the Fund may be applied and who are connected by residence or otherwise with England, Wales, Scotland and Northern Ireland respectively.

(4) References in this Part of this Act to the Trustees are to the body constituted by subsection (2) above; and Schedule 1 to this Act shall have effect with respect to the Trustees and the discharge of their functions. [11]

UNITED KINGDOM
I.e., Great Britain and Northern Ireland; see the Interpretation Act 1978, s. 5, Sch. 1, A.L.S. Vol. 258. "Great Britain" means England, Scotland and Wales by virtue of the Union with Scotland Act 1706, preamble, Art. I, as read with the Interpretation Act 1978, s. 22 (1), Sch. 2, para. 5(*a*). Neither the Channel Islands nor the Isle of Man is within the United Kingdom.

NATIONAL LAND FUND
This fund was established by the Finance Act 1946, s. 48, A.L.S. Vol. 37 (repealed by ss. 15 (1) and 18 (5) and Sch. 2, *post*).

APPLICABLE FOR THE PURPOSES SPECIFIED IN THIS PART
I.e., Part I (ss. 1 – 7) of this Act. As to the purposes for which the Fund may be applied, see ss. 3 and 4, *post*.

BODY CORPORATE
For the general law relating to corporations, see 9 Halsbury's Laws (4th Edn.), paras. 1201 *et seq*.

TRUSTEES OF THE NATIONAL HERITAGE MEMORIAL FUND
As to the transfer of certain Ministerial functions to the Trustees, see s. 14, *post*.

ENGLAND; WALES
For meanings, see the Interpretation Act 1978, s. 5, Sch. 1.

FURTHER PROVISIONS
See, further, in connection with the National Heritage Memorial Fund and its Trustees (in addition to Sch. 1, *post*), s. 2, *post* (payments into the Fund; s. 3, *post* (grants and loans from the Fund); s. 4, *post* (other expenditure out of the Fund); s. 5, *post* (acceptance of gifts); s. 6, *post* (powers of investment); and s. 7, *post* (annual reports and accounts).

2. Payments into the Fund

(1) The Secretary of State and the Chancellor of the Duchy of Lancaster (in this Act referred to as "the Ministers") shall pay into the Fund in the first month of each financial year a sum determined by them before the beginning of the year; and the Ministers may at any time pay into the Fund such further sum or sums as they may from time to time determine.

(2) There shall also be paid into the Fund any other sums received by the Trustees in consequence of the discharge of their functions.   [12]

SECRETARY OF STATE
I.e., one of Her Majesty's Principal Secretaries of State; see the Interpretation Act 1978, s. 5, Sch. 1, A.L.S. Vol. 258. The Secretary of State here concerned is the Secretary of State for the Environment or as respects Wales the Secretary of State for Wales.

CHANCELLOR OF THE DUCHY OF LANCASTER
This is a reference to the Chancellor in his capacity as a Minister of the Crown with responsibility for the Arts; see s. 18 (3), *post*.

PAY INTO THE FUND . . . A SUM, ETC
Money paid into the Fund under sub-s. (1) above may be invested in any manner approved by the Treasury; see s. 6 (2) *post*. "The Fund" is the National Heritage Memorial Fund established under s. 1 (1), *ante*.

THERE SHALL ALSO BE PAID INTO THE FUND, ETC
In connection with sub-s. (2) above note the provisions restricting acceptance of gifts in s. 5 (2), *post*.

DEFINITIONS
For "the Trustees", see s. 1 (4), *ante*; for "financial year", see s. 18 (2), *post*. Note as to "the Ministers", sub-s. (1) above.

3. Grants and loans from the Fund

(1) Subject to the provisions of this section, the Trustees may make grants and loans out of the Fund to eligible recipients for the purpose of assisting them to acquire, maintain or preserve—

(*a*) any land, building or structure which in the opinion of the Trustees is of outstanding scenic, historic, aesthetic, architectural or scientific interest;

(*b*) any object which in their opinion is of outstanding historic, artistic or scientific interest;

(*c*) any collection or group of objects, being a collection or group which taken as a whole is in their opinion of outstanding historic, artistic or scientific interest;

(d) any land or object not falling within paragraph (a), (b) or (c) above the acquisition, maintenance or preservation of which is in their opinion desirable by reason of its connection with land or a building or structure falling within paragraph (a) above; or

(e) any rights in or over land the acquisition of which is in their opinion desirable for the benefit of land or a building or structure falling within paragraph (a) or (d) above.

(2) The Trustees shall not make a grant or loan under this section in respect of any property unless they are of opinion, after obtaining such expert advice as appears to them to be appropriate, that the property (or, in the case of land or an object falling within paragraph (d) of subsection (1) above, the land, building or structure with which it is connected or, in the case of rights falling within paragraph (e) of that subsection, the land, building or structure for whose benefit they are acquired) is of importance to the national heritage.

(3) In determining whether and on what terms to make a grant or loan under this section in respect of any property the Trustees shall have regard to the desirability of securing, improving or controlling public access to, or the public display of, the property.

(4) In making a grant or loan under this section in respect of any property the Trustees may impose such conditions as they think fit, including—

(a) conditions with respect to—

(i) public access to, or the public display of, the property;

(ii) the maintenance, repair, insurance and safe keeping of the property;

(iii) the disposal or lending of the property; and

(b) conditions requiring the amount of a grant and the outstanding amount of a loan to be repaid forthwith on breach of any condition.

(5) A grant under this section for the purpose of assisting in the maintenance or preservation of any property may take the form of a contribution to a trust established or to be established for that purpose.

(6) Subject to subsection (7) below, the eligible recipients for the purposes of this section are—

(a) any museum, art gallery, library or other similar institution having as its purpose or one of its purposes the preservation for the public benefit of a collection of historic, artistic or scientific interest;

(b) any body having as its purpose or one of its purposes the provision, improvement or preservation of amenities enjoyed or to be enjoyed by the public or the acquisition of land to be used by the public;

(c) any body having nature conservation as its purpose or one of its purposes;

(d) the Secretary of State acting in the discharge of his functions under section 5 of the Historic Buildings and Ancient Monuments Act 1953 or section 11 (1) or 13 of the Ancient Monuments and Archaeological Areas Act 1979; and

(e) the Department of the Environment for Northern Ireland acting in the discharge of its functions under so much of section 1 (1) of the Historic Monuments Act (Northern Ireland) 1971 as relates to the acquisition of historic monuments by agreement, section 4 of that Act or Article 84 of the Planning (Northern Ireland) Order 1972.

(7) The institutions referred to in paragraph (*a*) of subsection (6) above include any institution maintained by a Minister or Northern Ireland department; but neither that paragraph nor paragraph (*b*) or (*c*) of that subsection applies to any institution or body established outside the United Kingdom or established or conducted for profit.   [13]

SUB-S. (1): MAKE GRANTS AND LOANS . . . TO ELIGIBLE RECIPIENTS
    As to the meaning of this phrase, see s. 18 (4), *post*; and for the meaning of "eligible recipients", note sub-s. (6) above.

THE FUND
    I.e., the National Heritage Memorial Fund established under s. 1 (1), *ante*.

LAND
    For definition, see the Interpretation Act 1978, s. 5, Sch. 1, A.L.S. Vol. 258.

OPINION
    For a discussion as to the effect of the use of the words "in the opinion" and similar expressions, such as "it appears to the Secretary of State" or "the Secretary of State is satisfied", on the power of the courts to review administrative action, see 1 Halsbury's Laws (4th Edn.), para. 22.

SUB-S. (3): PUBLIC
    See the note "The public" to sub-s. (6) below.

SUB-S. (4): THINKS FIT
    See the note "opinion" to sub-s. (1) above.

FORTHWITH
    A provision to the effect that a thing must be done "forthwith" or "immediately" means that it must be done as soon as possible in the circumstances, the nature of the act to be done being taken into account; see *Re Southam, Ex parte Lamb* (1818), 19 Ch. D. 169, C.A.; [1881−5] All E.R. Rep. 391; *Re Muscovitch, Ex parte Muscovitch*, [1939] Ch. 694; [1939] 1 All E.R. 135, C.A.; and *Sameen* v. *Abeyewickrema*, [1963] A.C. 597; [1963] 3 All E.R. 382, P.C. Provided, however, that no harm is done, "forthwith" means "at any reasonable time thereafter", and in the absence of some detriment suffered by the person affected, failure to act "forthwith" does not invalidate the action taken; see *London Borough of Hillingdon* v. *Cutler*, [1968] 1 Q.B. 124; [1967] 2 All E.R. 361, C.A. See, further, on the meaning of "forthwith", 37 Halsbury's Laws (3rd Edn.), p. 103 and 2 Words and Phrases (2nd Edn.) 273−275.

SUB-S. (6): PUBLIC BENEFIT; THE PUBLIC
    For cases on the meaning of "public", "the public" and "member of the public" in various contexts, see *Tatem Steam Navigation Co., Ltd.* v. *Inland Revenue Comrs.*, [1941] 2 K.B. 194; [1941] 2 All E.R. 616, C.A.; *Income Tax Comr.* v. *Bjordal*, [1955] A.C. 309; [1955] 1 All E.R. 401, P.C.; *Director of Public Prosecutions* v. *Milbanke Tours, Ltd.*, [1960] 2 All E.R. 467; *Morrisons Holdings, Ltd.* v. *Inland Revenue Comrs.* [1966] 1 All E.R. 789; *Inland Revenue Comrs.* v. *Park Investments, Ltd.*, [1966] Ch. 701; [1966] 2 All E.R. 785, C.A.; *R.* v. *Delmayne*, [1970] 2 Q.B. 170; [1969] 2 All E.R. 980, C.A.; *Benyon* v. *Caerphilly Lower Licensing Justices*, [1970] 1 All E.R. 618; and *Attorney-General's Reference (No. 2 of 1977)*, [1978] 2 All E.R. 646, C.A. See also the decisions mentioned in the note "Performance in public" to the Copyright Act 1956, s. 2, A.L.S. Vol. 100.

SECRETARY OF STATE
    See the note to s. 2, *ante*.

SUB-S. (7): MINISTER
    It is thought that in sub-s. (7) this means any Minister of the Crown and not only one of "the Ministers" as defined by s. 18 (2), *post*.

UNITED KINGDOM
    See the note to s. 1, *ante*.

ESTABLISHED OR CONDUCTED FOR PROFIT
    It seems clear that an institution or body may have been established or conducted otherwise than for profit even though profits are made; see, in particular, *National Deposit Friendly Society Trustees* v. *Skegness Urban District Council*, [1959] A.C. 293; [1958] 2 All E.R. 601. In fact there

is authority for saying that the making of profits is irrelevant if it is only a subsidiary object, *viz.*, only a means whereby the main object of the body in question can be furthered or achieved; see, in particular, *National Deposit Friendly Society Trustees* v. *Skegness Urban District Council, supra*, at pp. 319, 320 and p. 612, respectively, *per* Lord Denning.

EXTENSION
Sub-ss. (2) and (3) above apply in relation to the application of any sums out of the Fund under s. 4, *post*, as they apply in relation to the making of a grant or loan under this section; see s. 4 (2), *post*.

DEFINITIONS
For "the Trustees", see s. 1 (4), *ante*. Note as to "eligible recipients", sub-s. (6) above.

HISTORIC BUILDING AND ANCIENT MONUMENTS ACT 1953, S. 5
See 24, Halsbury's Statutes (3rd edn.), p. 279.

ANCIENT MONUMENTS AND ARCHAEOLOGICAL AREAS ACT 1979, SS. 11 (1), 13
See 49, Halsbury's Statutes (3rd edn.), p. 975.

HISTORIC MONUMENTS ACT (NORTHERN IRELAND) 1971
1971 c. 17 (N.I.).

PLANNING (NORTHERN IRELAND) ORDER 1972
S.I. 1972 No. 1634.

4. Other expenditure out of the Fund

(1) Subject to the provisions of this section, the Trustees may apply the Fund for any purpose other than making grants or loans, being a purpose connected with the acquisition, maintenance or preservation of property falling within section 3 (1) above, including its acquisition, maintenance or preservation by the Trustees.

(2) Subsections (2) and (3) of section 3 above shall have effect in relation to the application of any sums out of the Fund under this section as they have effect in relation to the making of a grant or loan under that section.

(3) The Trustees shall not retain any property acquired by them under this section except in such cases and for such period as either of the Ministers may allow. **[14]**

THE FUND
I.e., the National Heritage Memorial Fund established under s. 1 (1), *ante*.

DEFINITIONS
For "the Trustees", see s. 1 (4), *ante*; for "the Ministers", see s. 18 (2), *post*.

5. Acceptance of gifts

(1) Subject to the provisions of this section, the Trustees may accept gifts of money or other property.

(2) The Trustees shall not accept a gift unless it is either unconditional or on conditions which enable the subject of the gift (and any income or proceeds of sale arising from it) to be applied for a purpose for which the Fund may be applied under this Part of this Act and which enable the Trustees to comply with subsection (3) below and section 2 (2) above.

(3) The Trustees shall not retain any property (other than money) accepted by them by way of gift except in such cases and for such period as either of the Ministers may allow.

(4) References in this section to gifts include references to bequests and devises. **[15]**

PURPOSE FOR WHICH THE FUND MAY BE APPLIED UNDER THIS PART
See ss. 3 and 4, *ante*.

DEFINITIONS
For "the Trustees", see s. 1 (4), *ante*; for "the Ministers", see s. 18 (2), *post*. Note as to "gifts", sub-s. (4) above.

6. Powers of investment

(1) Any sums in the Fund which are not immediately required for any other purpose may be invested by the Trustees in accordance with this section.

(2) Sums directly or indirectly representing money paid into the Fund under section 2 (1) above may be invested in any manner approved by the Treasury; and the Trustees —

    (*a*) shall not invest any amount available for investment which represents such money except with the consent of the Treasury; and

    (*b*) shall, if the Treasury so require, invest any such amount specified by the Treasury in such manner as the Treasury may direct.

(3) Any sums to which subsection (2) above does not apply may be invested in accordance with the Trustee Investments Act 1961; and sections 1, 2, 5, 6, 12 and 13 of that Act shall have effect in relation to such sums, and in relation to any investments for the time being representing such sums, as if they constituted a trust fund and the Trustees were the trustees of that trust fund.   [16]

THE FUND
I.e., the National Heritage Memorial Fund established under s. 1 (1), *ante*.

THE TRUSTEES
I.e., the body constituted by s. 1 (2), *ante*; see s. 1 (4), *ante*.

TREASURY
I.e., the Commissioners of Her Majesty's Treasury; see the Interpretation Act 1978, s. 5, Sch. 1, A.L.S. Vol. 258.

TRUSTEE INVESTMENTS ACT 1961, SS. 1, 2, 5, 6, 12, 13
A.L.S. Vol. 127.

7. Annual reports and accounts

(1) As soon as practicable after the end of each financial year the Trustees shall make a report to the Ministers on the activities of the Trustees during that year; and the Ministers shall cause the report to be published and lay copies of it before Parliament.

(2) It shall be the duty of the Trustees —

    (*a*) to keep proper accounts and proper records in relation to the accounts;

    (*b*) to prepare in respect of each financial year a statement of account in such form as the Ministers may with the approval of the Treasury direct; and

    (*c*) to send copies of the statement to the Ministers and the Comptroller and Auditor General before the end of the month of November next following the end of the financial year to which the statement relates.

(3) The Comptroller and Auditor General shall examine, certify and report on each statement received by him in pursuance of this section and lay copies of it and of his report before Parliament.   [17]

LAY . . . BEFORE PARLIAMENT
For meaning, see the Laying of Documents before Parliament (Interpretation) Act 1948, s. 1 (1), A.L.S. Vol. 56.

IT SHALL BE THE DUTY
As to the remedies for failure to perform a statutory duty, see generally 36 Halsbury's Laws (3rd Edn.), pp. 440 *et seq.*; and 1 Halsbury's Laws (4th Edn.), paras. 99, 195, 205.

TREASURY
See the note to s. 6, *ante*.

COMPTROLLER AND AUDITOR GENERAL
I.e., the officer appointed in pursuance of the Exchequer and Audit Department Act 1866; see the Interpretation Act 1978, s. 5, Sch. 1, A.L.S. Vol. 258. See, in particular, ss. 3 and 6 of the Act of 1866.

DEFINITIONS
For "the Trustees", see s. 1 (4), *ante*; for "financial year" and "the Ministers", see, s. 18 (2), *post*.

PART II

PROPERTY ACCEPTED IN SATISFACTION OF TAX

8. Payments by Ministers to Commissioners of Inland Revenue

(1) Where under paragraph 17 of Schedule 4 to the Finance Act 1975 the Commissioners of Inland Revenue have accepted any property in satisfaction of any amount of capital transfer tax, the Ministers may pay to the Commissioners a sum equal to that amount.

(2) Any sums paid to the Commissioners under this section shall be dealt with by them as if they were payments on account of capital transfer tax.

(3) Subsections (1) and (2) above shall apply in relation to estate duty chargeable on a death occurring before the passing of the said Act of 1975 as they apply in relation to capital transfer tax; and for that purpose the reference in subsection (1) to paragraph 17 of Schedule 4 to that Act shall be construed as a reference to —

(*a*) section 56 of the Finance (1909 – 1910) Act 1910;

(*b*) section 30 of the Finance Act 1953 and section 1 of the Finance (Miscellaneous Provisions) Act (Northern Ireland) 1954; and

(*c*) section 34 (1) of the Finance Act 1956, section 46 of the Finance Act 1973, Article 10 of the Finance (Northern Ireland) Order 1972 and Article 5 of the Finance (Miscellaneous Provisions) (Northern Ireland) Order 1973.

(4) References in this Part of this Act to property accepted in satisfaction of tax are to property accepted by the Commissioners under the provisions mentioned in this section. **[18]**

CAPITAL TRANSFER TAX
This tax is charged under the Finance Act 1975, Part III, A.L.S. Vol. 227, as amended and supplemented by provisions of subsequent Finance Acts.

THE MINISTERS
For meaning, see s. 18 (2), *post*. As to the transfer of the functions of the Ministers to the Trustees of the National Heritage Memorial Fund, see s. 14, *post*.

ESTATE DUTY
This duty was charged under the Finance Act 1894, Part I, as amended and supplemented by provisions of subsequent Finance Acts. It was abolished by the Finance Act 1975, s. 49, as respects deaths on or after the passing of that Act on 13th March 1975.

THIS PART OF THIS ACT
I.e., Part II (ss. 8 – 15) of this Act.

PROPERTY ACCEPTED IN SATISFACTION OF TAX
See also as to the meaning of this phrase, s. 13 (3), *post*.

EXTENSION
This section has effect where by virtue of s. 13, *post*, property is accepted in satisfaction of interest as it has effect where property is accepted in satisfaction of capital transfer tax or estate duty; see s. 13 (3), *post*.

FURTHER PROVISIONS
See, further, in particular, in connection with the enactments mentioned in this section, s. 9, *post* (disposal of property accepted by Commissioners); s. 10, *post* (receipts and expenses in respect of property accepted by Commissioners); s. 12, *post* (approval of property for acceptance in satisfaction of tax); and s. 13, *post* (acceptance of property in satisfaction of interest on tax).

FINANCE ACT 1975
For Sch. 4, para. 17, to that Act, see A.L.S. Vol. 227; that paragraph is amended by s. 12 (1), *post* (and see also s. 13 (1), *post*). The Act of 1975 was passed, *i.e.*, received the Royal Assent, on 13th March 1975.

FINANCE (1909–1910) ACT 1910, S. 56
That section and the enactments mentioned in sub-s. (3) (*b*) and (*c*) above were repealed by the Finance Act 1975, ss. 52 (2), 59 (5), Sch. 13, Part I, in relation to deaths occurring on or after 13th March 1975, and the enactments mentioned in sub-s. (3) (*a*)–(*c*) above are also affected by ss. 12 (2) and 13 (2), *post*, and those mentioned in sub-s. (3) (*b*) and (*c*) by s. 12 (3), *post*. The correct short title of the Act of 1910 is "the Finance (1909–10) Act 1910".

FINANCE ACT 1953, S. 30 A.L.S. Vol. 80
S. 30 (2) is repealed by s. 18 (5) and Sch. 2, *post*. See also the note on the Finance (1909–10) Act 1910 above.

FINANCE (MISCELLANEOUS PROVISIONS) ACT (NORTHERN IRELAND) 1954
1954 c. 3 (N.I.). See also the note on the Finance (1909–10) Act 1910 above.

FINANCE ACT 1956, S. 34 (1)
A.L.S. Vol. 95. See also the note on the Finance (1909–10) Act 1910 above.

FINANCE ACT 1973, S. 46
A.L.S. Vol. 213. See also the note on the Finance (1909–10) Act 1910 above.

FINANCE (NORTHERN IRELAND) ORDER 1972
S.I. 1972 No. 1100. See also the note on the Finance (1909–10) Act 1910 above.

FINANCE (MISCELLANEOUS PROVISIONS) (NORTHERN IRELAND) ORDER 1973
S.I. 1973 No. 1323. See also the note on the Finance (1909–10) Act 1910 above.

9. Disposal of property accepted by Commissioners

(1) Any property accepted in satisfaction of tax shall be disposed of in such manner as either of the Ministers may direct.

(2) Without prejudice to the generality of subsection (1) above, either Minister may in particular direct that any such property shall, on such conditions as he may direct, be transferred to any institution or body falling within section 3 (6) (*a*), (*b*) or (*c*) above which is willing to accept it, to the National Art Collections Fund or the Friends of the National Libraries if they are willing to accept it, to the Secretary of State or to the Department of the Environment for Northern Ireland.

(3) Where either of the Ministers has determined that any property accepted in satisfaction of tax is to be disposed of under this section to any such institution or body as is mentioned in subsection (2) above or to any other person who is willing to accept it, he may direct that the disposal shall be effected by means of a transfer direct to that institution or body or direct to that other person instead of being transferred to the Commissioners.

(4) Either of the Ministers may in any case direct that any property accepted

in satisfaction of tax shall, instead of being transferred to the Commissioners, be transferred to a person nominated by the Ministers; and where property is so transferred the person to whom it is transferred shall, subject to any directions subsequently given under subsection (1) or (2) above, hold the property and manage it in accordance with such directions as may be given by the Minister.

(5) In exercising their powers under this section in respect of an object or collection or group of objects having a significant association with a particular place, the Ministers shall consider whether it is appropriate for the object, collection or group to be, or continue to be, kept in that place, and for that purpose the Ministers shall obtain such expert advice as appears to them to be appropriate.

(6) The Ministers shall lay before Parliament as soon as may be after the end of each financial year a statement giving particulars of any disposal or transfer made in that year in pursuance of directions given under this section.

(7) References in this section to the disposal or transfer of any property include references to leasing, sub-leasing or lending it for any period and on any terms. **[19]**

SUB-S. (1): PROPERTY ACCEPTED IN SATISFACTION OF TAX
For the meaning of this phrase in this Part of this Act, see s. 8 (4), *ante*, and s. 13 (3), *post*.

THE MINISTERS
For meaning, see s. 18 (2), *post*. As to the transfer of the functions of the Ministers to the Trustees of the National Heritage Memorial Fund, see s. 14, *post*.

SUB-S. (2): PROPERTY SHALL . . . BE TRANSFERRED TO ANY INSTITUTION OR BODY, ETC
This includes the transferring of property to trustees for the institution or body involved; see s. 18 (4), *post*.

SECRETARY OF STATE
See the note to s. 2, *ante*.

SUB-S. (3): PERSON
This includes a body of persons corporate or unincorporate; see the Interpretation Act 1978, s. 5, Sch. 1, A.L.S. Vol. 258.

COMMISSIONERS
I.e., the Commissioners of Inland Revenue.

SUB-S. (5): APPEARS
See the note "Opinion" to s. 3, *ante*.

SUB-S. (6): LAY BEFORE PARLIAMENT
See the note to s. 7, *ante*.

STAMP DUTY
No stamp duty is payable on any conveyance or transfer of property made under this section to any institution or body mentioned in sub-s. (2) above or on any conveyance or transfer made under sub-s. (4) above; see s. 11, *post*.

DEFINITIONS
For "financial year" and "the Ministers", see s. 18 (2), *post*. Note as to the disposal or transfer of any property, sub-s. (7) above.

10. Receipts and expenses in respect of property accepted by Commissioners

(1) This section applies where property is accepted in satisfaction of tax and the Ministers have made a payment in respect of the property under section 8 above.

(2) Any sums received on the disposal of, or of any part of, the property (including any premium, rent or other consideration arising from the leasing, sub-leasing or lending of the property) and any sums otherwise received in

connection with the property shall be paid to the Ministers.

(3) Any expenses incurred in connection with the property so far as not disposed of under section 9 above, including in the case of leasehold property any rent payable in respect of it, shall be defrayed by the Ministers.   **[20]**

PROPERTY IS ACCEPTED IN SATISFACTION OF TAX
   For the meaning of this phrase in this Part of this Act, see s. 8 (4), *ante*, and s. 13 (3), *post*.

MINISTERS
   For meaning, see s. 18 (2), *post*. As to the transfer of the functions of the Ministers to the Trustees of the National Heritage Memorial Fund, see s. 14, *post*.

11. Exemption from stamp duty

No stamp duty shall be payable on any conveyance or transfer of property made under section 9 above to any such institution or body as is mentioned in subsection (2) of that section or on any conveyance or transfer made under subsection (4) of that section.   **[21]**

CONVEYANCE OR TRANSFER
   This includes a conveyance or transfer of property to trustees for any institution or body; see s. 18 (4), *post*.

12. Approval of property for acceptance in satisfaction of tax

(1) In paragraph 17 of Schedule 4 to the Finance Act 1975 —

   (*a*) in sub-paragraph (1) (power of Commissioners of Inland Revenue, if they think fit, to accept property in satisfaction of capital transfer tax) after the words "if they think fit" there shall be inserted the words "and the Ministers agree";

   (*b*) in sub-paragraphs (3) and (4) (approval by Treasury of objects to be accepted) for the words "the Treasury", in each place where they occur, there shall be substituted the words "the Ministers";

   (*c*) in sub-paragraph (5) (interpretation) after the words "In this paragraph" there shall be inserted the words "the Ministers' means the Secretary of State and the Chancellor of the Duchy of Lancaster and";

   (*d*) at the end of sub-paragraph (5) there shall be inserted the words "and, in determining under sub-paragraph (4) above whether an object or collection or group of objects is pre-eminent, regard shall be had to any significant association of the object, collection or group with a particular place."

(2) The power of the Commissioners of Inland Revenue to accept property in satisfaction of estate duty under the provisions mentioned in subsection (3) of section 8 above shall not be exercisable except with the agreement of the Ministers; and the Ministers shall exercise the functions conferred on the Treasury by the provisions mentioned in paragraphs (*b*) and (*c*) of that subsection (which correspond to paragraph 17 (3) and (4) of Schedule 4 to the said Act of 1975).

(3) Any question whether an object or collection or group of objects is pre-eminent shall be determined under the provisions mentioned in section 8 (3) (*b*) or (*c*) above in the same way as under the said paragraph 17 (4).   **[22]**

THE MINISTERS
   For meaning, see s. 18 (2), *post*, or the definition inserted by sub-s. (1) (*c*) above. As to the transfer of the functions of the Ministers to the Trustees of the National Heritage Memorial Fund, see s. 14, *post*.

SECRETARY OF STATE
See the note to s. 2, *ante*.

CHANCELLOR OF THE DUCHY OF LANCASTER
This is a reference to the Chancellor in his capacity as a Minister of the Crown with responsibility for the Arts; see s. 18 (3), *post*.

ESTATE DUTY
See the note to s. 8, *ante*.

TREASURY
See the note to s. 6, *ante*.

FINANCE ACT 1975, SCH. 4, PARA. 17
A.L.S. Vol. 227.

13. Acceptance of property in satisfaction of interest on tax

(1) In paragraph 19 of Schedule 4 to the Finance Act 1975 (interest on capital transfer tax) after sub-paragraph (5) there shall be inserted—

"(6) In paragraphs 17 (1) and 18 (1) above references to tax include references to interest payable under sub-paragraph (1) above."

(2) References to estate duty in—

(*a*) the provisions mentioned in section 8 (3) above; and

(*b*) section 32 of the Finance Act 1958 and section 5 of the Finance Act (Northern Ireland) 1958,

shall include references to interest payable under section 18 of the Finance Act 1896.

(3) Section 8 above shall have effect where by virtue of this section property is accepted in satisfaction of interest as it has effect where property is accepted in satisfaction of capital transfer tax or estate duty and references in this Part of this Act to property accepted in satisfaction of tax shall be construed accordingly. **[23]**

ESTATE DUTY; CAPITAL TRANSFER TAX
See the notes to s. 8, *ante*.

THIS PART OF THIS ACT
I.e., Part II (ss. 8—15) of this Act.

PROPERTY ACCEPTED IN SATISFACTION OF TAX
See also s. 8 (4), *ante*.

FINANCE ACT 1975, SCH. 4, PARAS. 17 (1), 18 (1), 19
A.L.S. Vol. 227. Sch. 4, para. 17 (1), to the Act of 1975 is amended by s. 12 (1), *ante*.

FINANCE ACT 1958, S. 32
A.L.S. Vol. 111. That section and the other enactments mentioned in sub-s. (2) above were repealed by the Finance Act 1975, ss. 52 (2), 59 (5), Sch. 13, Part I, in relation to deaths occurring on or after 13th March 1975.

FINANCE ACT (NORTHERN IRELAND) 1958
1958 c. 14 (N.I.). See also the note to the Finance Act 1975 above.

FINANCE ACT 1896, S. 18
See 12, Halsbury's Statutes (3rd edn.), p. 497. See also the note on the Finance Act 1975 above.

14. Transfer of Ministerial functions

(1) Her Majesty may by Order in Council provide for the transfer to the Trustees

of the National Heritage Memorial Fund of any functions exercisable by the Ministers or either of them under any of the provisions of this Part of this Act or of the provisions amended by section 12 above.

(2) An Order under this section may contain such incidental, consequential and supplemental provisions as may be necessary or expedient for the purpose of giving effect to the Order, including provisions adapting any of the provisions referred to in subsection (1) above.

(3) No Order shall be made under this section unless a draft of the Order has been laid before, and approved by a resolution of, each House of Parliament. [24]

TRUSTEES OF THE NATIONAL HERITAGE MEMORIAL FUND
    I.e., the body constituted by s. 1 (2), *ante*; cf. s. 1 (4), *ante*.

THE MINISTERS
    For meaning, see s. 18 (2), *post*.

THIS PART OF THIS ACT
    I.e., Part II (ss. 8 – 15) of this Act.

LAID BEFORE . . . PARLIAMENT
    See the corresponding note to s. 7, *ante*.

ORDERS IN COUNCIL UNDER THIS SECTION
    At the time of going to press no Order in Council had been made under this section.
        The power to make Orders in Council is exercisable by statutory instrument; see the Statutory Instruments Act 1946, s. 1 (1), A.L.S. Vol. 36.

15. Abolition of National Land Fund

(1) Sections 48, 50 and 51 of the Finance Act 1946 (which establish the National Land Fund for the purpose of making such payments as are mentioned in section 8 above and contain other provisions superseded by this Part of this Act) and section 7 of the Historic Buildings and Ancient Monuments Act 1953 (which enables payments to be made out of that Fund for various other purposes) shall cease to have effect.

(2) Subsection (1) above does not affect subsection (4) of the said section 48 (accounts) in relation to any receipts into or payments out of the National Land Fund at any time before that section ceases to have effect.

(3) The Treasury shall, within six months of the date on which the said section 48 ceases to have effect, cancel all investments of the National Land Fund in debt charged on the National Loans Fund. [25]

TREASURY
    See the note to s. 6, *ante*.

WITHIN SIX MONTHS OF, ETC
    The general rule in the computation of periods of time is that, unless there is a sufficient indication to the contrary, the day on which the initial event occurs is to be excluded and the last day is to be included and that fractions of a day are to be ignored; see generally 37 Halsbury's Laws (3rd Edn.), pp. 92, 100. "Months" means calendar months; see the Interpretation Act 1978, s. 5, Sch. 1, A.L.S. Vol. 258.

NATIONAL LOANS FUND
    The National Loans Fund was established by the National Loans Act 1968, s. 1.

FINANCE ACT 1946, SS. 48, 50, 51
    A.L.S. Vol. 37. Those sections are also repealed by s. 18 (5) and Sch. 2, *post*.

HISTORIC BUILDINGS AND ANCIENT MONUMENTS ACT 1953, S. 7
    See 24, Halsbury's Statutes (3rd edn.), p. 272. That section is also repealed by s. 18 (5) and Sch. 2, *post*.

PART III

MISCELLANEOUS AND SUPPLEMENTARY

16. Indemnities for objects on loan

(1) Subject to subsections (3) and (4) below, either of the Ministers may, in such cases and to such extent as he may determine, undertake to indemnify any institution, body or person falling within subsection (2) below for the loss of, or damage to, any object belonging to that institution, body or person while on loan to any other institution, body or person falling within that subsection.

(2) The institutions, bodies and persons referred to above are—

(a) a museum, art gallery or other similar institution in the United Kingdom which has as its purpose or one of its purposes the preservation for the public benefit of a collection of historic, artistic or scientific interest and which is maintained—

(i) wholly or mainly out of moneys provided by Parliament or out of moneys appropriated by Measure; or

(ii) by a local authority or university in the United Kingdom;

(b) a library which is maintained—

(i) wholly or mainly out of moneys provided by Parliament or out of moneys appropriated by Measure; or

(ii) by a library authority;

or the main function of which is to serve the needs of teaching and research at a university in the United Kingdom;

(c) the National Trust for Places of Historic Interest or Natural Beauty;

(d) the National Trust for Scotland for Places of Historic Interest or Natural Beauty; and

(e) any other body or person for the time being approved for the purposes of this section by either of the Ministers with the consent of the Treasury.

(3) Neither Minister shall give an undertaking under this section unless he considers that the loan will facilitate public access to the object in question or contribute materially to public understanding or appreciation of it.

(4) Neither Minister shall give an undertaking under this section unless the loan of the object in question is made in accordance with conditions approved by him and the Treasury and the Minister is satisfied that appropriate arrangements have been made for the safety of the object while it is on loan.

(5) Subsections (1) to (4) above shall apply in relation to the loan of an object belonging to an institution, body or person established or resident in Northern Ireland with the substitution for references to either of the Ministers and the Treasury of references to the Department of Education for Northern Ireland and the Department of Finance for Northern Ireland respectively.

(6) In subsection (2) above "library authority" means a library authority within the meaning of the Public Libraries and Museums Act 1964, a statutory library authority within the meaning of the Public Libraries (Scotland) Act 1955 or an Education and Library Board within the meaning of the Education and Libraries (Northern Ireland) Order 1972 and "university" includes a university college and a college, school or hall of a university.

(7) References in this section to the loss of or damage to, or to the safety of, an object while on loan include references to the loss of or damage to, or the safety of, the object while being taken to or returned from the place where it is to be or has been kept while on loan.   **[26]**

SUB-S. (1): **PERSON**
  See the note to s. 9, *ante.*

SUB-S. (2): UNITED KINGDOM
See the note to s. 1, *ante*.

PUBLIC BENEFIT
See the note "Public benefit; the public" to s. 3, *ante*.

WHOLLY OR MAINLY
The word "mainly" probably means "more than half"; see *Fawcett Properties, Ltd.* v. *Buckingham County Council,* [1961] A.C. 636, at p. 669; [1960] 3 All E.R. 503, H.L., at p. 512, *per* Lord Morton of Henryton. See also on the meaning of "wholly or mainly" (or "exclusively or mainly"), *Re Hatschek's Patents, Ex parte Zerenner,* [1909] 2 Ch. 68; *Miller* v. *Owners of Ottilie,* [1944] 1 K.B. 188; [1944] 1 All E.R. 277; *Franklin* v. *Gramophone Co., Ltd.,* [1948] 1 K.B. 542, at p. 555; [1948] 1 All E.R. 353, C.A., at p. 358, *per* Somervell, L.J.; and *Berthelemy* v. *Neale,* [1952] 1 All E.R. 437, C.A.

LOCAL AUTHORITY
This is not defined in this Act, but cf. the definition in the Local Government Act 1972, s. 270 (1), A.L.S. Vol. 209.

NATIONAL TRUST FOR PLACES OF HISTORIC INTEREST OR NATURAL BEAUTY
This body corporate commonly referred to as "the National Trust" was incorporated by the National Trust Act 1907, s. 3, 24, Halsbury's Statutes (3rd edn.), p. 288.

TREASURY
See the note to s. 6, *ante*.

SUB-S. (3): PUBLIC ACCESS; PUBLIC UNDERSTANDING, ETC
See the note "Public benefit; the public" to s. 3, *ante*.

SUB-S. (4): SATISFIED
See the note "Opinion" to s. 3, *ante*.

DEFINITIONS
For "the Minister", see s. 18 (2), *post*. Note as to "library authority" and "university", sub-s. (6) above, and as to "loss of or damage to" or "safety of an object while on loan", sub-s. (7) above.

PUBLIC LIBRARIES AND MUSEUMS ACT 1964
For the meaning of "library authority" in that Act, see s. 25 thereof, 19, Halsbury's Statutes (3rd edn.), p. 890.

PUBLIC LIBRARIES (SCOTLAND) ACT 1955
1955 c. 27.

EDUCATION AND LIBRARIES (NORTHERN IRELAND) ORDER 1972
S.I. 1972 No. 1263.

17. Expenses and receipts

Any sums required by any Minister for making payments under this Act shall be defrayed out of moneys provided by Parliament, and any sums received by any Minister under this Act shall be paid into the Consolidated Fund.   **[27]**

MINISTER
I.e., one of "the Ministers" as defined by s. 18 (2), *post*.

CONSOLIDATED FUND
The Consolidated Fund of the United Kingdom was established by the Consolidated Fund Act 1816, s. 1, 22, Halsbury's Statutes (3rd edn.), p. 916.

18. Short title, interpretation, repeals and extent

(1) This Act may be cited as the National Heritage Act 1980.
   (2) In this Act—

"financial year" means the twelve months ending with 31st March;
"the Ministers" means the Secretary of State and the Chancellor of the
Duchy of Lancaster.

(3) References in this Act and in the provisions amended by section 12 (1)
above to the Chancellor of the Duchy of Lancaster are references to the
Chancellor in his capacity as a Minister of the Crown with responsibility for the
Arts.

(4) References in this Act to the making of a grant or loan or the transfer or
conveyance of any property to any institution or body include references to the
making of a grant or loan or the transfer or conveyance of property to trustees for
that institution or body.

(5) The enactments mentioned in Schedule 2 to this Act are hereby repealed
to the extent specified in the third column of that Schedule.

(6) This Act extends to Northern Ireland. **[28]**

MONTHS
   I.e., calendar months; see the Interpretation Act 1978, s. 5, Sch. 1, A.L.S. Vol. 258.

THE MINISTERS
   As to the transfer of certain functions of the Ministers to the Trustees of the National Heritage
   Memorial Fund, see s. 14, *ante*.

SECRETARY OF STATE
   See the note to s. 2, *ante*.

CHANCELLOR IN HIS CAPACITY AS A MINISTER . . . WITH RESPONSIBILITY FOR THE ARTS
   The Chancellor of the Duchy of Lancaster originally acquired his functions as a Minister with
   responsibility for the Arts by virtue of the Transfer of Functions (Arts and Libraries) Order 1979,
   S.I. 1979 No. 907 (made under the Ministers of the Crown Act 1975, ss. 1, 2, 45, Halsbury's
   Statutes (3rd edn.), pp. 129, 131.

SCHEDULES

SCHEDULE 1

Section 1 (4).

The Trustees of the National Heritage Memorial Fund

Status

1. The Trustees shall not be regarded as acting on behalf of the Crown and neither they
nor their officers or servants shall be regarded as Crown servants.

2. Section 40 of the General Rate Act 1967 (relief for charities and other organisations),
section 4 of the Local Government (Financial Provisions etc.) (Scotland) Act 1962 (corresponding provisions for Scotland) and Article 41 of the Rates (Northern Ireland) Order
1977 (corresponding provisions for Northern Ireland) shall apply to any hereditament,
lands and heritages occupied by the Trustees for the purposes of this Act as they apply to a
hereditament, lands and heritages occupied by trustees for a charity.

Tenure of office of trustee

3.—(1) Subject to the provisions of this paragraph, a member of the body constituted
by section 1 (2) of this Act (in this Schedule referred to as "a trustee") shall hold and vacate
his office in accordance with the terms of his appointment.

(2) A person shall not be appointed a trustee for more than three years.

(3) A trustee may resign by notice in writing to the Prime Minister.

(4) The Prime Minister may terminate the appointment of a trustee if he is satisfied
that—

(*a*) for a period of six months beginning not more than nine months previously he has, without the consent of the other trustees, failed to attend the meetings of the trustees;

(*b*) he is an undischarged bankrupt or has made an arrangement with his creditors or is insolvent within the meaning of paragraph 9 (2) (*a*) of Schedule 3 to the Conveyancing and Feudal Reform (Scotland) Act 1970;

(*c*) he is by reason of physical or mental illness, or for any other reason, incapable of carrying out his duties; or

(*d*) he has been convicted of such a criminal offence, or his conduct has been such, that it is not in the Prime Minister's opinion fitting that he should remain a trustee.

(5) A person who ceases or has ceased to be a trustee may be re-appointed.

Tenure of office of chairman

4. —(1) Subject to the provisions of this paragraph, the chairman of the Trustees shall hold and vacate his office in accordance with the terms of his appointment.

(2) The chairman may resign his office by notice in writing to the Prime Minister.

(3) A trustee who ceases or has ceased to be chairman may be reappointed to that office.

(4) If the chairman ceases to be a trustee he shall also cease to be chairman.

Expenses and allowances

5. —(1) All administrative and other expenses incurred by the Trustees in discharging their functions under this Act shall be defrayed out of the Fund.

(2) There may be paid out of the Fund to a trustee such allowances as the Ministers may with the consent of the Minister for the Civil Service approve.

Staff

6. The Trustees may, after consultation with the Ministers, appoint such officers and servants as they think fit but the number appointed shall require the approval of the Ministers and the remuneration to be paid, any provisions as to superannuation and the other terms and conditions of service shall require the approval of the Ministers given with the consent of the Minister for the Civil Service.

Proceedings

7. —(1) Subject to the provisions of this Act —

(*a*) the Trustees shall discharge their functions in accordance with such arrangements as they may determine; and

(*b*) those arrangements may provide for any function to be discharged under the general direction of the Trustees by a committee or committees consisting of three or more trustees.

(2) Anything done by a committee under the arrangements shall, if the arrangements so provide, have effect as if done by the Trustees.

(3) The validity of any proceedings of the Trustees shall not be affected by any vacancy among the trustees or by any defect in the appointment of a trustee.

(4) The arrangements made under this paragraph may include provisions specifying a quorum for meetings of the Trustees and any committee; and until a quorum is so specified in relation to meetings of the Trustees the quorum for such meetings shall be such as may be determined by the Ministers. **[29]**

PARA. 1: SHALL NOT BE REGARDED AS ACTING ON BEHALF OF THE CROWN, ETC
   Para. 1 above appears to have been inserted *ex abundati cautela* since it is established that bodies of the kind set up by s. 1 (2), *ante*, are not servants or agents of the Crown unless it is expressly provided that they shall act on behalf of the Crown; see in particular, *Tamlin* v. *Hannaford*, [1950] 1 K.B. 18; [1949] 2 All E.R. 327, C.A. (British Transport Commission), and *British Broadcasting Corporation* v. *Johns (Inspector of Taxes)*, [1965] Ch. 32; [1964] 1 All E.R. 923.

PARA. 3: WRITING
   For meaning, see the Interpretation Act 1978, s. 5, Sch. 1, A.L.S. Vol. 258.

SATISFIED; OPINION
   See the note "Opinion" to s. 3, *ante*.

MONTHS
   I.e., calendar months; see the Interpretation Act 1978, s. 5, Sch. 1.

PARA. 5: FUND
   I.e., the National Heritage Memorial Fund established under s. 1 (1), *ante*.

PARA. 6: CONSULTATION
   On what constitutes consultation, see, in particular, *Rollo* v. *Minister of Town and Country Planning*, [1948] 1 All E.R. 13, C.A.; *Re Union of Whippingham and East Cowes Benefices, Derham* v. *Church Comrs. for England*, [1954] A.C. 245; [1954] 2 All E.R. 22, P.C.; and *Agricultural, Horticultural and Forestry Industry Training Board* v. *Aylesbury Mushrooms, Ltd.*, [1972] 1 All E.R. 280.

THINKS FIT
   See the note "Opinion" to s. 3, *ante*.

PARA. 7: QUORUM
   "The word 'quorum' in its ordinary significance has reference to the existence of a complete body of persons, of whom a certain specified number is competent to transact the business of the whole"; see *Faure Electric Accumulator Co., Ltd.* v. *Phillipart* (1888), 58 L.T. 525, st p. 527.

DEFINITIONS
   For "the Trustees", see s. 1 (4), *ante*; for "the Ministers", see s. 18 (2), *ante*. Note as to "a trustee", para. 3 (1) above.

GENERAL RATE ACT 1967, S. 40
   A.L.S. Vol. 166.

LOCAL GOVERNMENT (FINANCIAL PROVISIONS, ETC.) (SCOTLAND) ACT 1962
   1962 c. 9.

RATES (NORTHERN IRELAND) ORDER 1977
   S.I. 1977 No. 2157.

CONVEYANCING AND FEUDAL REFORM (SCOTLAND) ACT 1970
   1970 c. 35.

SCHEDULE 2

Section 18 (5).

REPEALS

Chapter	Short title	Extent of repeal
9 & 10 Geo. 6, c. 64	The Finance Act 1946	Section 48.
		Sections 50 and 51.
1 & 2 Eliz. 2, c. 34	The Finance Act 1953	Section 30 (2).
1 & 2 Eliz. 2, c. 49	The Historic Buildings and Ancient Monuments Act 1953	Section 7.
1969 c. 22	The Redundant Churches and other Religious Buildings Act 1969	Section 6.
1975 c. 7	The Finance Act 1975	In Schedule 12, paragraph 7.

THE BETTING, GAMING AND LOTTERIES (AMENDMENT) ACT 1980

(1980 c. 18)

PRELIMINARY NOTE

This Act, which came into force on receiving the Royal Assent on 31st March 1980, amends the Betting, Gaming and Lotteries Act 1963, s. 7, A.L.S. Vol. 140, and the Betting, Gaming and Lotteries (Amendment) Act 1971, s. 2, A.L.S. Vol. 199, in accordance with recommendations made in the Final Report of the Royal Commission on Gambling presented to Parliament in July 1978 (Cmnd 7200).

S. 1, *post*, amends the Betting, Gaming and Lotteries Act 1963, s. 7, by increasing the number of races on which betting may take place on any day on dog racecourses from eight to ten and on any special betting day from sixteen to twenty.

S. 2, *post*, amends the Betting, Gaming and Lotteries (Amendment) Act 1971, s. 2, by increasing the number of special betting days for any particular track from four to six with power for the Secretary of State from time to time to prescribe such other number as he thinks fit. **[31]**

An Act to amend the provisions of the Betting, Gaming and Lotteries Acts 1963 to 1971 in relation to the number of races on which betting may take place on dog racecourses on any day and in relation to the number of special betting days [31st March 1980]

NORTHERN IRELAND
This Act does not apply; see the Betting Gaming and Lotteries Act 1963, s. 58 (2), A.L.S. Vol. 140, and the Betting, Gaming and Lotteries (Amendment) Act 1971, s. 4, A.L.S. Vol. 199.

1. Restriction of betting on dog racecourses

Section 7 of the Betting, Gaming and Lotteries Act 1963 shall have effect as if: —

    (*a*) in subsection (1) (*a*) thereof (which restricts the number of races on which betting may take place on any day on a dog racecourse) for the word "eight" there were substituted the word "ten"; and

    (*b*) in subsection (2) (*a*) (which imposes a like restriction in respect of any special betting day) for the word "eight" there were substituted the word "ten" and for the word "sixteen" there were substituted the word "twenty". **[32]**

BETTING, GAMING AND LOTTERIES ACT 1963, S. 7 (1) (*a*), (2) (*a*)
A.L.S. Vol. 140.

2. Special betting days

Section 2 of the Betting, Gaming and Lotteries (Amendment) Act 1971 (which relates to the notification of special betting days) shall have effect as if—

  (i) in subsection (2) for the word "four" in each place where it occurs there were substituted the word "six"; and

  (ii) after subsection (2) there were inserted the following subsection: —

  "(2A) (*a*) The Secretary of State may from time to time by order provide that subsection (2) above shall have effect with the substitution, for the references to six days, of references to such other number of days as may be specified in the order.

  (*b*) An order under this subsection shall be made by statutory instrument and shall be subject to annulment in pursuance of a resolution of either House of Parliament.".   **[33]**

SECRETARY OF STATE
  I.e., one of Her Majesty's Principal Secretaries of State; see the Interpretation Act 1978, s. 5, Sch. 1,A.L.S. Vol. 258. The Secretary of State here concerned is the Secretary of State for the Home Department.

STATUTORY INSTRUMENT; SUBJECT TO ANNULMENT
  For provisions as to statutory instruments generally, see the Statutory Instruments Act 1946, A.L.S. Vol. 36, and as to statutory instruments which are subject to annulment, see ss. 5 (1) and 7 (1) of that Act.

BETTING, GAMING AND LOTTERIES (AMENDMENT) ACT 1971, S. 2 (2)
  A.L.S. Vol. 199.

ORDERS UNDER THIS SECTION
  At the time of going to press no order had been made under the Betting, Gaming and Lotteries (Amendment) Act 1971, s. 2 (2A), as inserted by this section.

3. Short title and citation

This Act may be cited as the Betting, Gaming and Lotteries (Amendment) Act 1980 and the Betting, Gaming and Lotteries Acts 1963 to 1971 and this Act may be cited together as the Betting, Gaming and Lotteries Acts 1963 to 1980.   **[34]**

THE LICENSED PREMISES (EXCLUSION OF CERTAIN PERSONS) ACT 1980

(1980 c. 32)

PRELIMINARY NOTE

This Act, which came into force on receiving the Royal Assent on 30th June 1980, empowers the courts to make exclusion orders prohibiting certain persons, who have been convicted of offences committed on licensed premises and who, in committing the offences, threatened or used violence, from entering those premises or any other specified licensed premises.

S. 1, *post*, empowers the courts to make exclusion orders, in addition to any other sentence or order, for a period of not less than three months nor more than two years.

S. 2, *post*, provides a penalty for breach of an exclusion order and for the termination or variation of such an order.

S. 3, *post*, empowers the licensee of licensed premises, with the aid of a constable, if necessary, to expel any person whom he reasonably suspects has entered the premises in breach of an exclusion order.

Ss. 4 and 5, *post*, contain provisions relating to interpretation and other supplemental provisions. **[35]**

An Act to empower the courts to make orders excluding certain categories of convicted persons from licensed premises   [30th June 1980]

NORTHERN IRELAND
  This Act does not apply; see s. 5 (2), *post*.

1. Exclusion orders

(1) Where a court by or before which a person is convicted of an offence committed on licensed premises is satisfied that in committing that offence he resorted to violence or offered or threatened to resort to violence, the court may, subject to subsection (2) below, make an order (in this Act referred to as an "exclusion order") prohibiting him from entering those premises or any other specified premises, without the express consent of the licensee of the premises or his servant or agent.

(2) An exclusion order may be made either —

> (*a*) in addition to any sentence which is imposed in respect of the offence of which the person is convicted; or

> (*b*) where the offence was committed in England or Wales, notwithstanding the provisions of sections 2, 7 and 13 of the Powers of Criminal Courts Act 1973 (cases in which probation orders and absolute and conditional discharges may be made, and their effect), in addition to a probation order or an order discharging him absolutely or conditionally; or

> (*c*) (*Applies to Scotland*);

but not otherwise.

(3) An exclusion order shall have effect for such period, not less than three months or more than two years, as is specified in the order, unless it is terminated under section 2 (2) below.   **[36]**

EXCLUSION ORDER
 For penalty for breach of an exclusion order, see s. 2 (1), *post*; for power to terminate or vary an exclusion order, see s. 2 (2), *post*; and for power of a licensee to expel person in breach of an exclusion order, see s. 3, *post*. A copy of the order must be sent to the licensee of the premises to which the order relates; see s. 4 (3), *post*.

SERVANT OR AGENT
 Whether one person is the servant of another is a question of fact (*Brady* v. *Giles* (1835), 1 Mood. & R. 494; *Jones* v. *Scullard,* [1898] 2 Q.B. 565), but, in general, a servant is a person who is subject to the commands of his master not only as to what work he is to do but also as to the manner in which it is to be done (*Yewens* v. *Neakes* (1880), 6 Q.B.D. 530, C.A., *per* Bramwell, L.J., at p. 532; *Simmons* v. *Heath Laundry Co.,* [1910] 1 K.B. 543, C.A., *per* Buckley, L.J., at p. 552). An agent is a person who has the authority, express or implied, to act on behalf of another, and who consents to act (*Pole* v. *Leask* (1863), 33 T.J. Ch. 155, at p. 161). See further, 1 Halsbury's Laws (4th Edn.), para. 701 and 16 Halsbury's Laws (4th edn.), paras. 501 *et seq.*

ENGLAND; WALES
 These expressions are defined by the Interpretation Act 1978, s. 5, Sch. 1, A.L.S. Vol. 258.

MONTHS
 I.e., calendar months; see the Interpretation Act 1978, s. 5, Sch. 1.

DEFINITIONS
 For "licensed premises", "licensee" and "specified premises", see s. 4 (1), *post*. Note as to exclusion order, sub-s. (1) above.

POWERS OF CRIMINAL COURTS ACT 1973, SS. 2, 7, 13
 See 43, Halsbury's Statutes (3rd edn.), pp. 291, 299, 306.

2. Penalty for non-compliance with exclusion order

(1) A person who enters any premises in breach of an exclusion order shall be guilty of an offence and shall be liable on summary conviction or, in Scotland, on conviction in a court of summary jurisdiction to a fine not exceeding £200 or to imprisonment for a term not exceeding one month or both.

(2) The court by which a person is convicted of an offence under subsection (1) above shall consider whether or not the exclusion order should continue in force, and may, if it thinks fit, by order terminate the exclusion order or vary it by deleting the name of any specified premises, but an exclusion order shall not otherwise be affected by a person's conviction for such an offence.   **[37]**

EXCLUSION ORDER
 For the power of the courts to make exclusion orders, see s. 1, *ante*.

SUMMARY CONVICTION
 Summary jurisdiction and procedure are mainly governed by the Magistrates' Courts Act 1952, the Magistrates' Courts Act 1957, A.L.S. Vol. 104, and certain provisions of the Criminal Justice Act 1967, A.L.S. Vol. 163, and of the Criminal Law Act 1977, A.L.S. Vol. 249. Procedural provisions are also contained in rules made under the Justices of the Peace Act 1949, s. 15, A.L.S. Vol. 64.

BY ORDER TERMINATE THE EXCLUSION ORDER, ETC
 A copy of an order terminating or varying an exclusion order must be sent to the licensee of the relevant premises; see s. 4 (3) *post*.

DEFINITIONS
 For "exclusion order", see s. 1 (1), *ante*; for "specified premises", see s. 4 (1), *post*.

3. Power to expel person from licensed premises

Without prejudice to any other right to expel a person from premises, the licensee of licensed premises or his servant or agent may expel from those premises any person who has entered or whom he reasonably suspects of having entered the premises in breach of an exclusion order; and a constable shall on the demand of the licensee or his servant or agent help to expel from licensed premises any person whom the constable reasonably suspects of having entered in breach of an exclusion order.   [38]

SERVANT OR AGENT
    See the note to s. 1, *ante*.

EXCLUSION ORDER
    For the power of the courts to make exclusion orders, see s. 1, *ante*.

CONSTABLE
    This means any person holding the office of constable (as to which, see 30 Halsbury's Laws (3rd Edn.), pp. 43 *et seq*.), not a member of a police force holding the rank of constable. As to the attestation of constables, see the Police Act 1964, s. 18, Sch. 2, A.L.S. Vol. 148, and as to their jurisdiction, see s. 19 of that Act.

DEFINITIONS
    For "exclusion order", see s. 1 (1) *ante*; for "licensed premises" and "licensee", see s. 4 (1), *post*.

4. Supplemental

(1) In this Act—

   "licensed premises", in relation to England and Wales, means premises in respect of which there is in force a justices' on-licence (within the meaning of section 1 of the Licensing Act 1964 . . .; and
   "licensee" in relation to any licensed premises means the holder of the licence granted in respect of those premises; and
   "specified premises", in relation to an exclusion order, means any licensed premises which the court may specify by name and address in the order.

   (2) (*Applies to Scotland.*)

   (3) Where a court makes an exclusion order or an order terminating or varying an exclusion order, the clerk of the court, or the appropriate officer of the Crown Court, as the case may be, shall send a copy of the order to the licensee of the premises to which the order relates.   [39]

The words omitted from the definition of "licensed premises" where indicated by dots apply to Scotland.

ENGLAND; WALES
    See the note to s. 1, *ante*.

EXCLUSION ORDER
    As to the making of such orders by the courts, see s. 1, *ante*.

ORDER TERMINATING OR VARYING AN EXCLUSION ORDER
    Such an order may be made under s. 2 (2), *ante*.

CROWN COURT
    I.e., the Crown Court constituted by the Courts Act 1971, s. 4, A.L.S. Vol. 200; see the Interpretation Act 1978, s. 5, Sch. 1, A.L.S. Vol. 258.

LICENSING ACT 1964, S. 1
    See 17, Halsbury's Statutes (3rd edn.), p. 1059.

5. Short title, citation and extent

(1) This Act shall be cited as the Licensed Premises (Exclusion of Certain Persons) Act 1980 . . .

    (2) This Act shall not extend to Northern Ireland.   **[40]**

The words omitted from sub-s. (1) where indicated by dots apply to Scotland.

THE INDUSTRY ACT 1980

(1980 c. 33)

PRELIMINARY NOTE

This Act, which came into force on receiving the Royal Assent on 30th June 1980, amends the Industry Act 1975, A.L.S. Vol. 241, and the Welsh Development Agency Act 1975. It modifies the functions of the National Enterprise Board ("NEB") and the Welsh Development Agency. It provides for the transfer of property held by the NEB and the Agency to private ownership or to the Secretary of State and empowers the Secretary of State to provide finance for companies in which a controlling interest has been transferred to him from the NEB. It makes amendments relating to the financial limits and financial powers of the NEB and of the Welsh Development Agency. It also provides for a financial limit relating to companies control of which is transferred to the Secretary of State from the NEB. It also makes further provision relating to the English Industrial Estates Corporation, reduces the powers of the Secretary of State to pay regional development grant under the Industry Act 1972, Part I, A.L.S. Vol. 204 amends s. 8 of that Act, (selective financial assistance to industry), and authorises the Secretary of State to provide advisory services for businesses. The Act also amends the Scottish Development Agency Act 1975.

The National Enterprise Board and the Welsh Development Agency

S. 1, *post*, amends the Industry Act 1975, s. 2, the Welsh Development Agency Act 1975, s. 1. It provides that the NEB shall cease to have the function of extending public ownership and provides that the NEB and the Welsh Development Agency shall cease to have the function of promoting industrial reorganisation and industrial democracy. The section gives a new function to the NEB and to the Agency of disposing of assets held by them in order to promote private ownership.

S. 2, *post*, empowers the NEB and the Welsh Development Agency to transfer assets held or controlled by them to the Secretary of State and extends his powers of direction to enable him to require them to transfer assets to him.

S. 3, *post*, empowers the Secretary of State to provide finance for companies in which a controlling interest has been transferred to him from the NEB. It also requires him to make annual reports to Parliament on the exercise of these powers and to lay before Parliament the accounts of the companies concerned.

S. 4, *post*, provides for the making of payments by the NEB and the Welsh Development Agency in reduction of their public dividend capital. The NEB and the Agency are empowered to make such payments with the agreement of the Secretary of State and must do so if required by him.

S. 5, *post*, removes the powers of the Secretary of State to increase the financial limits of the NEB and of the Welsh Development Agency. The section also sets a financial limit in relation to companies of which control is transferred to the Secretary of State and to which accordingly s. 3, *ante*, applies, empowers the Secretary of State to reduce the NEB's financial limit to a minimum of £750 million and provides that the aggregate of the financial limits of the Secretary of

State and of the NEB shall not exceed the present financial limit of the NEB, *i.e.*, £3,000 million.

S. 6, *post*, replaces the existing limits on the acquisition of share capital by the NEB and the Welsh Development Agency. The new limits are that the total expenditure on shares in any body corporate shall not exceed £5 million for the Board and £1 million for the Agency.

S. 7, *post*, reduces the maximum number of members of the NEB from 16 to 12 and relieves the Secretary of State of the duty to maintain a register of the financial interests of members of the NEB. It also provides that the chief executive of the NEB shall be disqualified from membership of the House of Commons and of the Northern Ireland Assembly.

S. 8, *post*, abolishes the Secretary of State's power to direct the NEB and the Welsh Development Agency to exercise his powers of giving selective financial assistance.

S. 9, *post*, provides that the NEB and the Welsh Development Agency shall no longer be able to furnish technical assistance outside the United Kingdom under the Overseas Aid Act 1966, 4, Halsbury's Statutes (3rd edn.), p. 557.

The English Industrial Estates Corporation

S. 10, *post*, gives new functions to the English Industrial Estates Corporation in relation to the provision and management of industrial or commercial premises in England and the disposal of its assets. It also strengthens the Secretary of State's powers of direction, and provides that the Corporation shall not after the enactment of the Act be regarded as a servant or agent of the Crown.

S. 11, *post*, vests in the Corporation land held by the Crown which is subject to a lease to the Corporation. It also ensures that the Secretary of State has power to acquire land (by compulsory purchase or otherwise) under the Local Employment Act 1972, s. 5, A.L.S. Vol. 204, with a view to transferring it to the Corporation.

S. 12, *post*, removes the limits on the number of the members of the Corporation.

S. 13, *post*, gives power to the Corporation to borrow from the Commission of the European Communities or from the European Investment Bank; and s. 14, *post*, provides for Treasury guarantees to be given on sums borrowed under s. 13.

S. 15, *post*, extends the Local Employment Act 1972, s. 11 (9), (expenses of the Corporation under that Act to be defrayed by the Secretary of State), to the Corporation's expenses under this Act.

Grants and other financial assistance for industry

S. 16, *post*, reflects changes already put into effect, in exercise of the Secretary of State's discretion under the Industry Act 1972, Part I, relating to regional development grants. The section provides that regional development grant shall no longer be payable in respect of expenditure incurred in providing (i) buildings and works on qualifying premises in intermediate areas, (ii) mining works in development areas, and (iii) machinery and plant in development areas used in construction activities. The section also consolidates the provisions of the Regional Development Grants (Variation of Prescribed Percentages) Order 1979, S.I. 1979 No. 975, which reduced the rate of grant payable in respect of the development areas.

S. 17 and Sch. 1, *post*, amend the provisions relating to financial assistance for industry contained in the Industry Act 1972, Part II. In particular the Secretary of State is enabled to give guarantees where the liability is in foreign currencies. Sterling liabilities are to be covered by the existing statutory limits (Sch. 1, para. 2). Liabilities in foreign currencies, which are to be excluded from the limit on individual projects in s. 8 (8) of the Act of 1972 will be subject to new limits specified in special drawing rights (Sch. 1, paras. 3, 4). The precise arrangement for computing liabilities is set out in the new section inserted in the Act of 1972 by Sch. 1, para. 6. Foreign currency liabilities (*i.e.,* before any payment is made) are to be converted into special drawing rights on the day they are undertaken and revalued each quarter; payments and receipts are to be valued on the day of the transaction. Sub-s. (6) of the new section specifies the circumstances in which liabilities are permitted in excess of the limit specified in Sch. 1, para. 3.

Miscellaneous and General

S. 18, *post*, empowers the Secretary of State to provide advisory services to those carrying on or proposing to carry on businesses.

S. 19, *post*, repeals the provisions of the Industry Act 1975, with regard to planning agreements and to the disclosure of information by companies.

S. 20, *post*, removes the obligation on the Secretary of State to keep a register of financial interests of members of British Shipbuilders.

S. 21 and Sch. 2, *post*, provide for repeals and transitional provisions.   [41]

ARRANGEMENT OF SECTIONS

The National Enterprise Board and the Scottish and Welsh Development Agencies

An Act to make further provisions in relation to the National Enterprise Board, the Scottish Development Agency, the Welsh Development Agency and the English Industrial Estates Corporation; to authorise the Secretary of State to acquire securities of, make loans to and provide guarantees for companies in which he acquires shares from the National Enterprise Board; to amend the Industry Act 1972 and the Industry Act 1975; to authorise the provision by the Secretary of State of an advisory service; to remove the requirement for a register of the financial interests of members of British Shipbuilders; and for connected purposes. [30th June 1980]

NORTHERN IRELAND
The Act except ss. 10 – 16, *post* and any other provision so far as it relates to the Scottish or Welsh Development Agency, applies; see s. 22 (2), (3), *post*.

The National Enterprise Board and the Scottish and Welsh Development Agencies

1. Functions of the Board and Agencies

(1) In section 2 (2) of the Industry Act 1975 —

    (*a*) in paragraph (*b*) the words "reorganisation or" and paragraphs (*c*) and (*d*) shall cease to have effect; and

    (*b*) after paragraph (*e*) there shall be added —

        "(*f*) promoting the private ownership of interests in industrial undertakings by the disposal of securities and other property held by the Board or any of their subsidiaries."

(2) (*Applies to Scotland.*)

(3) In section 1 of the Welsh Development Agency Act 1975 —

    (*a*) in subsection (2), in paragraph (*a*), at the end there shall be added the words ", and in that connection to provide, maintain or safeguard employment";

    (*b*) in subsection (3), after paragraph (*i*) there shall be added —

        "(*j*) to promote the private ownership of interests in industrial undertakings by the disposal of securities and other property held by the Agency or any of their subsidiaries.";

    (*c*) subsection (2)(*c*), in subsection (3)(*d*) the word "reorganisation", and subsection (3)(*e*) shall cease to have effect; and

    (*d*) in subsection (11) the words from "in connection" to "above" shall cease to have effect. **[42]**

SHALL CEASE TO HAVE EFFECT
The provisions which cease to have effect are also repealed by s. 21(1) and Sch. 2, *post*.

DEFINITIONS
For "the Board", see the Industry Act 1975, s. 1(1), A.L.S. Vol. 241; for "the Agency", see the Welsh Development Agency Act 1975, s. 1(1), for "industrial" and "subsidiary" see s. 37(1) of the former Act, or s. 27(1) of the latter Act.

INDUSTRY ACT 1975, S. 2(2)
A.L.S. Vol. 241.

TRANSITIONAL PROVISION
See p. 21 (2), *post*.

2. Transfer of property to Secretary of State

(1) Without prejudice to any power otherwise conferred on them and notwith-

standing anything in any other enactment, the National Enterprise Board, the Scottish Development Agency and the Welsh Development Agency may transfer securities or other property held by them, and may procure the transfer of securities or other property held by any of their subsidiaries, to the Secretary of State or to a nominee of his; and the power of the Secretary of State to give directions —

(a) to the National Enterprise Board under section 7 of the Industry Act 1975,

(b) (*applies to Scotland*), and

(c) to the Welsh Development Agency under section 1 (9) of the Welsh Development Agency Act 1975,

shall extend to the giving of directions as to the making and terms of a transfer.

(2) Stamp duty shall not be chargeable on any instrument which is certified to the Commissioners of Inland Revenue by the Secretary of State as having been made or executed for the purpose of the transfer of property to him or a nominee of his from, or from any subsidiary of, the National Enterprise Board, the Scottish Development Agency or the Welsh Development Agency.

(3) There may be defrayed out of money provided by Parliament any expenditure incurred by the Secretary of State in respect of the acquisition of property by him or a nominee of his from, or from a subsidiary of, the National Enterprise Board, the Scottish Development Agency or the Welsh Development Agency; and any sums received by him on the disposal of property so acquired shall be paid into the Consolidation Fund.

(4) In this section "subsidiary" means a subsidiary as defined by section 154 of the Companies Act 1948 or section 148 of the Companies Act (Northern Ireland) 1960. [43]

NATIONAL ENTERPRISE BOARD
For the establishment and powers of this Board, see the Industry Act 1975, ss. 1–10, Schs. 1, 2, A.L.S. Vol. 241; and note the amendments made by the present Act.

SCOTTISH DEVELOPMENT AGENCY
For the establishment and powers of this body, see the Scottish Development Agency Act 1975; (c. 69).

WELSH DEVELOPMENT AGENCY
For the establishment and powers of this body, see the Welsh Development Agency Act 1975; and note the amendments made by the present Act.

SECRETARY OF STATE
I.e., one of Her Majesty's Principal Secretaries of State; see the Interpretation Act 1978, s. 5, Sch. 1, A.L.S. Vol. 258. The Secretary of State here concerned is the Secretary of State for Industry or, as respects Wales the Secretary of State for Wales.

COMMISSIONERS OF INLAND REVENUE
This, or the Board of Inland Revenue, is the usual title of the Commissioners appointed under the Inland Revenue Regulation Act 1890, s. 1. For further provisions relating to the Commissioners see ss. 2 *et seq.* of that Act.

CONSOLIDATED FUND
The Consolidated Fund was established under the Consolidated Fund Act 1816, s. 1.

INDUSTRY ACT 1975, S. 7
A.L.S. Vol. 241.

3. Finance for companies transferred to Secretary of State

(1) This section applies to a company if the National Enterprise Board has at any time transferred to the Secretary of State a controlling interest in the company and

the Secretary of State has not since that time ceased to hold such an interest in it.

(2) Subject to subsection (3) below and section 5 of this Act, the Secretary of State may with the approval of the Treasury—

(a) acquire securities of a company to which this section applies,

(b) make loans to such a company on such conditions and at such rates of interest as he may with that approval determine, and

(c) guarantee obligations (arising out of loans or otherwise) incurred by such a company.

(3) The Secretary of State shall not determine a rate of interest in respect of a loan under subsection (2) (b) above which is lower than the lowest rate for the time being determined by the Treasury under section 5 of the National Loans Act 1968 in respect of comparable loans out of the National Loans Fund.

(4) Not later than six months after the end of any financial year in which this section has applied to one or more companies the Secretary of State shall prepare and lay before each House of Parliament a report on the exercise during that year of his powers under subsection (2) above; and the report shall specify in relation to each company which at the end of that year is a company to which this section applies—

(a) particulars of the securities of the company held by the Secretary of State at the end of that year,

(b) the amount then outstanding, otherwise than by way of interest, in respect of any loans to the company made under paragraph (b) of subsection (2) above,

(c) particulars of guarantees then subsisting which were given under paragraph (c) of that subsection in respect of obligations incurred by the company, and

(d) any sums paid to meet guarantees so given, to the extent that they have not by then been repaid.

(5) As soon as practicable after the holding of any general meeting of a company to which this section applies, the Secretary of State shall lay before each House of Parliament a copy of any accounts which, in accordance with any requirement of the Companies Acts 1948 to 1980, are laid before the company at that meeting, and of any documents which are annexed or attached to any such accounts.

(6) Any expenditure incurred by the Secretary of State under subsection (2) above may be defrayed out of money provided by Parliament; and any sums received by him by virtue of this section (including sums received on the disposal of securities acquired by virtue of this section) shall be paid into the Consolidated Fund.

(7) In this section and in section 5 of this Act—

"company" means a company within the meaning of the Companies Act 1948 or the Companies Act (Northern Ireland) 1960,

"controlling interest" means, in relation to a company, shares carrying in the aggregate more than half the voting rights exercisable at general meetings of the company,

"shares" includes stock,

"subsidiary" means a subsidiary as defined by section 154 of the said Act of 1948 or section 148 of the said Act of 1960,

and references to the transfer of securities to or the holding or acquisition of securities by the Secretary of State include references to the transfer of securities to or the holding or acquisition of securities by any nominee of his. **[44]**

SUB-S. (1): NATIONAL ENTERPRISE BOARD; SECRETARY OF STATE
See the notes to s. 2, *ante*.

TRANSFERRED TO THE SECRETARY OF STATE A CONTROLLING INTEREST IN THE COMPANY
Note that a new power to transfer property from the National Enterprise Board to the Secretary of
State is conferred by s. 2, *ante*.

SUB-S. (2): TREASURY
I.e., the Commissioners of H.M. Treasury; see the Interpretation Act 1978, s. 5, Sch. 1, A.L.S.
Vol. 258.

SUB-S. (3): NATIONAL LOANS FUND
This Fund was established by the National Loans Act 1968, s. 1.

SUB-S. (4): NOT LATER THAN SIX MONTHS AFTER
In calculating this period the *dies a quo* is not to be reckoned; see, in particular, *Goldsmiths' Co.* v.
West Metropolitan Rail. Co., [1904] 1 K.B. 1; [1900 – 3] All E.R. Rep. 667, C.A., and *Stewart* v.
Chapman, [1951] 2 K.B. 792; [1951] 2 All E.R. 613. "Months" means calendar months by virtue of
the Interpretation Act 1978, s. 5, Sch. 1, A.L.S. Vol. 258.

FINANCIAL YEAR
I.e., the twelve months ending with 31st March; see the Interpretation Act 1978, s. 5, Sch. 1.

LAY BEFORE . . . PARLIAMENT
For meaning, see the Laying of Documents before Parliament (Interpretation) Act 1948, s. 1(1),
A.L.S. Vol. 56.

SUB-S. (6): CONSOLIDATED FUND
See the note to s. 2, *ante*.

FURTHER PROVISIONS
As to financial limits for the purposes of this section, see s. 5(3) – (8), *post*.

COMPANIES ACT 1948 TO 1980
For the Acts which may be cited by this collective title, see the Companies Act 1980, s. 90(2),
A.L.S. Vol. 270.

COMPANIES ACT 1948
For the meaning of "company", see s. 455(1) of the Act of 1948.

COMPANIES ACT (NORTHERN IRELAND) 1960
1960 c. 22 (N.I.).

4. Public dividend capital

(1) In paragraph 5 of Schedule 2 to the Industry Act 1975 after sub-paragraph (3)
there shall be inserted —

> "(3A) The Board may with the agreement of the Secretary of State, and
> shall if the Secretary of State with the approval of the Treasury requires
> them to do so, make payments to the Secretary of State in reduction of the
> public dividend capital of the Board; and any sums received by the Secretary
> of State in pursuance of this sub-paragraph shall be paid into the
> Consolidated Fund."

(2) (*Applies to Scotland.*)

(3) In paragraph 1 of Schedule 3 to the Welsh Development Agency Act 1975
after sub-paragraph (3) there shall be inserted —

> "(3A) The Agency may with the agreement of the Secretary of State,
> and shall if the Secretary of State with the approval of the Treasury requires
> them to do so, make payments to the Secretary of State in reduction of
> the public dividend capital of the Agency; and any sums received by the

Secretary of State in pursuance of this sub-paragraph shall be paid into the Consolidated Fund." **[45]**

SECRETARY OF STATE; CONSOLIDATED FUND
    See the notes to s. 2, *ante*.

TREASURY
    See the note to s. 3, *ante*.

DEFINITIONS
    For "the Agency" see the Welsh Development Agency Act 1975, s. 1 (1); for "the Board", see the Industry Act 1975, s. 1 (1), A.L.S. Vol. 241; for "public dividend capital", see the Industry Act 1975, Sch. 2, para. 5 (1), or the Welsh Development Agency Act 1975, Sch. 3, para. 1 (1).

INDUSTRY ACT 1975, SCH. 2, PARA. 5(3)
    A.L.S. Vol. 241.

WELSH DEVELOPMENT AGENCY ACT 1975, SCH. 3, PARA. 1(3)
    See 45, Halsbury's Statutes (3rd edn.), p. 2367.

5. Financial limits

(1) In section 8 (2) of the Industry Act 1975, section 13 (3) of the Scottish Development Agency Act 1975 and section 18 (3) of the Welsh Development Agency Act 1975 (which set limits on the amounts outstanding in respect of certain borrowings and other liabilities of the National Enterprise Board and the Scottish and Welsh Development Agencies and their subsidiaries, but enable the Secretary of State to raise the limits) the words from "but" to the end shall cease to have effect.

(2) After section 8 (2) of the Industry Act 1975, there shall be inserted—

"(2A) The Secretary of State may by order provide for the limit specified in subsection (2) above to be reduced or further reduced to such amount not less than £750 million as may be specified in the order.

(2B) Notwithstanding section 38 (2) below, an order under subsection (2A) above may not be revoked or varied by a later order except in connection with the making of a further reduction in the limit specified in subsection (2) above.

(2C) No order shall be made under subsection (2A) above unless a draft of it has been approved by resolution of the House of Commons."

(3) Subject to subsection (4) below, the Secretary of State shall by order specify an amount as the financial limit for the purposes of section 3 of this Act, and may by order increase or further increase the amount so specified.

(4) The aggregate of the amounts for the time being specified under subsection (3) above and in section 8 (2) of the Industry Act 1975 shall not exceed £3,000 million.

(5) The power to make orders under subsection (3) above shall be exercisable by statutory instrument, and no such order shall be made unless a draft of it has been laid before and approved by resolution of the House of Commons.

(6) Subject to subsection (7) below, the aggregate of—

  (*a*) any sums paid by the Secretary of State under this Act in respect of the acquisition of shares in any company which before or immediately after the acquisition was a company to which section 3 of this Act applied,

  (*b*) the amounts outstanding, otherwise than by way of interest, in respect of the general external borrowing of companies to which that section applies, and

  (*c*) any sums paid by the Secretary of State to meet guarantees given under subsection (2) (*c*) of that section, to the extent that they have not been repaid,

shall not exceed the amount which is for the time being the financial limit for the purposes of that section.

(7) The sums paid by the Secretary of State under this Act in respect of the acquisition from the National Enterprise Board of shares in any company shall be treated for the purposes of subsection (6) above as reduced by an amount equal to so much of the debt of the Board assumed under paragraph 6 (1) of Schedule 2 to the Industry Act 1975 on their acquisition of securities of the company as was, immediately before section 3 of this Act applied to the company, treated by virtue of paragraph 5 (2) of that Schedule as part of the Board's public dividend capital.

(8) For the purposes of subsection (6) (*b*) above, the general external borrowing of a company is the aggregate of—

> (*a*) sums borrowed by the company otherwise than from any subsidiary of the company, and
>
> (*b*) sums borrowed by such a subsidiary otherwise than from the company or another such subsidiary.   **[46]**

SUB-S. (1): SHALL CEASE TO HAVE EFFECT
The words which cease to have effect are also repealed by s. 21 (1) and Sch. 2, *post*.

SUB-S. (2): SECRETARY OF STATE
See the note to s. 2, *ante*.

LIMIT SPECIFIED IN SUB-S. (2) ABOVE
The limit specified in the Industry Act 1975, s. 8 (2), A.L.S. Vol. 241, as amended by the Industry Act 1979, s. 1 (2), is £3,000 million.

SUB-S. (5): STATUTORY INSTRUMENT
For provisions as to statutory instruments generally, see the Statutory Instruments Act 1946, A.L.S. Vol. 36.

LAID BEFORE . . . THE HOUSE OF COMMONS
For meaning, see the Laying of Documents before Parliament (Interpretation) Act 1948, s. 1 (1), A.L.S. Vol. 56.

SUB-S. (7): SUMS PAID . . . IN RESPECT OF . . . SHARES, ETC
As to the transfer of property from the National Enterprise Board to the Secretary of State, see s. 2, *ante*; see also s. 3, *ante*.

NATIONAL ENTERPRISE BOARD
See the note to s. 2, *ante*.

PUBLIC DIVIDEND CAPITAL
I.e., public dividend capital as defined by the Industry Act 1975, Sch. 2, para. 5 (1).

DEFINITIONS
For "company", "shares" and "subsidiary" and as to the acquisition of securities by the Secretary of State, see s. 3 (7), *ante*. Note as to "general external borrowing", sub s. (8) above.

INDUSTRY ACT 1975, SS. 8 (2), 38 (2), SCH. 2, PARAS. 5 (2), 6 (1)
A.L.S. Vol. 241.

SCOTTISH DEVELOPMENT AGENCY ACT 1975
1975 c. 69.

WELSH DEVELOPMENT AGENCY ACT 1975, S. 18 (3)
See 45, Halsbury's Statutes (3rd edn.), p. 2354.

ORDERS
The Financial Limits (National Enterprise Board and Secretary of State) Order 1980, S.I. 1980 No. 1211.

6. Restrictions on powers to acquire shares

(1) In section 10 (1) (*b*) of the Industry Act 1975 (which restricts the acquisition of share capital by the Board and their subsidiaries where the value of the consideration, together with that for share capital previously acquired, would exceed £10,000,000) for the words "previously acquired, would exceed £10,000,000" there shall be substituted the words "already held by the Board or any of their subsidiaries, would exceed £5,000,000".

(2) (*Applies to Scotland*).

(3) In section 20 (1) (*b*) of the Welsh Development Agency Act 1975 (which makes similar provision in relation to the Welsh Development Agency, with a limit of £2,000,000) for the words "previously acquired, would exceed £2 million" there shall be substituted the words "already held by the Agency or any of their subsidiaries, would exceed £1,000,000".

(4) Section 10 (3) of the Industry Act 1975, section 14 (3) of the Scottish Development Agency Act 1975 and section 20 (3) of the Welsh Development Agency Act 1975 (savings for powers to form bodies corporate) shall cease to have effect.   **[47]**

SHALL CEASE TO HAVE EFFECT
> The subsections which cease to have effect are also repealed by s. 21 (1) and Sch. 2, *post*.

DEFINITIONS
> For "the Board", see the Industry Act 1975, s. 1 (1), A.L.S. Vol. 241; for "the Agency", see the Welsh Development Agency Act 1975, s. 1 (1); for "subsidiary", see s. 37 (1) of the former Act, or s. 27 (1) of the latter Act.

INDUSTRY ACT 1975, S. 10 (1) (b), (3)
> A.L.S. Vol. 241.

WELSH DEVELOPMENT AGENCY ACT 1975, S. 20 (1) (b), (3)
> See 45, Halsbury's Statutes (3rd edn.), p. 2356.

SCOTTISH DEVELOPMENT AGENCY ACT 1975
> 1969 c. 69.

7. Members and chief executive of the Board

(1) In section 1 of the Industry Act 1975 —

    (*a*) in subsection (2) (membership of the National Enterprise Board) for the word "sixteen" there shall be substituted the word "twelve"; and

    (*b*) subsection (8) (register of members' financial interests) shall cease to have effect.

(2) In Part III of Schedule 1 to the House of Commons Disqualification Act 1975 and in Part III of Schedule 1 to the Northern Ireland Assembly Disqualification Act 1975 there shall be inserted, at the appropriate place in alphabetical order —

"Chief executive of the National Enterprise Board".   **[48]**

NATIONAL ENTERPRISE BOARD
> See the note to s. 2, *ante*.

INDUSTRY ACT 1975, S. 1 (2), (8)
> A.L.S. Vol. 241. S. 1 (8) of that Act is also repealed by s. 21 (1) and Sch. 2, *post*.

HOUSE OF COMMONS DISQUALIFICATION ACT 1975, SCH. 1, PART III
> See 45, Halsbury's Statutes (3rd edn.), p. 1607.

NORTHERN IRELAND ASSEMBLY DISQUALIFICATION ACT 1975, SCH. 1, PART III
See 45, Halsbury's Statutes (3rd edn.), p. 1520.

8. Selective financial assistance under the Industry Act 1972

(1) The Secretary of State shall not after the commencement of this Act give any direction under section 3 of the Industry Act 1975 (exercise by the National Enterprise Board of powers to give selective financial assistance under the Industry Act 1972) other than a direction varying or revoking an earlier direction.

(2) Section 5 of the Scottish Development Agency Act 1975 and section 12 of the Welsh Development Agency Act 1975 (which make corresponding provision in relation to the Scottish and Welsh Development Agencies) shall cease to have effect.   [49]

SECRETARY OF STATE
See the note to s. 2, *ante*.

COMMENCEMENT OF THIS ACT
This Act came into force on receiving the Royal Assent on 30th June 1980.

INDUSTRY ACT 1975, S. 3
A.L.S. Vol. 241.

INDUSTRY ACT 1972
A.L.S. Vol. 204.

SCOTTISH DEVELOPMENT AGENCY ACT 1975
1975 c. 69.

WELSH DEVELOPMENT AGENCY ACT 1975, S. 12
See 45, Halsbury's Statutes (3rd edn.), p. 2349.
That section also repealed by s. 21(1) and Sch. 2, *post*

9. Overseas aid

Section 4 of the Industry Act 1975, section 18 of the Scottish Development Agency Act 1975 and section 3 of the Welsh Development Agency Act 1975 shall cease to have effect.   [50]

SHALL CEASE TO HAVE EFFECT
The sections which cease to have effect are also repealed by s. 21 (1) and Sch. 2, *post*.

INDUSTRY ACT 1975, S. 4
A.L.S. Vol. 241.

SCOTTISH DEVELOPMENT AGENCY ACT 1975
1975 c. 69.

WELSH DEVELOPMENT AGENCY ACT 1975, S. 3
See 45, Halsbury's Statutes (3rd edn.), p. 2346.

The English Industrial Estates Corporation

10. Functions and status of the Corporation

(1) The English Industrial Estates Corporation may, in accordance with directions given under subsection (3) below, —

(*a*) provide, facilitate the provision of, and manage sites and premises in

England for occupation by industrial or commercial undertakings,

(*b*) provide, and facilitate the provision of, means of access, services and other facilities required in connection with sites and premises in England occupied or to be occupied by such undertakings, and

(*c*) dispose for any purpose of land and other property held by the Corporation.

(2) Subject to directions given under subsection (3) below, the Corporation may do anything, whether in England or elsewhere, which is calculated to facilitate or is conducive or incidental to the discharge of their functions, and in particular, without prejudice to the generality of the preceding provisions of this subsection, may—

(*a*) act alone or with other persons, either in partnership or otherwise,

(*b*) acquire land, plant, machinery and equipment and other property,

(*c*) form, or acquire interests in, bodies corporate, and

(*d*) make loans and guarantee obligations (arising out of loans or otherwise) incurred by other persons.

(3) The Secretary of State may give the Corporation general or specific directions and the Corporation shall comply with any such directions.

(4) After the commencement of this Act—

(*a*) the Corporation shall not be regarded as the servant or agent of the Crown or as enjoying any status, immunity or privilege of the Crown, or as exempt from any tax, duty, rate, levy or other charge whatsoever, whether general or local, and

(*b*) the property of the Corporation shall not be regarded as the property of, or property held on behalf of, the Crown.

(5) Planning permission shall be deemed to have been granted under section 29 of the Town and Country Planning Act 1971 in respect of any development initiated by the Corporation before the end of March 1981.

(6) In this section references to the provision of premises include references to the carrying out of any works, and the provision of any plant, machinery or equipment, on or for the purposes of any premises; and references to an industrial or commercial undertaking include references to any activity providing employment.

(7) Subsections (1) to (3) of section 11 of the Local Employment Act 1972 (which are superseded by this section) shall cease to have effect.   [51]

SUB-S. (1): ENGLISH INDUSTRIAL ESTATES CORPORATION
As to the constitution and functions of this Corporation, see the Local Employment Act 1972, ss. 10, 11, Sch. 1, A.L.S. Vol. 204; and note the amendments, etc., made by the present section and ss. 11 *et seq.*, *post*.

ENGLAND
This is defined by the Interpretation Act 1978, s. 5, Sch. 1, A.L.S. Vol. 258.

SUB-S. (2): PERSONS
The expression "person" includes any body of persons, corporate or unincorporate; see the Interpretation Act 1978, s. 5, Sch. 1.

BODIES CORPORATE
For the general law relating to corporations, see 9 Halsbury's Laws (4th Edn.) paras. 1201 *et seq*.

SUB-S. (3): SECRETARY OF STATE
See the note to s. 2, *ante*.

DIRECTIONS
As to directions to the English Industrial Estates Corporation with respect to the power of that

body to borrow from the Commission of the European Communities or from the European Investment Bank, see s. 13, *post*.

SUB-S. (4): COMMENCEMENT OF THIS ACT
This Act came into force on receiving the Royal Assent on 30th June 1980.

TOWN AND COUNTRY PLANNING ACT 1971, S. 29
A.L.S. Vol. 212.

LOCAL EMPLOYMENT ACT 1972, S. 11 (1)–(3)
A.L.S. Vol. 204. Those subsections are also repealed by s. 21 (1) and Sch. 2, *post*.

11. Transfer of land to the Corporation

(1) Any land which, immediately before the commencement of this Act, is vested in a Minister of the Crown subject to a lease to the English Industrial Estates Corporation shall by virtue of this Act vest in the Corporation, subject to all rights, liabilities and obligations relating to it (except those arising out of the lease).

(2) The power to acquire land conferred on the Secretary of State by section 5 of the Local Employment Act 1972 (provision of sites and premises) shall include power to acquire land with a view to transferring it to the English Industrial Estates Corporation.   [52]

LAND . . . SUBJECT TO A LEASE TO THE ENGLISH INDUSTRIAL ESTATES CORPORATION
As to the leasing of land to the Corporation by the Secretary of State, see the Local Employment Act 1972, s. 11 (1), A.L.S. Vol. 204 (repealed by s. 10 (7), *ante*, and s. 21 (1) and Sch. 2, *post*).

COMMENCEMENT OF THIS ACT
This Act came into force on receiving the Royal Assent on 30th June 1980.

ENGLISH INDUSTRIAL ESTATES CORPORATION
See the note to s. 10, *ante*.

LOCAL EMPLOYMENT ACT 1972, S. 5
A.L.S. Vol. 204.

12. Members of the Corporation

In section 10 (2) of the Local Employment Act 1972 (which provides that the English Industrial Estates Corporation shall consist of a chairman and four other members appointed by the Secretary of State) for the words from "four" to "and the members" there shall be substituted the words "such number of other members as the Secretary of State thinks fit; and the members shall be appointed by the Secretary of State and".   [53]

ENGLISH INDUSTRIAL ESTATES CORPORATION
See the note to s. 10, *ante*.

SECRETARY OF STATE
See the note to s. 2, *ante*.

LOCAL EMPLOYMENT ACT 1972, S. 10 (2)
A.L.S. Vol. 204.

13. Power for the Corporation to borrow

(1) The English Industrial Estates Corporation may, in accordance with directions under section 10 (3) of this Act given with the approval of the Treasury,

borrow in any currency from the Commission of the European Communities or from the European Investment Bank, but subject to subsection (2) below.

(2) The aggregate amount outstanding in respect of the principal of sums borrowed under this section shall not exceed £30 million or such greater sum not exceeding £50 million as the Secretary of State may with the approval of the Treasury by order specify.

(3) The power to make orders under this section shall be exercisable by statutory instrument, and no such order shall be made unless a draft of it has been laid before and approved by resolution of the House of Commons.

(4) In section 11 (8) of the Local Employment Act 1972 (receipts of Corporation, with certain exceptions, to be paid over to Secretary of State) after paragraph (*a*) there shall be inserted—

"(*aa*) receipts consisting of sums borrowed under section 13 of the Industry Act 1980; and". **[54]**

ENGLISH INDUSTRIAL ESTATES CORPORATION
See the note to s. 10, *ante*.

TREASURY
See the note to s. 3, *ante*.

BORROW
For Treasury guarantees, see s. 14, *post*.

COMMISSION OF THE EUROPEAN COMMUNITIES
As to the Commission, see the Merger Treaty, Chapter II, Vol. 42A, pp. 350 *et seq*.

EUROPEAN INVESTMENT BANK
As to this Bank, see the E.E.C. Treaty, Articles 129, 130, 42A, Halsbury's Statutes (3rd edn.), p. 138, and the Protocol on the Statute of the European Investment Bank, *ibid.*, p. 139.

SECRETARY OF STATE
See the note to s. 2, *ante*.

STATUTORY INSTRUMENT
See the note to s. 5, *ante*.

LOCAL EMPLOYMENT ACT 1972, S. 11 (8)
A.L.S. Vol. 204.

ORDERS UNDER THIS SECTION
At the time of going to press no order had been made under sub-s. (2) above.

14. Treasury guarantees

(1) The Treasury may guarantee, in such manner and on such condition as they think fit, repayment of the principal of, and the payment of interest on, any sums borrowed under section 13 of this Act.

(2) Immediately after a guarantee is given under this section, the Treasury shall lay a statement of the guarantee before each House of Parliament; and where any sum is issued for fulfilling a guarantee so given the Treasury shall, as soon as possible after the end of each financial year (beginning with that in which the sum is issued and ending with that in which all liability in respect of the principal of the sum and in respect of interest thereon is finally discharged) lay before each House of Parliament a statement relating to that sum.

(3) Any sums required by the Treasury for fulfilling a guarantee under this section shall be charged on and issued out of the Consolidated Fund.

(4) If any sums are issued in fulfilment of a guarantee given under this section,

the Corporation shall make to the Treasury, at such times and in such manner as the Treasury may from time to time direct, payments of such amounts as the Treasury may so direct in or towards repayment of the sums so issued and payments of interest at such rate as the Treasury may so direct on what is outstanding for the time being in respect of sums so issued.

(5) Any sums received under subsection (4) above by the Treasury shall be paid into the Consolidated Fund.   **[55]**

TREASURY; LAY BEFORE . . . PARLIAMENT; FINANCIAL YEAR
See the notes to s. 3, *ante.*

CONSOLIDATED FUND
See the note to s. 2, *ante.*

THE CORPORATION
I.e., the English Industrial Estates Corporation.

15. Expenses of the Corporation

In subsection (9) of section 11 of the Local Employment Act 1972 (certain expenses of the English Industrial Estates Corporation incurred under that section to be defrayed by the Secretary of State) after the word "section" there shall be inserted the words "or under the Industry Act 1980".   **[56]**

LOCAL EMPLOYMENT ACT 1972, S. 11 (9)
A.L.S. Vol. 204.

Grants and other financial assistance for industry

16. Regional development grants

(1) For the Table in section 1 of the Industry Act 1972 (which sets out the expenditure towards which, and the rates at which, grants may be made under that section) there shall be substituted—

Expenditure incurred in	Prescribed percentage
1. Providing a building as part of, or providing works on, qualifying premises in a development area	If the qualifying premises are in a special development area: 22 per cent. If not: 15 per cent.
2. Providing new machinery or plant for use in qualifying premises in a development area	If the qualifying premises are in a special development area: 22 per cent. If not: 15 per cent.

(2) The Regional Development Grants (Variation of Prescribed Percentages) Order 1979 (which is superseded by subsection (1) above) is hereby revoked.

(3) Subsections (1) and (2) above shall not have effect in relation to—

(*a*) expenditure incurred in providing an asset, other than mining works, as part of, or on or for use in, qualifying premises if—

(i) the asset is provided before 1st August 1980, or

(ii) the expenditure was defrayed before 18th July 1979;

(*b*) expenditure incurred in providing a building as part of, or providing works on, qualifying premises in a derelict land clearance area, if the construction of the building or the carrying out of the works was begun before 22nd March 1974;

(*c*) expenditure incurred in providing mining works if—

(i) the works were provided before 1st April 1977, or

(ii) the expenditure was defrayed before 6th August 1976;

(*d*) expenditure incurred in providing new machinery or plant for use in activities which are within Order XX of the Standard Industrial Classification (construction industry) if the machinery or plant was provided before 1st April 1977.

(4) Where, apart from this subsection, the amount of a grant under Part I of the Industry Act 1972 towards expenditure falling within subsection (5) below would be less than 20 per cent. of the expenditure, the amount shall instead be 20 per cent. of the expenditure.

(5) The expenditure falling within this subsection is expenditure incurred—

(*a*) in providing an asset as part of, or on or for use in, qualifying premises in a relevant special development area in such circumstances that, by reason of Article 5 (1) and (4) (*d*) or Article 5A (2) and (5) (*b*) of the Assisted Areas Order 1979, any grant under Part I of the Industry Act 1972 towards the expenditure is to be made at the rate appropriate to a development area which is not a special development area, or

(*b*) in providing a building or works at any time as part of or on qualifying premises in a relevant development area in such circumstances that, by reason of Article 5 (2) and (4) (*d*) of that order, no grant may be made under Part I of that Act towards any expenditure incurred in providing machinery or plant at that time for use in those premises.

(6) In subsection (5) above—

(*a*) "relevant special development area" means an area which became a special development area on the coming into operation of the Assisted Areas Order 1977, the Assisted Areas Order 1979 or the Assisted Areas (Amendment) Order 1979, and

(*b*) "relevant development area" means an area which became a development area on the coming into operation of the Assisted Areas Order 1977, the Assisted Areas (No. 2) Order 1977 or the Assisted Areas Order 1979.

(7) Expressions used in this section and in Part I of the Industry Act 1972 have the same meanings in this section as in that Act.   **[57]**

DEFINITIONS
By virtue, where required, of sub-s. (7) above, for "special development area", see the Industry Act 1972, s. 1 (4), A.L.S. Vol. 204; for "qualifying premises", see s. 2 (1) of that Act; as to "asset provided as part of, or on, or for use in; qualifying premises", see s. 2 (8) of that Act, for "building" and as to "providing a building"; see s. 6 (1) of that Act; for "asset", "derelict land clearance area", "expenditure", "machinery or plant", "mining works", "new", "Standard Industrial Classification" and "works", see s. 6 (2) of that Act; for "development area", see s. 15 of that Act.

INDUSTRY ACT 1972, PART I, S. 1
A.L.S. Vol. 204.

REGIONAL DEVELOPMENT GRANTS (VARIATION OF PRESCRIBED PERCENTAGES) ORDER 1979
S.I. 1979 No. 975. That order was made under the Industry Act 1972, s. 3 (1).

ASSISTED AREAS ORDER 1979
S.I. 1979 No. 837. That order and the other orders mentioned below were made under the Local Employment Act 1972, s. 1, A.L.S. Vol. 204, and the Industry Act 1972, s. 1 (4).

ASSISTED AREAS ORDER 1977
S.I. 1977 No. 683. That order was revoked by the Assisted Areas Order 1979, S.I. 1979 No. 837; see also the note on that order above.

ASSISTED AREAS (AMENDMENT) ORDER 1979
S.I. 1979 No. 1642. That order amends the Assisted Areas Order 1979, S.I. 1979 No. 837; see also the note on that order above.

ASSISTED AREAS (NO. 2) ORDER 1977
S.I. 1977 No. 706. That order was revoked by the Assisted Areas Order 1979, S.I. 1979 No. 837; see also the note on that order above.

17. Assistance under Part II of the Industry Act 1972

(1) For subsection (4) of section 7 of the Industry Act 1972 there shall be substituted —

"(4) Financial assistance shall not be given under this section in the way described in subsection (3) (*a*) above unless the Secretary of State is satisfied that it cannot, or cannot appropriately, be so given in any other way, and the Secretary of State, in giving financial assistance in the way so described, shall not acquire any shares or stock in a company without the consent of that company."

(2) In section 8 (1) of that Act, after paragraph (*b*) there shall be added —

"and

(*c*) the financial assistance cannot, or cannot appropriately, be so provided otherwise than by the Secretary of State."

(3) For subsection (3) of section 8 of that Act there shall be substituted —

"(3) Financial assistance shall not be given under this section in the way described in subsection (3) (*a*) of the last preceding section unless the Secretary of State is satisfied that it cannot, or cannot appropriately, be so given in any other way, and the Secretary of State, in giving financial assistance in the way so described, shall not acquire any shares or stock in a company without the consent of that company".

(4) The provisions of Schedule 1 to this Act (which relate to the limits on the financial assistance that may be given by the Secretary of State under section 8 of that Act) shall have effect. [58]

SECRETARY OF STATE
See the note to s. 2, *ante*.

INDUSTRY ACT 1972, SS. 7 (4), 8
A.L.S. Vol. 204.

Miscellaneous and general

18. Advice for businesses

(1) The Secretary of State may make provision for the giving of advice (whether free of charge or otherwise) to persons carrying on or proposing to carry on a business.

(2) Any expenditure incurred by the Secretary of State by virtue of this section

may be defrayed out of money provided by Parliament.

(3) Not later than six months after the end of any financial year in which this power is used the Secretary of State shall prepare and lay before Parliament a report on the exercise during the year of his powers under this section. **[59]**

SECRETARY OF STATE
See the note to s. 2, *ante*.

PERSONS
See the note to s. 10, *ante*.

NOT LATER THAN SIX MONTHS AFTER; FINANCIAL YEAR; LAY BEFORE PARLIAMENT
See the note to s. 3, *ante*.

19. Planning agreements and disclosure of information

Sections 21 (planning agreements) and 28 to 34 (disclosure of information by companies) of the Industry Act 1975 shall cease to have effect. **[60]**

INDUSTRY ACT 1975, SS. 21, 28–34
A.L.S. Vol. 241. Those sections are also repealed by s. 21 (1) and Sch. 2, *post*.

20. British Shipbuilders: members' interests

Sections 1 (9) and 18 (5) of the Aircraft and Shipbuilding Industries Act 1977 (register of members' financial interests to be kept by Secretary of State) shall cease to have effect in respect of British Shipbuilders. **[61]**

BRITISH SHIPBUILDERS
I.e., one of the bodies constituted under the Aircraft and Shipbuilding Industries Act 1977, s. 1, 47, Halsbury's Statutes (3rd edn.), p. 1368.

21. Repeals and transitional provisions

(1) The enactments mentioned in Schedule 2 to this Act are hereby repealed to the extent specified in column 3 of that Schedule.

(2) Notwithstanding the repeal by this Act of any provision of section 2 (2) of the Industry Act 1975, section 2 (2) of the Scottish Development Agency Act 1975 or section 1 (3) of the Welsh Development Agency Act 1975, the National Enterprise Board, the Scottish Development Agency and the Welsh Development Agency may continue to hold property held by them, and to carry on activities in which they are engaged, at the commencement of this Act. **[62]**

NATIONAL ENTERPRISE BOARD; SCOTTISH DEVELOPMENT AGENCY; WELSH DEVELOPMENT AGENCY
See the notes to s. 2, *ante*.

INDUSTRY ACT 1975, S. 2 (2)
A.L.S. Vol. 241. That subsection is partly repealed by s. 1 (1) (*a*), *ante*, and sub-s. (1) above and Sch. 2, *post*.

SCOTTISH DEVELOPMENT AGENCY ACT 1975
1975 c. 69.

WELSH DEVELOPMENT AGENCY ACT 1975, S. 1 (3)
See 45, Halsbury's Statutes (3rd edn.), p. 2343. That subsection is partly repealed by s. 1 (3) (*c*), *ante*, and sub-s. (1) above and Sch. 2, *post*.

22. Short title and extent

(1) This Act may be cited as the Industry Act 1980.

(2) The provisions of this Act so far as they relate to the Scottish Development Agency extend to Scotland only.

(3) Subject to subsection (2) above, the provisions of this Act except—

    (*a*) sections 10 to 16, and

    (*b*) any other provision so far as it relates to the Welsh Development Agency, extend to Northern Ireland. **[63]**

SCOTTISH DEVELOPMENT AGENCY; WELSH DEVELOPMENT AGENCY
  See the notes to s. 2, *ante*.

SCHEDULES

SCHEDULE 1

Section 17

LIMITS ON FINANCIAL ASSISTANCE UNDER INDUSTRY ACT 1972 SECTION 8

1. Part II of the Industry Act 1972 shall be amended as follows.

2. In subsection (6) of section 8—

    (*a*) after the word "section" in paragraph (*a*) there shall be inserted the words ", other than sums paid in respect of foreign currency guarantees,";

    (*b*) after the word "guaranteed" in paragraph (*b*) there shall be inserted the words "and of any liability under a foreign currency guarantee";

    (*c*) after the words "guarantee under this section" there shall be inserted the words "(other than a foreign currency guarantee)".

3. After subsection (7) of that section there shall be inserted—

"(7A) Subject to section 8A of this Act, the aggregate of—

    (*a*) the liabilities of the Secretary of State under foreign currency guarantees (exclusive of any liability in respect of interest on a principal sum guaranteed by him under this section) and

    (*b*) any sums paid by the Secretary of State in respect of foreign currency guarantees,

less any sums received by the Secretary of State by way of repayment of principal sums paid to meet foreign currency guarantees, shall not at any time exceed the limit specified in subsection (7B) below.

(7B) The said limit shall be 1,000 million special drawing rights, but the Secretary of State may, on not more than four occasions, by order made with the consent of the Treasury increase or further increase that limit by an amount specified in the order, being an amount not exceeding 500 million special drawing rights.

An order under this subsection shall be contained in a statutory instrument, and such an order shall not be made unless a draft of the order has been approved by a resolution of the Commons House of Parliament."

4. In subsection (8) of that section after the word "project" there shall be inserted the words ", excluding sums paid or to be paid in respect of foreign currency guarantees,".

5. After subsection (8) of that section there shall be inserted—

"(9) In this section—

'foreign currency" means any currency other than sterling, including special drawing rights;

'foreign currency guarantee' means a guarantee given under this section by the Secretary of State under which his liability is measured in a foreign currency, whether or not it is to be discharged in a foreign currency, and for this purpose—

    (*a*) a liability measured in sterling but expressed to be subject to a limit in a foreign currency shall be taken to be measured in foreign currency, and

    (*b*) a liability measured in foreign currency but expressed to be subject to a limit

in sterling shall be taken to be measured in sterling;
'guarantee' includes any form of insurance."

6. After section 8 there shall be inserted—

8A. "Limit on foreign currency liabilities: supplementary provisions

(1) The amount to be taken into account under section 8 (7A) of this Act at any time in respect of a liability of the Secretary of State shall, if the amount of the liability is not expressed in special drawing rights, be the equivalent at that time in special drawing rights of the amount of the liability.

(2) The equivalent in special drawing rights of the amount of a liability shall be determined by the Secretary of State—

   (a) by reference to the day on which the guarantee is given, and
   (b) by reference to the last day of each quarter at the end of which the guarantee remains in force,

and shall be so determined having regard to what appears to him to be the appropriate rate of exchange.

(3) A determination made under subsection (2) (a) above shall take effect as from the day by reference to which it is made and (unless it ceases to be required at an earlier date) shall remain in force until the end of the quarter in which the guarantee is given.

(4) A determination made by reference to the last day of the quarter under subsection (2) (b) above shall take effect as from the end of that quarter and (unless it ceases to be required at an earlier date) shall remain in force throughout the next succeeding quarter.

(5) The amount to be taken into account under section 8 (7A) of this Act in respect of a sum paid or received by the Secretary of State otherwise than in special drawing rights shall be an amount determined by him, by reference to the day of payment or receipt and having regard to what appears to him to be the appropriate rate of exchange, as being the equivalent in special drawing rights of that sum.

(6) The limit imposed by section 8 (7A) of this Act may be exceeded if the excess is attributable only to, or to a combination of,—

   (a) a quarterly revaluation;
   (b) the Secretary of State's liability under a guarantee given in pursuance of a previous undertaking of his, so far as the amount to be taken into account for the purposes of the limit in respect of the liability exceeds what it would have been if determined by reference to the day on which the undertaking was given;
   (c) a payment made by the Secretary of State under a guarantee, so far as the amount to be taken into account for the purposes of the limit in respect of the payment exceeds what it would have been if determined by reference to the day on which the guarantee was given.

(7) In this section—

'guarantee' has the same meaning as in section 8 of this Act;
'quarter' means a quarter ending with 31st March, 30th June, 30th September or 31st December in any year;
'quarterly revaluation' means a determination made under subsection (2) (b) above."

[64]

SECRETARY OF STATE
   See the note to s. 2, *ante*.

SPECIAL DRAWING RIGHTS
   This refers to special drawing rights within the meaning of the Articles of Agreement of the International Monetary Fund. For the main provisions relating to special drawing rights, see Articles XV *et seq*. of the Second Amendment to the Articles of Agreement adopted on 24th March 1976 (Cmnd. 7331).

TREASURY
   See the note to s. 3, *ante*.

STATUTORY INSTRUMENT
See the note to s. 5, *ante*.

INDUSTRY ACT 1972, PART II, S. 8
A.L.S. Vol. 204.

ORDERS
At the time of going to press no order had been made under the Industry Act 1972, s. 8 (7B), as inserted by para. 3 above.

SCHEDULE 2

REPEALS   Section 21

Chapter	Short title	Extent of Repeal
1972 c. 5.	The Local Employment Act 1972.	In section 11— subsections (1) to (3); in subsection (4), the words from "but" to "Secretary of State"; subsections (6), (7) and (10) (*a*). In section 13— in subsection (1), the words from "or vested" to "1960"; in subsection (2), the words from "or vested" to "1960" and the words "or vested in". In Schedule 2, paragraph 2.
1972 c. 63.	The Industry Act 1972.	In section 3 (2) (*a*), the words from "or vary the" to "this Act". In section 9, the subsection (5) inserted by paragraph 3 of Schedule 4 to the Scottish Development Agency Act 1975. Section 13 (6). In section 16 (1) (*a*), the words from "and section 5" to "Agency Act 1975".
1975 c. 68.	The Industry Act 1975.	Section 1 (8). In section 2 (2), in paragraph (*b*) the words "reorganisation or", and paragraphs (*c*) and (*d*). Section 4. In section 8, in subsection (2) the words from "but" to the end, and subsection (3). Section 10 (3). Section 21. In section 22, the words from "and" to the end. Sections 28 to 34.

Chapter	Short title	Extent of Repeal
1975 c. 68 (*cont'd*)	The Industry Act 1975 (*cont'd*)	In section 37 (1), the definitions of "the Ministers" and "planning agreement". In section 39 (5), paragraph (*b*) and the word "and" immediately preceding it, and the words from "and the latter Act" to the end. In Schedule 2, paragraph 8 (3). In Schedule 4, paragraphs 1 (*a*), 2 (*a*), 2 (*b*) (i), 3 and 4, and Part II. In Schedule 5, paragraph 9. Schedule 6.
1975 c. 69.	The Scottish Development Agency Act 1975.	Section 2 (1) (*b*). In section 2 (2)— in paragraph (*c*) the word "reorganisation"; paragraph (*f*); at the end of paragraph (*h*), the word "and". Section 5. In section 13— in subsection (2) (*d*), the words from "otherwise" to "Act"; in subsection (3), the words from "but" to the end; subsection (4); in subsection (5) (*a*), subparagraph (iii) and the word "or" immediately preceding it. Section 14 (3). In section 17, the words from "with" to the end. Section 18. In section 20 (5), the words "section 5 of this Act and". In Schedule 2— in paragraph 3 (1), the words from "other than" to "Act"; in paragraph 7 (2), paragraph (*b*) and the word "or" immediately preceding it; paragraph 7 (5). In Schedule 4, paragraphs 3 and 4.
1975 c. 70.	The Welsh Development Agency Act 1975.	Section 1 (2) (*c*). In section 1 (3)— in paragraph (*d*) the word "reorganisation"; paragraph (*e*); at the end of paragraph (*h*), the word "and". In section 1 (11), the words from "in connection" to "above".

Chapter	Short title	Extent of Repeal
1975 c. 70 (*cont'd*)	The Welsh Development Agency Act 1975 (*cont'd*)	Section 3. Section 12. In section 18— in subsection (2) (*d*), the words "otherwise than under section 12 above"; in subsection (3), the words from "but" to the end; subsection (4); in subsection (5) (*a*), subparagraph (iii) and the word "or" immediately preceding it. In section 19, in subsection (3) the words "Subject to subsection (4) below", and subsection (4). Section 20 (3). In Schedule 3— in paragraph 2 (*a*), the words from "without" to "above"; paragraph 3 (4); in paragraph 7 (2), paragraph (*b*) and the word "or" immediately preceding it; paragraph 7 (5); in paragraph 9 (3), the words from "which was" to "but".

[65]

THE TRANSPORT ACT 1980

(1980 c. 34)

PRELIMINARY NOTE

This Act received the Royal Assent on 30th June 1980. For commencement dates for the various Parts of the Act see s. 70 (3), *post*, and the notes thereto. The Act makes various changes in the law relating to transport and road traffic. It replaces (in part re-enacting with amendment) the principal existing provisions relating to public service vehicles in Great Britain, provides for the transfer of the undertaking of the National Freight Corporation to a company limited by shares and makes changes in the arrangements by which Government support is provided for certain pensions obligations of the British Railways Board and the National Freight Corporation.

PUBLIC SERVICE VEHICLES

Part I (ss. 1 – 44) of the Act is concerned with public service vehicles, and s. 1, *post*, sets out the main purposes for which Part I is enacted and repeals certain provisions of the Road Traffic Act 1960, Part III, A.L.S. Vol. 124 and the whole of the Transport Act 1968, s. 30, A.L.S. Vol. 178, which are superseded.

Definition and classification of public service vehicles

S. 2, as read with Sch. 1, *post*, defines "public service vehicle" in a new way which excludes from licensing small vehicles (no more than eight passenger seats) in which passengers are carried otherwise than in the course of a business of carrying passengers. Journeys in such small vehicles on which the fares taken do not exceed the running costs are treated as not being made in the course of a business of carrying passengers.

S. 3, as read with Sch. 1, *post*, reclassifies stage, express and contract carriages. Express carriages are newly defined, in particular by reference to a minimum length of passenger journey (30 miles). Restrictions are removed which prevent certain vehicles carrying passengers at separate fares from being treated as contract carriages where any of the passengers makes the journey frequently or as a matter of routine. Restrictions on advertising by certain travel clubs are removed.

Road service licences

Ss. 4 – 11, *post*, replace the provisions in the Road Traffic Act 1960, ss. 134 – 140, A.L.S. Vol. 124, relating to road service licences.

S. 4, *post* requires road service licences to be obtained for the operation of stage carriage services. The requirement of the Road Traffic Act 1960, s. 134, A.L.S. Vol. 124, for licences for the operation of express carriage services is removed.

S. 5, *post*, deals with the grant of road service licences; it revises the criteria to which traffic commissioners must have regard in exercising their licensing function and creates a presumption in favour of the applicant.

Ss. 6 and 7, *post*, empower the commissioners to attach, vary or remove conditions to road service licences in certain circumstances. S. 7, *post*, limits the power to attach conditions about fares to particular cases where it is essential in the interests of the public either to prevent a licence holder using his position unreasonably or to regulate the terms of competition between services sharing a route.

S. 8, *post*, provides for the automatic grant of road service licences for services on routes where the traffic commissioners are satisfied that there are no other transport facilities available (replacing the Transport Act 1968, s. 30, A.L.S. Vol. 178.

S. 9, *post*, provides for the automatic grant of road service licences where the traffic commissioners are satisfied that the service would be an excursion or tour and either would not compete with other licensed services (other than excursions or tours) or would operate only to enable passengers to attend special events.

S. 10, *post*, contains provisions for the revocation or suspension of a road service licence.

S. 11, *post*, extends from three to five years the normal duration of a road service licence.

Trial areas

Ss. 12−15, *post*, enable trial areas to be designated in which road service licences are not to be required.

S. 12, as read with Sch. 2, *post*, enables the Minister of Transport to designate trial areas on application from a county council. The local authority is required to publish its proposals before making an application. An order may be varied or revoked by the Minister, but only on application from the local authority concerned and after such minimum period (of between two and five years) as is specified in the order.

S. 13, *post*, provides that in a trial area no road service licence is required for a stage carriage service.

S. 14, *post*, requires the operator of any stage carriage service in a trial area to notify to the local authority and the relevant district councils, and to publish details of the service he intends to provide and of any change in it or any discontinuance of it.

S. 15, *post*, provides that in a trial area there is to be a relaxation of the public passenger transport operators' duties to co-operate with and afford information to one another.

Fitness of public service vehicles

Ss. 16−18, *post*, are concerned with the fitness of public service vehicles.

S. 16, *post* (following provisions in the Road Traffic Act 1960, s. 128 (3), A.L.S. Vol. 124 empowers certifying officers and public service vehicle examiners to inspect public service vehicles and for that purpose to detain vehicles and to enter premises where vehicles are. The Minister is also empowered to provide stations (and equipment) where inspections may be carried out and to designate premises for that purpose.

S. 17, *post* (replacing the provisions of the Road Traffic Act 1960, s. 129, A.L.S. Vol. 124, which relate to certificates of fitness) requires all public service vehicles to have a certificate of initial fitness or a certificate that the vehicle conforms to an approved type.

S. 18, *post*, empowers certifying officers and public service vehicle examiners to prohibit the driving of unfit public service vehicles. This replaces the comparable power in the Road Traffic Act 1960, s. 133, A.L.S. Vol. 124 (suspension of the public service vehicle licence) which falls with the replacement of public service vehicle licensing by operator licensing. The power is similar to that given to goods vehicle examiners by the Road Traffic Act 1972, ss. 56 – 58, A.L.S. Vol. 208, as amended. The section also contains provisions as to the removal of prohibition and appeals in respect of a refusal to make such a removal.

Public service vehicle operators' licences

Ss. 19 – 27, *post*, provide for a system of public service vehicle operator licensing. This replaces the present system of public service vehicle licensing under the Road Traffic Act 1960, s. 127, A.L.S. Vol. 124.

S. 19, *post*, requires vehicles used as stage, express or contract carriages to be used under a PSV operator's licence and empowers the traffic commissioners to grant such licences.

S. 20, *post*, divides PSV operators' licences into standard and restricted licences. Restricted licences are valid only for the use of vehicles with under nine passenger seats, and vehicles with between nine and sixteen passenger seats if not used commercially or not used by a person whose main occupation is carrying passengers in vehicles.

S. 21, as read with Sch. 3, *post*, requires the traffic commissioners to be satisfied of the applicant's good repute, financial standing and (in the case of a standard licence) of his professional competence. There are also requirements relating to the operators' vehicle maintenance facilities and arrangements for securing compliance with the law relating to the driving and operation of vehicles. The normal duration of a licence is five years but the commissioners may fix a shorter term.

S. 22, *post*, enables the commissioners to attach conditions to licences and to vary such conditions.

S. 23 as read with Sch. 3, *post*, provides that the commissioners by whom a standard licence was granted shall revoke the licence if it appears to them that the holder ceases to satisfy any of the requirements of good repute, financial standing and professional competence, and that the commissioners may, on certain specified grounds, revoke, suspend or curtail any licence (standard or restricted) or vary certain conditions attached to it or attach new conditions.

S. 24, *post*, requires that vehicles being used in circumstances such that PSV operators' licences are required should display an operator's disc with prescribed particulars on it.

S. 25, *post*, requires an applicant or licence-holder to inform the commissioners of any relevant conviction of himself or his employees, of any bankruptcy of the holder or similar event, and of any change in the identity of his transport manager.

S. 26, *post*, follows the Road Traffic Act 1960, S. 132, A.L.S. Vol. 124, in requiring notification to the traffic commissioners of damage to, or structural alteration in, a public service vehicle. It also requires a holder of an operator's licence to give the commissioners such information as they may require about the public service vehicles owned by him.

S. 27, *post*, enables persons who wish to carry on a road passenger transport business or to be the transport manager of such a business in any other member state of the EEC or in Northern Ireland to apply to the commissioners for an appropriate certificate of qualification.

Supplementary provisions relating to licences

Ss. 28 – 31, *post*, deal with supplementary matters relating to road service licences and PSV operator's licences.

S. 28, *post*, provides for rights of appeal to the Minister for applicants for licences or licence-holders, and for certain other persons having standing in the matter, against decisions of the traffic commissioners.

S. 29, *post*, provides for further appeals to the High Court on points of law.

S. 30, *post*, provides that regulations may be made modifying the statutory provisions relating to public services in their application to the operation of vehicles by persons in partnership, and that licences are not to be granted to unincorporated bodies or joint ventures except where permitted by regulations.

S. 31, *post*, provides that licences are not assignable and outlines the circumstances in which licences are to terminate.

Other matters

Ss. 32−44, *post*, deal with other matters connected with public service vehicles.

S. 32, *post*, provides that a local education authority may use a school bus to carry fare-paying passengers or to provide a local bus service.

S. 33, *post*, amends the Minibus Act 1977, A.L.S. Vol. 254, to bring that Act in line with the new concepts introduced by this Act.

S. 34, *post*, removes, by amendment to the Road Traffic Act 1972, s. 44 (4), A.L.S. Vol. 208, the exemption of public service vehicles adapted to carry eight or more passengers from the requirements of ss. 43 and 44 of that Act, 1686, which relate to obligatory test certificates. This will allow regulations to be made requiring the annual testing of all large passenger vehicles, including public service vehicles.

S. 35, *post*, inserts new sections in the Transport (London) Act 1969, which provide for an appeal to the Minister against a refusal by the London Transport Executive to enter into an agreement to enable another person to provide a London bus service, or to vary an existing agreement, and for further appeals to the High Court on points of law.

S. 36, *post*, abolishes the licensing of conductors of public service vehicles.

S. 37, *post*, provides for the reduction of the minimum age for driving large passenger vehicles from 21 to 18 but only in certain specified circumstances.

S. 38, *post*, provides for the charging of fees on application for and grant of the licences and certificates provided for under the Act, and for tests (where these are required) for applicants for public service driver licences.

S. 39, *post*, revises the arrangements for appointing traffic commissioners.

S. 40 and Sch. 4, *post*, increase the penalties for various offences under the Road Traffic Act 1960, A.L.S. Vol. 124.

S. 41, *post*, provides that directors and managers, etc., of companies may be held liable for any offence under Part I of the Act or Part III of the Act of 1960, A.L.S. Vol. 124 committed with their consent, etc.

S. 42, *post*, makes certain defences available to persons charged with certain offences under Part I of the Act or under the Act of 1960.

S. 43 (1) and Sch. 5, *post*, amend the Act of 1960 and various other Acts to take account of the changes made by this Act, and s. 43 (2), *post*, gives the Minister power to modify or revoke any existing restriction or prohibition on the running of public service vehicles which is contained in a local Act or an instrument.

S. 44, *post*, contains general provisions relating to the interpretation of Part I of the Act.

TRANSFER OF UNDERTAKING OF NATIONAL FREIGHT CORPORATION

Part II (ss. 45−51) of the Act deals with the transfer of the undertaking of the National Freight Corporation to a company limited by shares.

S. 45 and Sch. 6, *post*, provide for the transfer, on a day to be appointed, of the undertaking of the National Freight Corporation, to a successor company formed and nominated for this purpose by the Minister and for the extinguishment immediately before that day of the Corporation's commencing capital debt and outstanding loans from the Minister.

S. 46, *post*, provides for the successor company to issue securities to the Minister or his nominees in consideration of the transfer of the Corporation's undertaking and requires the consent of the Treasury to any disposal of such securities.

S. 47, *post*, contains provisions relating to the treatment of reserves and dividends by the successor company following the transfer of the Corporation's undertaking.

S. 48, *post*, provides for the dissolution of the National Freight Corporation on the appointed day and requires the successor company to prepare a statement of the Corporation's final accounts and to arrange for their auditing.

S. 49, *post*, enables proceeds of the sale of securities of the successor company, which would otherwise fall to be paid into the Consolidated Fund under s. 46 (5), *post*, to be applied towards funding of certain of the obligations of the company or of its subsidiaries to its pension schemes which have not been funded at the time of the sale.

S. 50, *post*, defines the obligations which may thus be funded. They are, with certain exceptions, obligations of the successor company or of its subsidiaries which were obligations of the Corporation or of the subsidiaries concerned at 1st April 1975, and obligations arising after that date to pay increases in pensions not exceeding the increases granted to public service pensioners under the Pensions (Increase) Act 1971, 41, Halsbury's Statutes (3rd edn.) p. 1065.

S. 51 and Sch. 7, *post*, contain provisions relating to the interpretation of Part II of the Act and consequential amendments of the Transport Act 1968.

RAILWAY ETC. PENSIONS

Part III (ss. 52–60) of the Act alters the method by which Government financial assistance is being provided towards the fulfilment of certain obligations (the "relevant pension obligations") owed by the British Railways Board and the National Freight Corporation to certain of their pension schemes.

S. 52, *post*, places an obligation on the Minister to make payments each year to the persons responsible for administering each of the pension schemes in respect of which there are relevant pension obligations. The amount of the payment in respect of any scheme and of any year is to be a fixed proportion (the unfunded proportion determined under s. 54, *post*) of the pensions payments which are made by the scheme in that year and which correspond to the relevant pension obligations.

S. 53, *post*, defines the relevant pension obligations as, with certain exceptions the obligations owed by the Board on 1st January 1975 and by the Corporation on 1st April 1975 in connection with the pension schemes listed in s. 60 and Sch. 8, *post*, obligations of the Board and of the Corporation or the successor company arising after those dates to pay increases in pensions not exceeding those payable on official pensions under the Pensions (Increase) Act 1971, 41, Halsbury's Statutes (3rd edn.), p. 1065, and, in the case of the Corporation, obligations arising between 1st April 1975 and 1st January 1980 as a result of statutory instruments made under the Transport Act 1962, 26, Halsbury's Statutes (3rd edn.) p. 925. In the case of the Corporation, the obligations are limited to obligations relating to employees and former employees in that part of the Corporation's business which was transferred to the Corporation from the Board under the Transport Act 1968, A.L.S. Vol. 178.

S. 54, *post*, provides for the Minister or the actuary to the scheme to determine, for each of the pension schemes concerned, the proportion of the relevant pension obligations which is unfunded.

S. 55, *post*, provides for the determination, in relation to each pension scheme concerned and to each financial year, of the total amount of the pensions payments made by the scheme in that year and of the proportion of that total which corresponds to the relevant pension obligations in relation to the scheme.

S. 56, *post*, provides that, in certain circumstances, where a pension scheme has been certified by its actuary to be in surplus, in relation to a B.R. or N.F.C. pension scheme, the obligation to pay increases of pensions payable under that other pension scheme is to be disregarded as a relevant pension obligation for the purposes of any determination under s. 55 (1), *post*.

S. 57, *post*, provides that the transfer of pension rights from B.R. or N.F.C. pension scheme to other pension schemes is to be disregarded with respect to certain determinations.

S. 58, *post*, repeals the Railways Act 1974, ss. 5, 6, 44, Halsbury's Statutes (3rd edn.) pp. 1297, 1299 and the Transport Act 1978, ss. 19, 20, A.L.S. Vol. 265, and orders made thereunder which are superseded by Part III and provides for payments made under those provisions on or after 1st April 1980 to be treated as advance payments under s. 52, *post*.

S. 59, *post*, contains supplemental provisions to secure the continuance of the relevant pension obligations and to permit the rules of schemes to be amended to bring them into conformity with Part III.

S. 60 and Sch. 8, *post*, define certain terms used in Part III and list the pension schemes in relation to which there are relevant pension obligations.

MISCELLANEOUS AND GENERAL

Part IV (ss. 61 – 70) of the Act contains miscellaneous and general provisions.

S. 61, *post*, by amendment to the Road Traffic Act 1972, s. 148, A.L.S. Vol. 208 provides that any insurance policy or security which insures a vehicle with respect to its private use is to cover the use of that vehicle under car-sharing arrangements.

S. 62, *post*, redefines the vehicles which qualify for new bus grant and the services which qualify for fuel duty rebate in consequence of the changes in classification in s. 3, *post*, and excludes services not available to the general public from qualifying.

S. 63, *post*, provides that certain articulated passenger vehicles should be treated as single motor vehicles thus making them eligible to be treated as public service vehicles. They are distinguished from articulated vehicles generally by specified structural characteristics.

S. 64, *post*, provides that outside the metropolitan police district and the City of London, vehicles which are not taxis are not to carry roof signs which suggest that the vehicle is a taxi.

S. 65, *post*, repeals the Transport Charges etc. (Miscellaneous Provisions) Act 1954, s. 2, Sch. 1, A.L.S. Vol. 88 which relate to charges on certain tramways, trolley vehicles and railways of the nature of a tramway.

S. 66, *post*, abolishes the Freight Integration Council and repeals provisions of the Transport Act 1968, Part V, A.L.S. Vol. 178, which deal with special authorisations for the use of large goods vehicles but which were never brought into force.

S. 67, *post*, abolishes the Railways and Coastal Shipping Committee.

S. 69 and Sch. 9, *post*, make repeals consequential on the foregoing provisions of the Act.   **[66]**

ARRANGEMENT OF SECTIONS

PART I

PUBLIC SERVICE VEHICLES

Preliminary

PART II

TRANSFER OF UNDERTAKING OF NATIONAL FREIGHT CORPORATION

Transfer of undertaking of National Freight Corporation to a company limited by shares

Funding of certain pension obligations

Supplementary

PART III

RAILWAY ETC. PENSIONS

PART IV

MISCELLANEOUS AND GENERAL

An Act to amend the law relating to public service vehicles; to make provision for and in connection with the transfer of the undertaking of the National Freight Corporation to a company; to provide for the making of payments by the Minister of Transport in aid of certain railway and other pension schemes; to amend Part VI of the Road Traffic Act 1972 as regards car-sharing arrangements; to make amendments about articulated vehicles; to prohibit the display of certain roof-signs on vehicles other than taxis; to abolish the Freight Integration Council and the Railways and Coastal Shipping Committee; to repeal certain provisions about special authorisations for the use of large goods vehicles and about charges on independent tramways, trolley vehicles and the like; and for connected purposes [30th June 1980]

NORTHERN IRELAND
This Act applies in part as indicated in s. 70 (7), *post*.

PART I

PUBLIC SERVICE VEHICLES

Preliminary

1. Preliminary

(1) The purposes for which this Part is enacted include—

- (*a*) redefining and reclassifying public service vehicles;
- (*b*) abolishing road service licences for express carriages as redefined;
- (*c*) making it easier for applicants to obtain road service licences, and restricting the power to attach thereto conditions as to fares;
- (*d*) providing for the designation of areas as trial areas in which road service licences are not required for stage carriage services;
- (*e*) making new provision for securing the fitness of public service vehicles;
- (*f*) substituting a system of public service vehicle operators' licences for the system of public service vehicle licences; and
- (*g*) providing an appeal against a refusal by the London Transport Executive to enter into an agreement with a person other than the Executive for the provision of a London bus service;

and accordingly the provisions mentioned in subsection (2) (which, except so far as they are re-enacted with or without alteration in this Part, are no longer required) shall cease to have effect.

(2) Those provisions are—

- (*a*) in the Road Traffic Act 1960—

  - (i) sections 117 and 118 and Schedule 12 (classification of public service vehicles);
  - (ii) sections 127, 129 and 132 to 133A (licensing and fitness of public service vehicles); and
  - (iii) sections 134 to 140 (road service licences);

- (*b*) section 30 of the Transport Act 1968 (permits for certain bus services in lieu of road service licences).

(3) This Part and the 1960 Act shall be construed and have effect as if this Part (except so far as it textually amends any enactment) were contained in Part III of that Act; and section 44 of this Act shall apply for the interpretation of the said Part III as well as for the interpretation of this Part.

(4) Without prejudice to subsection (3), any reference to, or to Part III of, the 1960 Act in any statutory provision not contained in this Part or the 1960 Act shall, unless the context otherwise requires, be construed as including a reference to this Part. **[67]**

COMMENCEMENT
See s. 70 (5), *post*, and the note "Orders under this section" thereto.

THIS PART
 I.e., Part I (ss. 1 – 44) of this Act. Note that the expression "this Part" in sub-ss. (3) and (4) above
is to include a reference to the Transport Act 1978, s. 5, as substituted by s. 43 (1) and Sch. 5, Part
II, *post*; see s. 5 (8) of that Act as so substituted.

REDEFINING AND RECLASSIFYING PUBLIC SERVICE VEHICLES
 See ss. 2 and 3, *post*.

ABOLISHING ROAD SERVICE LICENCES FOR EXPRESS CARRIAGES AS REDEFINED
 For the public service vehicles which require a road service licence, see s. 4, *post*.

MAKING IT EASIER . . . AS TO FARES
 For the granting of road service licences, see ss. 5, 8 and 9, *post*; and for the attachment to road
service licences of conditions as to fares, see s. 7, *post*.

PROVIDING FOR THE DESIGNATION OF AREAS AS TRIAL AREAS . . . STAGE CARRIAGE SERVICES
 See s. 12, *post*.

MAKING NEW PROVISION FOR SECURING THE FITNESS OF PUBLIC SERVICE VEHICLES
 See ss. 16 – 18, *post*.

SUBSTITUTING A SYSTEM OF PUBLIC SERVICE VEHICLES OPERATORS' LICENCES, ETC
 See ss. 19 – 26, *post*.

PROVIDING AN APPEAL AGAINST A REFUSAL BY THE LONDON TRANSPORT EXECUTIVE, ETC
 See s. 35, *post*.

DEFINITIONS
 For "public-service vehicle", see s. 2, *post*, for "express carriage", see s. 3 (1) (*b*), *post*; for "trial
area", see s. 12 (1), *post*; for "road service licence" and "stage carriage service", see s. 44 (1), *post*;
for "statutory provision", see s. 70 (2), *post*; for "fares", see, by virtue of sub-s. (3) above, the Road
Traffic Act 1960, s. 257 (1), A.L.S. Vol. 124.

ROAD TRAFFIC ACT 1960
 For Part III and ss. 117, 118, 127, 129, 132, 133, 134 – 140 of, and Sch. 12 to, that Act, see A.L.S.
Vol. 124; s. 133A was added by the Road Traffic Act 1974, s. 10 (7), Sch. 2, para. 5, A.L.S.
Vol. 226. The provisions which cease to have effect are also repealed by s. 69 and Sch. 9, Part I,
post.

TRANSPORT ACT 1968, S. 30
 See A.L.S. Vol. 178. That section is also repealed by s. 69 and Sch. 9, Part I, *post*.

1960 ACT
 I.e., the Road Traffic Act 1960; see s. 44 (1), *post*. See, further, the note on that Act above.

Definition and classification of public service vehicles

2. Definition of "public service vehicle"

(1) Subject to the provisions of this section, in this Part "public service vehicle"
means a motor vehicle (other than a tramcar) which —

   (*a*) being a vehicle adapted to carry more than eight passengers, is used for
          carrying passengers for hire or reward; or
   (*b*) being a vehicle not so adapted, is used for carrying passengers for hire or
          reward at separate fares in the course of a business of carrying
          passengers.

   (2) For the purposes of subsection (1) a vehicle "is used" as mentioned in paragraph (*a*) or (*b*) of that subsection if it is being so used or if it has been used as mentioned in that paragraph and that use has not been permanently discontinued.
   (3) A vehicle carrying passengers at separate fares in the course of a business of

carrying passengers, but doing so in circumstances in which the conditions set out in Part I, II or III of Schedule 1 are fulfilled, shall be treated as not being a public service vehicle unless it is adapted to carry more than eight passengers.

(4) For the purposes of this section a journey made by a vehicle in the course of which one or more passengers are carried at separate fares shall not be treated as made in the course of a business of carrying passengers if —

(*a*) the fare or aggregate of the fares paid in respect of the journey does not exceed the amount of the running costs of the vehicle for the journey; and

(*b*) the arrangements for the payment of fares by the passenger or passengers so carried were made before the journey began;

and for the purposes of paragraph (*a*) the running costs of a vehicle for a journey shall be taken to include an appropriate amount in respect of depreciation and general wear.

(5) For the purposes of this section, section 3 and Schedule 1 —

(*a*) a vehicle is to be treated as carrying passengers for hire or reward if payment is made for, or for matters which include, the carrying of passengers, irrespective of the person to whom the payment is made and, in the case of a transaction effected by or on behalf of a member of any association of persons (whether incorporated or not) on the one hand and the association or another member thereof on the other hand, notwithstanding any rule of law as to such transactions;

(*b*) a payment made for the carrying of a passenger shall be treated as a fare notwithstanding that it is made in consideration of other matters in addition to the journey and irrespective of the person by or to whom it is made;

(*c*) a payment shall be treated as made for the carrying of a passenger if made in consideration of a person's being given a right to be carried, whether for one or more journeys and whether or not the right is exercised.

(6) Where a fare is paid for the carriage of a passenger on a journey by air, no part of that fare shall be treated for the purposes of subsection (5) as paid in consideration of the carriage of the passenger by road by reason of the fact that, in case of mechanical failure, bad weather or other circumstances outside the operator's control, part of that journey may be made by road. **[68]**

COMMENCEMENT
See s. 70 (5), *post*, and the note "Orders under this section" thereto.

SUB-S. (1): THIS PART
I.e., Part I (ss. 1 – 44) of this Act.

PUBLIC SERVICE VEHICLE
As to the classification of public service vehicles as stage, express or contract carriages, see s. 3, *post*, and for provisions relating to the fitness of public service vehicles, see ss. 16 – 18, *post*.

At any time when a vehicle would, apart from sub-s. (3) above, be a public service vehicle, it is to continue to be treated as such for the purpose only of provisions contained in a local Act or in the Local Government (Miscellaneous Provisions) Act 1976, Part II, A.L.S. Vol. 252, as amended by s. 43 (1) and Sch. 5, Part II, *post*, which regulate the use of private hire vehicles provided for hire with the services of a driver for the purpose of carrying passengers and exclude public service vehicles from the scope of that regulation; see the Transport Act 1978, s. 7 (3), A.L.S. Vol. 265, so amended.

MOTOR VEHICLE
As to the treatment of articulated vehicles for the purposes of this Part of this Act, see the Road Traffic Act 1972, s. 191, as substituted by s. 63, *post*.

VEHICLE . . . USED FOR CARRYING PASSENGERS FOR HIRE OR REWARD
As to roof signs which may not be displayed on vehicles used for carrying passengers for hire or reward other than taxis, see s. 64, *post*

ADAPTED
This term is ambiguous inasmuch as it may either have the meaning of changed or altered or transformed (see, e.g., *Davidson* v. *Birmingham Industrial Co-operative Society* (1920), 90 L.J.K.B. 206; and see also *Flower Freight Co., Ltd.,* v. *Hammond,* [1963] 1 Q.B. 275; [1962] 3 All E.R. 950, and the cases there cited) or that of fit or apt or suitable (see e.g. *Herrmann* v. *Metropolitan Leather Co., Ltd.,* [1942] Ch. 248; [1942] 1 All E.R. 294; *Maddox* v. *Storer,* [1963] 1 Q.B. 451; [1962] 1 All E.R. 831; *Burns* v. *Currell,* [1963] 2 Q.B. 433; [1963] 2 All E.R. 297; *Wurzal* v. *Addison,* [1965] 2 Q.B. 131; [1965] 1 All E.R. 20). It is thought that in this context "adapted" means "fit or apt or suitable".

IN THE COURSE OF A BUSINESS OF CARRYING PASSENGERS
Note as to this expression sub-s. (4) above. Something is done "in the course of" a business if it is done as part of its activities; cf. *Charles R. Davidson & Co.* v. *M'Robb (or Officer),* [1918] A.C. 304, at p. 321, *per* Lord Dunedin. See also *London Borough of Havering v. Stevenson,* [1970] 3 All E.R. 609, and *Wycombe Marsh Garages, Ltd.* v. *Fowler,* [1972] 3 All E.R. 248. On the meaning of "business", see 38 Halsbury's Laws (3rd Edn.), pp. 10, 11 and 1 Words and Phrases (2nd Edn.), pp. 100 *et seq.*

SUB-S. (3): SHALL BE TREATED AS NOT BEING A PUBLIC SERVICE VEHICLE
Where, in the case of any private or commercial vehicle, the use of the vehicle within any particular area, or on any particular journey, is covered by an authorisation under the Passenger Vehicles (Experimental Areas) Act 1977, s. 2, A.L.S. Vol. 254, then in relation to its use in that area or on that journey in circumstances in which the relevant conditions are fulfilled, the vehicle in question is not to be treated as a public service vehicle for the purposes of this Part of this Act; see the Passenger Vehicles (Experimental Areas) Act 1977, s. 2 (8), (which also defines "the relevant conditions"), as amended by s. 43 (1) and Sch. 5, Part II, *post,* and as construed in accordance with s. 1 (4), *ante.* See also the note "Experimental areas" to s. 14, *post.*
If a small passenger-carrying vehicle is used for carrying passengers for hire or reward, it is nevertheless to be treated as not being a public service vehicle if and so long as the conditions set out in the Minibus Act 1977, s. 1 (1) (*a*) — (*c*), A.L.S. Vol. 254, are satisfied; see s. 1 (1) of that Act as amended by s. 33 (1), *post;* and for the meaning of "small passenger-carrying vehicles", see s. 4 (2) (*bb*) of that Act as inserted by s. 33 (7), *post.*

SUB-S. (5): CARRYING PASSENGERS FOR HIRE OR REWARD
Sub-s. (5) (*a*) is applied by the Passenger Vehicles (Experimental Areas) Act 1977, s. 2 (9), A.L.S. Vol. 254, as amended by s. 43 (1) and Sch. 5, Part II, *post,* and the Minibus Act 1977, s. 4 (2) (*c*), A.L.S. Vol. 254, as so amended.

PERSON
This expression includes a body of persons corporate or unincorporate; see the Interpretation Act 1978, s. 5, Sch. 1, A.L.S. Vol. 258.

IN CONSIDERATION OF OTHER MATTERS IN ADDITION TO THE JOURNEY
This covers the case of passengers travelling with market produce for the transport of which no separate charge is made; see *Drew* v. *Dingle,* [1934] 1 K.B. 187; [1933] All E.R. Rep. 518. (Note that in that case the same charges would, it was said, have been made if the market produce alone had been carried.)

IRRESPECTIVE OF THE PERSON BY OR TO WHOM IT IS MADE
For illustrations of the application of this part of sub-s. (5) (*b*), see *Wurzal* v. *Addison,* [1965] 2 Q.B. 131; [1965] 1 All E.R. 20, and *Wurzal* v. *Wilson,* [1965] 1 All E.R. 26.

DEFINITIONS
For "operator", see s. 44 (2), (3), *post;* by virtue of s. 1 (3), *ante,* for "motor vehicle", see the Road Traffic Act 1960, s. 253 (1), A.L.S. Vol. 124, and for "fares", "road" and "tramcar", see s. 257 (1) of that Act. Note also as to "is used", sub-s. (2) above, and as to "carrying passengers for hire or reward", "fare" and "payment made for the carrying of a passenger", sub-s. (5) above.

3. Classification of public service vehicles as stage, express or contract carriages

(1) For the purpose of this Part —

(*a*) a "stage carriage" is a public service vehicle being used in the operation of a local service;

(*b*) an "express carriage" is a public service vehicle being used in the operation of an express service; and

(*c*) a "contract carriage" is a public service vehicle being used to carry passengers otherwise than at separate fares;

and references in this Part to use as a stage, express or contract carriage shall be construed accordingly.

(2) In this section —

(*a*) "local service" means a service for the carriage of passengers by road at separate fares, not being an express service;

(*b*) "express service" means a service for the carriage of passengers by road at separate fares, being a service as regards which the conditions specified in subsection (3) are satisfied.

(3) The conditions referred to in subsection (2) (*b*) are —

(*a*) except in the case of an emergency, either of the following requirements as to length of journey is satisfied in respect of every passenger using the service, namely —

(i) the place where he is set down is 30 miles or more, measured in a straight line, from the place where he was taken up; or

(ii) some point on the route between those places is 30 miles or more, measured in a straight line, from either of those places; and

(*b*) either —

(i) the service is an excursion or tour; or

(ii) the prescribed particulars of the service (including the route and the timetable) and of every change of any prescribed kind made in the service have, not later than the prescribed time for doing so, been notified in the prescribed manner to the traffic commissioners in whose area the place specified in the notification as the beginning of the route is situated.

(4) Where, in the case of any service for the carriage of passengers by road at separate fares, the condition specified in subsection (3) (*a*) is satisfied as regards any part of the service taken in isolation, but not as regards the service as a whole —

(*a*) that part of the service shall be treated for the purposes of subsections (2) (*b*) and (3) as a separate service (and will accordingly be an express service if the condition specified in subsection (3) (*b*) is satisfied as regards it); and

(*b*) any part of the service which is not an express service by virtue of the preceding paragraph shall be treated for the purposes of this section as a separate local service.

(5) A public service vehicle carrying passengers at separate fares shall be treated as a contract carriage, and not as a stage carriage or an express carriage, when used in circumstances in which the conditions set out in Part II or III of Schedule 1 are fulfilled.   [69]

COMMENCEMENT
see s. 70 (5), *post*, and the note "Orders under this section" thereto.

SUB-S. (1): THIS PART
I.e., Part I (ss. 1 – 44) of this Act.

Before operating a stage carriage service, a person generally has to comply with the following provisions of this Part of this Act—

    (i) ss. 4, *et seq., post* (obtaining a road service licence); see s. 4 (1), *post.*
    (ii) s. 17, *post* (obtaining a certificate of initial fitness (or equivalent)); see s. 17 (1), *post.*
    (iii) ss. 19 *et seq., post* (obtaining a PSV operator's licence); see s. 19 (1), *post.*

As to grants towards duty charged on bus fuel used in operating a stage carriage service which qualifies as "bus service" within the meaning of the Finance Act 1965, s. 92 (8), as substituted by s. 62 (1), *post,* see s. 92 of that Act, A.L.S. Vol. 151 as amended by ss. 43 (1) and 62 (1) and Sch. 5, Part II, *post,* and as partly repealed by s. 69 and Sch. 9, Part I, *post*; and as to grants towards the cost of providing new vehicles for use wholly or mainly in the operation of a stage carriage service which qualifies as a "bus service" within the meaning of s. 92 (8) of the Act of 1965 as substituted by s. 62 (1), *post,* see the Transport Act 1968, s. 32, A.L.S. Vol. 178, as amended by s. 62 (2), *post.*

As to the use of a school bus to provide a stage carriage service other than a service as regards which the condition specified in sub-s. (3) (*a*) above is satisfied, see s. 32, *post.*

EXPRESS CARRIAGE; CONTRACT CARRIAGE

Before operating an express carriage service or a contract carriage service, a person generally has to comply with the provisions of this Part of this Act mentioned in heads (ii) and (iii) of the first paragraph of the preceding note.

SUB-S. (3): PRESCRIBED

I.e., prescribed by regulations made under the Road Traffic Act 1960, s. 160, A.L.S. Vol. 124; see, by virtue of s. 1 (3), *ante,* s. 160 (2) of that Act. See the Public Service Vehicles (Road Service Licences and Express Services) Regulations 1980, S.I. 1980 No. 1354.

TRAFFIC COMMISSIONERS

As to the constitution and function of the traffic commissioners, see the Road Traffic Act 1960, s. 120, A.L.S. Vol. 124.

DEFINITIONS

For "public service vehicle", see s. 2, *ante*; for "excursion or tour", see s. 44 (1), *post*; by virtue of s. 1 (3), *ante,* for "the traffic commissioners", see the Road Traffic Act 1960, s. 120 (4), A.L.S. Vol. 124, for "prescribed", see s. 160 (2) of that Act, for "road", see s. 257 (1) of that Act, and for "fares", see s. 257 (1) of that Act, (and see also s. 2 (5) (*b*), *ante*). Note as to "stage carriage", "express carriage" and "contract carriage", sub-s. (1) above (and note also sub-s. (5) above), and as to "local service" and "express service", sub-s. (2) above.

Road service licences

4. Road service licences

(1) Subject to section 13 and to the provisions of section 23 of the Transport (London) Act 1969 as to London bus services, a stage carriage service shall not be provided except under a road service licence granted in accordance with the following provisions of this Part.

(2) The authority having power to grant a road service licence in respect of a stage carriage service is the traffic commissioners for any traffic area in which the service is proposed to be provided, not being an area in which passengers will be neither taken up nor set down in the course of the service; and a road service licence authorises the holder to provide the service specified in the licence in the area of the traffic commissioners by whom it was granted and in any other traffic area in which passengers are neither taken up nor set down in the course of the service.

(3) Where a stage carriage service is proposed to be provided on a route running through more than one traffic area, a separate road service licence is required for each traffic area in which passengers will be either taken up or set down in the course of the service.

(4) Subject to subsection (5) and section 9 (2), a road service licence granted by the traffic commissioners for any traffic area shall be of no effect at any time at

which the holder does not also hold a PSV operator's licence granted by the commissioners for that or any other traffic area, not being a licence which is at that time of no effect by reason of its suspension.

(5) Subsection (4) does not apply —

> (*a*) to a road service licence held by a local education authority or, in Scotland, an education authority;
>
> (*b*) to a road service licence granted in respect of a community bus service within the meaning of section 5 of the Transport Act 1978.

(6) If a stage carriage service is provided in contravention of subsection (1), the operator of the service shall be liable on summary conviction to a fine not exceeding £200.

(7) If a condition attached under section 6 or 7 to a road service licence is contravened, the holder of the licence shall be liable on summary conviction to a fine not exceeding £200.

(8) A road service licence is required for a stage carriage service notwithstanding that the provision of such a service is authorised under Part V of the Road Traffic Act 1930 or by a special Act or an order having the force of an Act.   **[70]**

COMMENCEMENT
See s. 70 (5), *post*, and the note "Orders under this section" thereto.

SUB-S. (1): FOLLOWING PROVISIONS OF THIS PART
As to road service licences, see, in particular, ss. 5 *et seq., post*.

SUB-S. (2): TRAFFIC COMMISSIONERS
See the note to s. 3, *ante*.

TRAFFIC AREA
As to the constitution of traffic areas, see the Road Traffic Act 1960, s. 119, A.L.S. Vol. 124.

SUB-S. (5): LOCAL EDUCATION AUTHORITY
Local education authorities are defined by the Education Act 1944, s. 6 (1), Sch. 1, Part I, 11, Halsbury's Statutes (3rd edn.), pp. 159, 265, together with the London Government Act 1963, s. 30, A.L.S. Vol. 138A and the Local Government Act 1972, ss. 1 (10), 20 (6), 792 (1).

SUB-S. (6): SHALL BE LIABLE
Any offence under this Part of this Act is a traffic offence for the purposes of the Road Traffic Act 1972, s. 8, A.L.S. Vol. 208; see s. 8 (8) of that Act, as construed in accordance with s. 1 (4), *ante*.

It is a defence for a person charged with an offence under sub-s. (6) or (7) above or s. 17 (3), 18 (8) (*b*), 19 (5), 22 (7) or 24 (4), *post*, to prove that he took all reasonable precautions and exercised all due diligence to avoid the commission of the offence; see s. 42 (3), (4), *post*.

As to offences by bodies corporate, see s. 41, *post*.

SUMMARY CONVICTION
Summary jurisdiction and procedure are mainly governed by the Magistrates' Courts Act 1952, A.L.S. Vol. 125, the Magistrates' Courts Act 1957, A.L.S. Vol. 104, and certain provisions of the Criminal Justice Act 1967, A.L.S. Vol. 163 and of the Criminal Law Act 1977, A.L.S. Vol. 249. Procedural provisions are also contained in rules made under the Justices of the Peace Act 1949, s. 15, A.L.S. Vol. 224. The relevant enactments are repealed and replaced by the Magistrates' Courts Act 1980 (to be included in a later issue of this service), as from a day to be appointed under s. 155 (7) of that Act.

SUB-S. (7): OF A CONDITION, ETC
Sub-s. (7) above applies also in relation to a condition attached under the Transport Act 1978, s. 5 (2), as substituted by s. 43 (1) and Sch. 5, Part II, *post*; see s. 5 (6) of that Act as so substituted.

SHALL BE LIABLE
See the note to sub-s. (6) above.

STANDS FOR HACKNEY CARRIAGES

Hackney carriage stands are not to be appointed so as to impede the use of any points authorised to be used in connection with a road service licence or PSV operator's licence granted under this Part of this Act as points for the taking up or setting down of passengers, see the Local Government (Miscellaneous Provisions Act 1976, s. 63 (3), A.L.S. Vol. 252, as amended by s. 43 (1) and Sch. 5, Part II, *post*).

PASSENGER TRANSPORT AREAS

By the Transport Act 1968, s. 19 (1), A.L.S. Vol. 178, the following provisions apply to any passenger transport area (designated area) designated by s. 9 (1) of the Act of 1968, as modified by the Local Government Act 1972, s. 202, A.L.S. Vol. 209, where the Minister of Transport by order so directs: —

(i) no person other than the Passenger Transport Executive established by order under s. 9 (1) of the Act of 1968, A.L.S. Vol. 178 or s. 202 (4) of the Act of 1972, A.L.S. Vol. 209 or a subsidiary of theirs may provide an area bus service (as defined by s. 159 (1) of the Act of 1968, in that area except in pursuance of an agreement with that Executive or, in the case of an existing service (as defined by Sch. 6, para. 1, to that Act), with the consent of the Executive granted under that Schedule (s. 19 (2) of the Act of 1968; see also the second limb of that subsection and s. 19 (4) of that Act.

(ii) notwithstanding anything in the Road Traffic Act 1960, Part III, A.L.S. Vol. 124, or, by virtue of s. 1 (4), *ante*, in this part of this Act, no road service licence is to be required for the provision of any bus service (as defined by s. 159 (1) of the Act of 1968 as substituted by s. 43 (1) and Sch. 5, Part II, *post*) operated wholly within the designated area in question, and where such a licence is granted in respect of a bus service operated in part as an area bus service (as so defined) in the designated area, no condition is to be attached to the licence with respect to the carriage of passengers who are both taken up and set down in that area (s. 19 (3) of the Act of 1968).

PUBLIC SERVICE VEHICLES PROVIDING INTERNATIONAL PASSENGER SERVICES

By the Road Transport (International Passenger Services) Regulations 1973, S.I. 1973 No. 806 (made under the European Communities Act 1972, s. 2 (2), A.L.S. Vol. 205 and the Road Traffic Act 1960, s. 160 (1), Parts III, IV, Sch. 2, as amended by the Road Transport (International Passenger Services) (Amendment) Regulations 1979, S.I. 1979, No. 654, regs. 5 — 9, and as construed in accordance with the Interpretation Act 1978, ss. 17 (2) (*a*), 23 (2), A.L.S. Vol. 258:

(i) Part III of the Act of 1960, A.L.S. Vol. 124 and, by virtue of s. 1 (4), *ante*, this part of this Act have effect in relation to public service vehicles which are used to provide international passenger services of a certain kind, as though this section and s. 144 of the Act of 1960, as amended by ss. 36, 37 (1), 40 and 43 (1) and Sch. 4 and Sch. 5, Part I, para. 4, *post*, were omitted therefrom, and as though the requirements of s. 19, *post*, were, in some cases, nullified, and, in others, replaced;

(ii) Part III of the Act of 1960, A.L.S. Vol. 124 and by virtue of s. 1 (4), *ante*, this Part of this Act have effect in relation to public service vehicles which are brought temporarily into Great Britain for the purpose of the international carriage of passengers, as though this section and s. 144 of the Act of 1960, as amended by ss. 36, 37 (1), 40 and 43 (1) and Sch. 4 and Sch. 5, Part I, para. 4, *post*, were omitted therefrom, and as though the requirements of s. 19, *post*, were, in some cases, nullified, and, in others, replaced.

FURTHER PROVISIONS

See, further, in connection with road service licences, s. 5, *post* (grant of road service licences); s. 6, *post* (attachment to road service licences of conditions as to matters other than fares); s. 7, *post* (attachment to road service licences of conditions as to fares); s. 8, *post* (grant of road service licences for services on routes not otherwise served); s. 9, *post* (grant of road service licences for certain excursions or tours); s. 10, *post* (revocation and suspension of road service licences); s. 11, *post* (duration of road service licences); and s. 31, *post* (death, bankruptcy, etc., of licence-holder).

EXCLUSIONS

If a large passenger-carrying vehicle is used for carrying passengers for hire or reward, then, if and so long as the conditons set out in the Minibus Act 1977, s. 1 (*a*) — (*c*), A.L.S. Vol. 254 are ratified, this section and s. 19 (1), *post*, do not apply to the driving or use of the vehicle; see s. 1 (1A) of that Act as inserted by s. 33 (1), *post*; and for the meaning of "large passenger-carrying vehicle", see s. 4 (2) (*bb*) of that Act as inserted by s. 33 (7), *post*.

DEFINITIONS

For "contravention", "contravene", "PSV operator's licence", "road service licence" and "stage carriage service", see s. 44 (1), *post*; for "operator", see s. 44 (2), (3), *post*; for "the traffic commissioners", see, by virtue of s. 1 (4), *ante*, the Road Traffic Act 1960, s. 120 (4), A.L.S. Vol. 124.

TRANSPORT (LONDON) ACT 1969, S. 23
See A.L.S. Vol. 185. That section is amended by s. 43 (1) and Sch. 5, Part II, *post*, and is partly repealed by s. 69 and Sch. 9, Part I, *post*.

TRANSPORT ACT 1978, S. 5
As to the meaning of "community bus service", see sub-s. (8) of that section as substituted by s. 43 (1) and Sch. 5, Part II, *post*.

ROAD TRAFFIC ACT 1930, PART V
See A.L.S. Vol. 79.

5. Grant of road service licences

(1) An application for a road service licence shall be made in such form as the traffic commissioners may require, and an applicant shall give the commissioners such information as they may reasonably require for disposing of the application.

(2) Where an application for the grant of a road service licence is made, the traffic commissioners —

> (a) shall grant the licence unless they are satisfied that to do so would be against the interests of the public; and
>
> (b) if they grant the licence, shall do so in accordance with the application except to the extent that they are satisfied that to do so would be against the interests of the public.

(3) In considering under subsection (2) whether the grant of a licence would be against the interests of the public, or the extent to which the grant of a licence in accordance with the application would be against those interests, the traffic commissioners shall in particular have regard to —

> (a) the transport requirements of the area as a whole (including so much as is relevant not only of the commissioners' own traffic area but also of adjoining traffic areas) and of particular communities in the area;
>
> (b) any transport policies or plans which have been made by the local authorities concerned and have been drawn to the commissioners' attention by those authorities; and
>
> (c) any objections or other representations made to the commissioners in the prescribed manner which in their opinion are relevant.

(4) In subsection (3) "the local authorities concerned" means —

> (a) in Greater London, the Greater London Council;
>
> (b) elsewhere in England and Wales, county councils; and
>
> (c) *(applies to Scotland)*.

(5) The traffic commissioners, on granting a road service licence, shall send notice thereof, including particulars of the services to be provided thereunder, to the chief officer of police of every police district in which any such service is to be provided and to each of the following councils in whose area any such service is to be provided, that is to say —

> (a) the Greater London Council, any London borough council and the Common Council of the City of London;
>
> (b) any county council or district council in England or Wales; and
>
> (c) *(applies to Scotland)*.

[71]

COMMENCEMENT
See s. 70 (5), *post*, and the note "Orders under this section" thereto.

SUB-S. (1): TRAFFIC COMMISSIONERS
As to the appropriate traffic commissioners, see s. 4 (2), *ante*. See, also, the note to s. 3, *ante*.

SUB-S. (2): GRANT THE LICENCE
A road service licence is not to be granted to an unincorporated body as such or to more than one person jointly except in cases permitted by regulations under s. 30, *post*; see s. 30 (2), *post*.

SATISFIED
For a discussion concerning the effect of the use of this and similar expressions such as "appears" or "in the opinion" on the power of the court to review administrative action, see 1 Halsbury's Laws (4th Edn.), para. 22.

AGAINST THE INTERESTS OF THE PUBLIC
Note, in this connection, the provisions of sub-s. (3) above. See also, for cases on the meaning of "public", "the public" and "member of the public" in various contexts, *Tatem Steam Navigation Co., Ltd.* v. *Inland Revenue Comrs.*, [1941] 2 K.B. 194; [1941] 2 All E.R. 616, C.A.; *Income Tax Comrs.* v. *Bjordal*, [1955] A.C. 309; [1955] 1 All E.R. 401, P.C.; *Director of Public Prosecutions* v. *Milbanke Tours, Ltd.*, [1960] 2 All E.R. 467; *Morrisons Holdings, Ltd.* v. *Inland Revenue Comrs.* [1966] 1 All E.R. 789; *Inland Revenue Comrs.* v. *Park Investments, Ltd.*, [1966] Ch. 701; [1966] 2 All E.R. 785, C.A.; *R.* v. *Delmayne*, [1970] 2 Q.B. 170; [1969] 2 All E.R. 980, C.A.; *Beynon* v. *Caerphilly Lower Licensing Justices*, [1970] 1 All E.R. 618; and *Attorney-General's Reference (No. 2 of 1977)*, [1978] 2 All E.R. 646, C.A.

SUB-S. (3): TRAFFIC AREA
See the note to s. 4, *ante*.

PRESCRIBED
I.e., prescribed by regulations made under the Road Traffic Act 1960, s. 160, A.L.S. Vol. 124; see, by virtue of s. 1 (3), *ante*, s. 160 (2) of that Act. See The Public Service Vehicles (Road Service Licences and Express Services) Regulations 1980, S.I. 1980 No. 1354.

SUB-S. (4): GREATER LONDON
I.e., the London boroughs, the City of London and the Inner and Middle Temples; see the London Government Act 1963, s. 2 (1), A.L.S. Vol. 138A.

GREATER LONDON COUNCIL
This council is constituted by the Local Government Act 1972, s. 8, Sch. 2, A.L.S. Vol. 209.

ENGLAND; WALES
For meanings, see the Interpretation Act 1978, s. 5, Sch. 1, A.L.S. Vol. 258.

COUNTY COUNCILS
See the note "County council; district council" to sub-s. (5) below.

SUB-S. (5): SHALL SEND NOTICE, ETC
As to the notice which the traffic commissioners must send on revoking or suspending a road service licence, see s. 10 (3), *post*.

CHIEF OFFICER OF POLICE; POLICE DISTRICT
These expressions are defined by the Police Act 1964, s. 62, Sch. 8, A.L.S. Vol. 148.

LONDON BOROUGH COUNCIL
As to London boroughs, see the Interpretation Act 1978, s. 5, Sch. 1, A.L.S. Vol. 258; and as to the London boroughs and their councils, see the London Government Act 1963, s. 1, Sch. 1, A.L.S. Vol. 138A, and the Local Government Act 1972, s. 8, Sch. 2, A.L.S. Vol. 209.

COMMON COUNCIL OF THE CITY OF LONDON
I.e., the mayor, aldermen and commons of the City of London in common council assembled; see the City of London (Various Powers) Act 1958, s. 5, 20, Halsbury's Statutes (3rd edn.), p. 398.

COUNTY COUNCIL; DISTRICT COUNCIL
As to counties and districts and their councils, see the Local Government Act 1972, ss. 1 (1) − (4), 2, Sch. 1, Parts I, II, A.L.S. Vol. 209 (England) and ss. 20 (1) − (3), 21, Sch. 4, Parts I, II, (Wales).

APPEALS
As to appeals from decisions of the traffic commissioners, see ss. 28 and 29, *post*.

By s. 4 (1), *ante*, the necessity of obtaining a road service licence for London is subject to the provisions of the Transport (London) act 1969, s. 23, A.L.S. Vol. 185, as amended by s. 43 (1) and Sch. 5, Part II, *post*, and as partly repealed by s. 69 and Sch. 9, Part I, *post*. Note also that this section and ss. 6 – 11 and 28, *post*, are excluded by Sch. 4, para. 1, to that Act, as construed in accordance with the Interpretation Act 1978, s. 17 (2) (*a*), A.L.S. Vol. 258.

PASSENGER TRANSPORT AREA
See the note to s. 4, *ante*.

CONDITIONS
For the attachment to road service licences of conditions as to matters other than fares, see s. 6, *post*; and for the attachment to road service licences of conditions as to fares, see s. 7, *post*.

COMMUNITY BUS SERVICE
For provisions which apply where a road service licence is granted under this section in respect of a community bus service, see the Transport Act 1978, s. 5 (1) – (9), as substituted by s. 43 (1) and Sch. 5, Part II, *post*.

FEES
As to the fees which are to be charged by the traffic commissioners in respect of applications for, and the grant of, road service licences and PSV operators' licences and in respect of applications for, and the issue of certificates of initial fitness under s. 17, *post*, see the Road Traffic Act 1960, s. 159 (1) (*a*) (i), (ii), as substituted by s. 38, *post*. For the actual fees payable in respect of road service licences, PSV operators' licences and certificates of initial fitness, see the Public Service Vehicles (Licences and Certificates) Regulations 1952, S.I. 1952 No. 900, regs. 44 (as amended by S.I. 1976 No. 1113 and S.I. 1980 No. 635), 17 (as substituted by S.I. 1957 No. 1118 and amended by S.I. 1962 No. 1058, S.I. 1969 No. 32, S.I. 1976 No. 1113 and S.I. 1980 No. 635), 24 (as amended by S.I. 1957 No. 1118, S.I. 1969 No. 32, S.I. 1976 No. 1113 and S.I. 1980 No. 635), respectively; 22 Halsbury's Statutory Instruments, title Transport (Part 2c), which will, if still in force when those provisions come into operation, have effect for the purposes of this section and ss. 17 and 21, *post*.
If the relevant fees have been paid, the traffic commissioners may decline to proceed with the application in question; see s. 159 (1A) of the Act of 1960 as substituted by s. 38, *post*.

EXTENSION
This section and s. 6, *post*, apply, with modifications, to the grant of road service licences for services on routes not otherwise served; see s. 8 (1), *post*.

EXCLUSION
Sub-ss. (2) – (4) above and ss. 6 and 7, *post*, do not apply to the grant of road service licences for certain excursions or tours; see s. 9 (1), *post*.

PARTNERSHIPS
Provision may be made by regulations for modifying the provisions of this Part in their application to the operation of vehicles and the provision of services by persons in partnership; see s. 30 (1), *post*.

DEFINITIONS
For "road service licence", see s. 44 (1), *post*; by virtue of s. 1 (3), *ante*, for "the traffic commissioners", see the Road Traffic Act 1960, s. 120 (4), A.L.S. Vol. 124, and for "prescribed", see s. 160 (2) of that Act. Note as to "the local authorities concerned", sub-s. (4) above.

6. Attachment to road service licences of conditions as to matters other than fares

(1) Subject to subsection (2) and to any regulations, traffic commissioners granting a road service licence may attach to the licence such conditions as they think fit having regard to the interests of the public, and in particular to the matters mentioned in section 5 (3) (*a*) to (*c*), and may in particular attach thereto such conditions as they think fit (having regard as aforesaid) for securing —

    (*a*) that suitable routes are used in providing any service which may be provided under the licence;

(*b*) that copies of the timetable and fare-table are carried and are available for inspection in vehicles used on any such service;

(*c*) that passengers are not taken up or are not set down except at specified points, or are not taken up or not set down between specified points,

and generally for securing the safety and convenience of the public, including persons who are disabled.

(2) No such condition as to fares as is mentioned in section 7 (1) shall be attached under this section to a road service licence.

(3) The traffic commissioners by whom a road service licence was granted may at any time while it is in force vary the licence by—

(*a*) altering, in such manner as they think fit having regard to the interests of the public, any condition attached to the licence; or

(*b*) removing any condition attached to the licence, if they think fit having regard to those interests; or

(*c*) attaching to the licence any such condition or additional condition as they think fit having regard to those interests.

(4) Where the holder of such a licence makes an application to the traffic commissioners requesting them to exercise their powers under subsection (3), the commissioners shall exercise those powers in accordance with the application except to the extent that they are satisfied that to do so would be against the interests of the public.

(5) Compliance with any condition attached to a road service licence under this section may be temporarily dispensed with by the traffic commissioners by whom the licence was granted if they are satisfied—

(*a*) that compliance with the condition would be unduly onerous by reason of circumstances not foreseen when the condition was attached or, if the condition has been altered, when it was last altered; and

(*b*) that such a dispensation would not be against the interests of the public.

[72]

COMMENCEMENT
See s. 70 (5), *post*, and the note "Orders under this section" thereto.

SUB-S. (1): TRAFFIC COMMISSIONERS GRANTING A ROAD SERVICE LICENCE
I.e., under s. 5, *ante*, or s. 8, *post*.

THINK FIT
See the note "Satisfied" to s. 5, *ante*.

INTERESTS OF THE PUBLIC
See the note "Against the interests of the public" to s. 5, *ante*.

OFFENCE
For the offence of contravening a condition attached under this section, ss. 4 (7), *ante*.

PASSENGER TRANSPORT AREAS
See the note to s. 4, *ante*.

APPEALS; LONDON; PARTNERSHIPS
See the notes to s. 5, *ante*.

PERMISSIBLE RELAXATIONS OF ROAD TRAFFIC AND TRANSPORT LAW
A person acting under and in accordance with a general or special authority granted by the Secretary of State under the Energy Act 1976, s. 4 (2), 46, Halsbury's Statutes (3rd edn.), p. 2066, may provide any stage carriage service or use any vehicle on a road as a stage carriage, an express carriage or a contract carriage notwithstanding that any conditions attached to any licence under this Part are not complied with; see Sch. 1, para. 1 (1), to that Act, as amended by s. 43 (1) and Sch. 5, Part II, *post*.

EXTENSION
See the note to s. 5, *ante*.

EXCLUSIONS
See the note "Exclusion" to s. 5, *ante*, and note that the powers conferred by sub-ss. (3) and (5) above to alter, remove or dispense from compliance with conditions attached to a road service licence do not apply to conditions attached to a road service licence granted in respect of a community bus service under the Transport Act 1978, s. 5 (2), as substituted by s. 43 (1) and Sch. 5, Part II, *post*; see the last limb of the said s. 5 (2).

DEFINITIONS
For "road service licence", see s. 44 (1), *post*; by virtue of s. 1 (3), *ante*, for "the traffic commissioners", see the Road Traffic Act 1960, s. 120 (4), A.L.S. Vol. 124 and for "regulations", see s. 160 (2) of that Act.

REGULATIONS UNDER THIS SECTION
See The Public Service Vehicles (Road Service Licences and Express Services) Regulations 1980, S.I. 1980 No. 1354.
By virtue of s. 1 (3), *ante*, for general provisions as to regulations, see the Road Traffic Act 1960, ss. 160, 260, A.L.S. Vol. 124, as amended by s. 43 (1) and Sch. 5, Part I, paras. 11 and 15, respectively, *post*, and as partly repealed, in the case of s. 160, by s. 69 and Sch. 9, Part I, *post*.

7. Attachment to road service licences of conditions as to fares

(1) Subject to subsection (3) and any regulations, traffic commissioners may (whether at the time when the licence is granted or at any time thereafter, and whether or not in response to any particulars received by them under this Part) attach to a road service licence granted by them conditions or additional conditions as to the fares, or the minimum or maximum fares, which may be charged for services provided under the licence.

(2) Subject to subsection (3), the traffic commissioners by whom a road service licence was granted may at any time while it is in force vary the licence by—

   (a) altering in such manner as they think fit any condition as to fares attached under subsection (1) to the licence; or

   (b) removing any condition as to fares so attached to the licence.

(3) The traffic commissioners shall not exercise their powers under subsection (1) or their powers of alteration under subsection (2) in any particular case unless satisfied that the proposed exercise of those powers in that case is essential in the interests of the public—

   (a) to protect the public from unreasonable use by the holder of the licence of his position as such; or

   (b) to regulate the terms of competition between stage carriage services on any route or routes.

(4) Where the holder of a road service licence makes an application to the traffic commissioners requesting them to exercise their powers (whether of alteration or removal) under subsection (2), the commissioners—

   (a) shall remove all the conditions attached under subsection (1) to the licence except to the extent that they are satisfied that it is essential in the interests of the public to maintain them, with or without alteration, for one or both of the purposes mentioned in paragraphs (a) and (b) of subsection (3); and

   (b) shall not exercise their powers of alteration under subsection (2) unless satisfied that the proposed exercise of those powers is consistent with their reasons for not removing all the conditions attached under subsection (1) to the licence.

(5) Compliance with any condition attached to a road service licence under

subsection (1) may be temporarily dispensed with by the traffic commissioners by whom the licence was granted if they are satisfied—

(*a*) that compliance with the condition would be unduly onerous by reason of circumstances not foreseen when the condition was attached or, if the condition has been altered, when it was last altered; and

(*b*) that such a dispensation would not be against the interests of the public.

(6) Where it is proposed to make any change in the fares charged for any service provided under a road service licence, it shall be the duty of the holder of the licence to supply to the traffic commissioners, not later than the prescribed time before the date of the proposed change, the prescribed particulars of the proposed change.

(7) A person who fails to supply within the prescribed time any particulars which he is required to supply under subsection (6) shall be liable on summary conviction to a fine not exceeding £200.

(8) A person who in purporting to comply with subsection (6) supplies any particulars which he knows to be false or does not believe to be true shall be liable on summary conviction to a fine not exceeding £500.   **[73]**

COMMENCEMENT
See s. 70 (5), *post*, and the note "Orders under this section" thereto.

SUB-S. (1): TRAFFIC COMMISSIONERS
See the note to s. 3, *ante*.

THIS PART
I.e., Part I (ss. 1 − 44) of this Act.

ROAD SERVICE LICENCE GRANTED BY THEM
I.e., under s. 5, *ante*, or s. 8, *post*.

CONDITIONS
The conditions mentioned in sub-s. (1) above are not to be attached to road service licences under s. 6, *ante*; see s. 6 (2), *ante*.

SUB-S. (2): THINK FIT
See the note "Satisfied" to s. 5, *ante*.

SUB-S. (3): SATISFIED
See the note to s. 5, *ante*.

INTERESTS OF THE PUBLIC
See the note "Against the interests of the public" to s. 5, *ante*.

PRESCRIBED
I.e., prescribed by regulations made under the Road Traffic Act 1960, s. 160, A.L.S. Vol. 124; see, by virtue of s. 1 (3), *ante*, s. 160 (2) of that Act. See The Public Service Vehicles (Road Service Licences and Express Services) Regulations 1980, S.I. 1980 No. 1354.

SUB-S. (7): PERSON
See the note to s. 2, *ante*.

SHALL BE LIABLE
See the first and third paragraphs of the note to s. 4, *ante*.
It is a defence for a person charged with an offence under sub-s. (7) above or s. 14 (6), 25 (5) or 26 (4), *post*, to prove that there was a reasonable excuse for the act or omission in respect of which he is charged; see s. 42 (1), (2), *post*.

SUMMARY CONVICTION
See the note to s. 4, *ante*.

SUB-S. (8): FALSE
A statement may be false on account of what it omits even though it is literally true; see *R.* v. *Lord Kylsant*, [1932] 1 K.B. 442; [1931] All E.R. Rep. 179, and *R.* v. *Bishirgian*, [1936] 1 All E.R. 586; and cf. *Curtis* v. *Chemical Cleaning and Dyeing Co., Ltd.*, [1951] 1 K.B. 805; [1951] 1 All E.R. 631, C.A., at pp. 808, 809 and 634, respectively. Whether or not gain or advantage accrues from the false statement is irrelevant; see *Jones* v. *Meatyard*, [1939] 1 All E.R. 140, and *Stevens and Steeds, Ltd. and Evans* v. *King*, [1943] 1 All E.R. 314.

PASSENGER TRANSPORT AREAS
See the note to s. 4, *ante*.

APPEALS; LONDON; PARTNERSHIPS; EXCLUSION
See the corresponding notes to s. 5, *ante*.

PERMISSIBLE RELAXATIONS OF ROAD TRAFFIC AND TRANSPORT LAW
See the note to s. 6, *ante*.

OFFENCE
For the offence of contravening a condition attached to this section, see s. 4 (7), *ante*.

DEFINITIONS
For "road service licence" and "stage carriage service", see s. 44 (1), *post*; by virtue of s. 1 (3), *ante*, for "the traffic commissioners", see the Road Traffic Act 1960, s. 120 (4), A.L.S. Vol. 124, and for "prescribed" and "regulations", see s. 160 (2) of that Act.

REGULATIONS UNDER THIS SECTION
See The Public Service Vehicles (Road Service Licences and Express Services) Regulations 1980, S.I. 1980 No. 1354.
By virtue of s. 1 (3), *ante*, for general provisions as to regulations, see the Road Traffic Act 1960, ss. 160, 260, A.L.S. Vol. 124 as amended by s. 43 (1) and Sch. 5, Part I, paras. 11 and 15, respectively; *post*, and as partly repealed, in the case of s. 160, by s. 69 and Sch. 9, Part I, *post*.

8. Grant of road service licences for services on routes not otherwise served

(1) If, in the case of any application for a road service licence, the traffic commissioners are satisfied that there are no other transport facilities available to meet the reasonable needs of the route on which the service which the applicant proposes to provide under the licence would operate —

    (*a*) the commissioners shall grant the applicant a road service licence in respect of that route, and shall do so in accordance with the application except to the extent that they are satisfied that to do so would be against the interests of the public; and

    (*b*) in relation to the application and to the licence granted on it, sections 5 and 6 shall have effect as if section 5 (2) to (4) and, in section 6 (1), the words "and in particular to the matters mentioned in section 5 (3) (*a*) to (*c*)" were omitted.

(2) Every road service licence granted in pursuance of this section shall include a statement that it is so granted.

(3) No appeal shall lie under section 28 from a decision of the traffic commissioners to refuse to grant a road service licence in pursuance of this section.　　**[74]**

COMMENCEMENT
See s. 70 (5), *post*, and the note "Orders under this section" thereto.

APPLICATION FOR A ROAD SERVICE LICENCE
For general provisions as to applications for road service licences, see s. 5, *ante*; but note sub-s. (1) (*b*) above.

TRAFFIC COMMISSIONERS
See the note to s. 3 *ante*. For the purpose of determining whether the traffic commissioners are

satisfied in accordance with sub-s. (1) above or s. 9 (1), *post*, the requirement in the Road Traffic Act 1960, s. 153 (3), A.L.S. Vol. 124, as amended by s. 43 (1) and Sch. 5, Part I, para. 9 (3), *post*, that not less than two commissioners be present at the hearing of an application is excluded; see s. 153 (5) of that Act as inserted by s. 43 (1) and Sch. 5, Part I, para. 9 (5), *post*.

SATISFIED; AGAINST THE INTERESTS OF THE PUBLIC
See the notes to s. 5, *ante*.

PASSENGER TRANSPORT AREAS
See the note to s. 4, *ante*.

LONDON; PARTNERSHIPS
See the notes to s. 5, *ante*.

DEFINITIONS
For "road service licence", see s. 44 (1), *post*; by virtue of s. 1 (3), *ante*, for "the traffic commissioners", see the Road Traffic Act 1960, s. 120 (4), A.L.S. Vol. 124.

9. Grant of road service licences for certain excursions or tours

(1) If, in the case of any application for a road service licence, the traffic commissioners are satisfied that the service which the applicant proposes to provide under the licence ("the proposed service") would be an excursion or tour and are also satisfied either —

(*a*) that the proposed service would not compete directly with —

(i) any other road service for which a road service licence has been granted, not being an excursion or tour, or

(ii) any London bus service within the meaning of section 23 of the Transport (London) Act 1969, or

(iii) any service being provided by means of one or more tramcars; or

(*b*) that the proposed service would operate only to enable passengers to attend special events,

the commissioners shall grant the applicant a road service licence in accordance with the application and, in relation to the application and to the licence granted on it, sections 5 (2) to (4), 6 and 7 shall not apply.

(2) Section 4 (4) does not prevent a road service licence granted in pursuance of this section from having effect for the purposes of the provision of a service by means of a vehicle whose operator holds a PSV operator's licence granted by the traffic commissioners for any traffic area, not being a licence which is for the time being of no effect by reason of its suspension.

(3) Every road service licence granted in pursuance of this section shall include a statement that it is so granted.

(4) No appeal shall lie under section 28 from a decision of the traffic commissioners to refuse to grant a road service licence in pursuance of this section.   [75]

COMMENCEMENT
See s. 70 (5), *post*, and the note "Orders under this section" thereto.

APPLICATION FOR A ROAD SERVICE LICENCE
For general provisions as to applications for road service licences, see s. 5, *ante*; but note sub-s. (1) above.

TRAFFIC COMMISSIONERS
See the note to s. 3, *ante*; and the note to s. 8, *ante*.

SATISFIED
See the note to s. 5, *ante*.

TRAFFIC AREA
See the note to s. 4, *ante*.

PASSENGER TRANSPORT AREA
See the note to s. 4, *ante*.

LONDON; PARTNERSHIPS
See the note to s. 5, *ante*.

DEFINITIONS
For "excursion or tour", "PSV operator's licence" and "road service licence", see s. 44 (1), *post*; for "operator", see s. 44 (2), (3), *post*; by virtue of s. 1 (3), *ante*, for "the traffic commissioners", see the Road Traffic Act 1960, s. 120 (4), A.L.S. Vol. 124, and for "tramcar", see s. 257 (1) of that Act. Note as to "the proposed service", sub-s. (1) above.

TRANSPORT (LONDON) ACT 1969, S. 23
See A.L.S. Vol. 185.

10. Revocation and suspension of road service licences

(1) Subject to subsection (2), a road service licence may be revoked or suspended by the traffic commissioners who granted the licence on the ground that there has been a contravention of any condition attached to it.

(2) The traffic commissioners shall not revoke or suspend a road service licence unless, owing to the frequency of the breach of conditions, or to the breach having been committed intentionally, or to the danger to the public involved in the breach, the commissioners are satisfied that the licence should be revoked or suspended.

(3) On revoking or suspending a road service licence the traffic commissioners shall send notice thereof—

   (*a*) to the chief officer of police of every policy district in which the service to which the licence relates was provided; and

   (*b*) to each of the councils mentioned in section 5 (5) (*a*) to (*c*) in whose area that service was provided.

(4) A road service licence suspended under this section shall during the time of suspension be of no effect.   **[76]**

COMMENCEMENT
See s. 70 (5), *post*, and the note "Orders under this section" thereto.

LICENCE MAY BE REVOKED OR SUSPENDED, ETC
The powers of the traffic commissioners under sub-s. (1) above are purely permissive and even their permissive jurisdiction only begins when one or other of the matters set out in sub-s. (2) above arises (*G. Newton, Ltd.* v. *Smith. W. C. Standerwick, Ltd.* v. *Smith*, [1962] 2 All E.R. 19, at p. 23).

TRAFFIC COMMISSIONERS WHO GRANTED THE LICENCE
As to the appropriate traffic commissioners, see s. 4 (2), *ante*; and as to the granting of road service licences, see ss. 5, 8 and 9, *ante*. See, also, the note "Traffic Commissioners" to s. 3, *ante*.

CONDITION ATTACHED TO IT
I.e., under s. 6 or 7, *ante*.

THE PUBLIC
See the note "Against the interests of the public" to s. 5, *ante*.

SATISFIED
See the note to s. 5, *ante*.

CHIEF OFFICER OF POLICE; DISTRICT
These expressions are defined by the Police Act 1964, s. 62, Sch. 8, A.L.S. Vol. 148.

PASSENGER TRANSPORT AREAS
    See the note to s. 4, *ante*.

APPEALS; LONDON; PARTNERSHIPS
    See the note to s. 5, *ante*.

APPLICATION TO EXPIRED LICENCES
    This section applies to road service licences which continue in force after their date of expiry in the cases specified in ss. 11 (3) and 28 (2), *post*.

DEFINITIONS
    For "contravention" and "road service licence", see s. 44 (1), *post*; by virtue of s. 1 (3), *ante*; for "the traffic commissioners", see the Road Traffic Act 1960, s. 120 (4), A.L.S. Vol. 124.

11. Duration of road service licences

(1) Regulations shall specify the dates in the year on which road service licences are to expire.

(2) Subject to subsection (3), a road service licence shall, unless previously revoked, continue in force up to and including that one of the dates so specified which occurs next before the expiration of five years from the date on which the licence is expressed to take effect unless at the time of the granting of the licence the traffic commissioners for special reasons determine that it shall continue in force only up to and including an earlier date (being one of those so specified), in which case it shall, unless previously revoked, continue in force only up to and including that date.

(3) If, on the date on which a road service licence is due to expire, proceedings are pending before the traffic commissioners on an application for the grant of a new licence in substitution for it, the existing licence shall continue in force until the application is disposed of, but without prejudice to the exercise in the meantime of the powers conferred by section 10.

(4) Nothing in this section shall prevent—

(*a*) the grant of a road service licence in respect of a service limited to one or more particular periods or occasions; or

(*b*) the attachment to a road service licence of a condition that the service shall be so limited.   **[77]**

COMMENCEMENT
    See s. 70 (5), *post*, and the note "Orders under this section" thereto.

EXPIRATION OF FIVE YEARS FROM, ETC
    The general rule in the computation of periods of time is that, unless there is a sufficient indication to the contrary, the day on which the initial event occurs is to be excluded and the last day is to be included and that fractions of a day are to be ignored; see generally 37 Halsbury's Laws (3rd Edn.), pp. 92, 100.

TRAFFIC COMMISSIONERS
    See the note to s. 3, *ante*.

APPLICATION FOR THE GRANT OF A NEW LICENCE
    See s. 5, 8 or 9, *ante*.

PREVENT
    There is high authority for saying that "prevent" means make impossible; see *Tennants (Lancashire), Ltd.* v. *C. S Wilson & Co., Ltd.*, [1917] A.C. 495, at p. 518 *per* Lord Atkinson.

PASSENGER TRANSPORT AREAS
    See the note to s. 4, *ante*.

APPEALS; LONDON; PARTNERSHIPS
  See the notes to s. 5, *ante*.

DEFINITIONS
  For "road service licence", see s. 44 (1), *post*; by virtue of s. 1 (3), *ante*, for "the traffic commissioners", see the Road Traffic Act 1960, s. 120 (4), A.L.S. Vol. 124, and for "regulations", see s. 160 (2) of that Act.

REGULATIONS UNDER THIS SECTION
  See the Public Service Vehicles (Road Service Licences and Express Services) Regulations 1980, S.I. 1980 No. 1354, reg. 14, prescribing the last days of February, June and November as the expiry dates.
  By virtue of s. 1 (3), *ante*, for general provisions as to regulations, see the Road Traffic Act 1960, ss. 160, 260, as amended by s. 43 (1) and Sch. 5, Part I, paras. 11 and 15, respectively, *post*, and as partly repealed, in the case of s. 160, by s. 69 and Sch. 9, Part I, *post*.

Trial areas

12. Designation of trial areas

(1) For the purposes of this Part a trial area is any area in Great Britain (outside Greater London) for the time being designated in accordance with the following provisions of this section as an area in which road service licences are not required for stage carriage services.

(2) The Minister may, if he thinks fit, make an order (in this section referred to as a "designation order") so designating any area consisting of the whole or part of the area of a local authority, but shall not make such an order in respect of any area except on an application made to him by the local authority concerned.

(3) An application for a designation order shall specify the area which the local authority concerned wishes to be designated by the order; and the area designated by such an order as originally made—

    (*a*) shall not include any area outside the area specified in the application on which the order is made; and

    (*b*) shall not consist of less than the whole of the area so specified unless the reduction is made with the consent of the local authority concerned.

(4) Subject to subsection (5), the Minister may by order vary or revoke a designation order but shall not do so except on an application made to him by the local authority concerned; and the Minister—

    (*a*) on an application for an order varying a designation order, may at his discretion refuse the application or make the order applied for either with or without modifications; and

    (*b*) on an application for an order revoking a designation order may at his discretion refuse the application or make the order applied for.

(5) A designation order—

    (*a*) shall not be revoked before the end of the period specified in the order, as originally made, as the minimum period for which the order is to be in force, being a period of not less than two and not more than five years beginning with the day on which it comes into force;

    (*b*) shall not before the end of that period be varied so as to exclude from the area designated by it any part of the area originally so designated; and

    (*c*) shall at no time be varied so as to include in the area designated by it any area outside the area originally so designated.

(6) The preceding provisions of this section have effect subject to the provisions of Schedule 2 (which relate to the making of applications for, and the variation and revocation of, designation orders).

(7) Any order under this section shall be made by statutory instrument subject to annulment in pursuance of a resolution of either House of Parliament.

(8) In this section and Schedule 2—

"designation order" has the meaning given by subsection (2) (but does not include an order under this section altering the area designated by a designation order);

"local authority" means, for England and Wales, a county council and, for Scotland, a regional or islands council;

"the local authority concerned", in relation to any area designated or proposed to be designated under this section, means the local authority whose area is or contains that area.   **[78]**

COMMENCEMENT
See s. 70 (5), *post*, and the note "Orders under this section" thereto.

SUB-S. (1): THIS PART
I.e., Part I (ss. 1—44) of this Act.

GREAT BRITAIN
I.e., England, Scotland and Wales; see the Union with Scotland Act 1706, preamble, Art. I, 6, Halsbury's Statutes (3rd edn.), p. 502, as read with the Interpretation Act 1978, s. 22 (1), Sch. 2, para. 5 (*a*), A.L.S. Vol. 258.

GREATER LONDON
See the note to s. 5, *ante*.

SUB-S. (2): THINKS FIT
See the note "satisfied" to s. 5, *ante*.

SUB-S. (5): TWO (FIVE) YEARS BEGINNING WITH, ETC
The use of the phrase "beginning with" makes it clear that in computing the relevant period the day from which it runs is to be included; see *Hare* v. *Gocher*, [1962] 2 Q.B. 641; [1962] 2 All E.R. 763, and *Trow* v. *Ind Coope (West Midlands), Ltd.*, [1967] 2 Q.B. at p. 909; [1967] 2 All E.R. 900, C.A.

SUB-S. (7): STATUTORY INSTRUMENT; SUBJECT TO ANNULMENT
For provisions as to statutory instruments generally, see the Statutory Instruments Act 1946, A.L.S. Vol. 36 and as to statutory instruments which are subject to annulment, see ss. 5 (1) and 7 (1) of that Act.

SUB-S. (8): ENGLAND; WALES
For meanings, see the Interpretation Act 1978, s. 5, Sch. 1, A.L.S. Vol. 258.

COUNTY COUNCIL
See the note "County council; district council" to s. 5, *ante*.

FURTHER PROVISIONS
See, further, in connection with trial areas, s. 13, *post* (stage carriage services in trial areas); s. 14, *post* (duty to publish particulars of stage carriage services in trial areas); and s. 15, *post* (relaxation in trial areas of operators' duties to co-operate and exchange information).

DEFINITIONS
For "road service licence" and "stage carriage service", see s. 44 (1), *post*; for "the Minister", see s. 70 (2), *post*. Note as to "designation order", sub-ss. (2) and (8) above, and as to "local authority" and "the local authority concerned", sub-s. (8) above.

ORDERS UNDER THIS SECTION
At the time of going to press no order had been made under this section.

13. Stage carriage services in trial areas

(1) A road service licence is not required for the provision of a stage carriage service within a trial area.

(2) Where a stage carriage service operates partly within one or more trial areas and partly not within a trial area —

    (*a*) a road service licence is not required in respect of so much of the service as operates not within a trial area but within a traffic area in which (except in any trial area) passengers are neither taken up nor set down in the course of the service; and

    (*b*) any conditions attached to a road service licence under which any part of that service is provided shall not apply in relation to so much of the service as operates within any trial area.

(3) So much of subsection (3) of section 1 of the Road Traffic Regulation Act 1967 as provides that no prohibition or restriction on waiting imposed by a traffic regulation order under that section shall apply to a stage carriage shall not operate within a trial area. **[79]**

COMMENCEMENT
See s. 70 (5), *post*, and the note "Orders under this section" thereto.

ROAD SERVICE LICENCE IS NOT REQUIRED, ETC
In general such a licence is required by s. 4 (1), *ante*.

TRAFFIC AREA
See the note to s. 4, *ante*.

ANY CONDITIONS ATTACHED TO A ROAD SERVICE LICENCE
I.e., under s. 6 or 7, *ante*.

COMMUNITY BUS SERVICE
Where any community bus service is provided in whole or in part within a trial area, regulations may provide that the Transport Act, s. 5 (1) – (6), as substituted by s. 43 (1) and Sch. 5, Part II, *post*, with such additions, omissions, alterations or other modifications as may be prescribed, is to have effect; see s. 5 (7) of that Act as so substituted.

DEFINITIONS
For "stage carriage", see s. 3 (1) (*a*), *ante*; for "trial area", see s. 12 (1), *ante*; for "road service licence" and "stage carriage service", see s. 44 (1), *post*.

ROAD TRAFFIC REGULATION ACT 1967, S. 1 (3)
See A.L.S. Vol. 165. Note that that subsection is partly repealed by ss. 43 (1) and 69 and Sch. 5, Part II, and Sch. 9, Part I, *post*.

14. Duty to publish particulars of stage carriage services in trial areas

(1) This section applies to any stage carriage service which operates wholly within a trial area; but where a stage carriage service operates only partly within a trial area, so much of it as operates within that area shall for the purposes of this section be treated as a separate service to which this section applies.

    (2) Before —

    (*a*) starting to provide a new service to which this section applies; or

    (*b*) making, otherwise than temporarily, any changes in a service to which this section applies; or

    (*c*) discontinuing a service to which this section applies,

the operator of the service shall —

        (i) give to the local authority concerned, and to every district council in whose area passengers will be or are taken up or set down in the course of the service in question (including, in a case within paragraph (*b*), the service as proposed to be changed), a notice giving the prescribed information about the new service, the changes or the discontinuance, as the case may be; and

(ii) publish in a local newspaper circulating in the locality served or to be served by the service a notice giving the prescribed information about the new service, the changes or the discontinuance, as the case may be.

(3) Subject to subsection (4), any notice required by subsection (2) shall be given or published not later than the prescribed time before the operator does as mentioned in subsection (2) (*a*), (*b*) or (*c*), as the case may be.

(4) Where the operator of a service to which this section applies does as mentioned in subsection (2) (*a*), (*b*) or (*c*) in consequence of unforeseen circumstances making it impracticable for him to give or, as the case may be, publish in accordance with subsection (3) a notice required by subsection (2), subsection (3) shall not apply to that notice, but instead the notice in question shall be given or, as the case may be, published (with any necessary modifications) as soon as is practicable.

(5) If, at the time when any area becomes a trial area, there is being provided under a road service licence a stage carriage service which operates wholly or partly within that area, that service shall for the purposes of subsection (1) be treated as one which operates wholly or, as the case may be, partly within a trial area.

(6) A person who fails to give or publish as required by this section any notice which this section requires him to give or publish shall be liable on summary conviction to a fine not exceeding £200.

(7) Where more than one person falls to be regarded as the operator of a service to which this section applies, the requirements of this section are complied with if the requisite notices are given and published by any of those persons.

(8) In this section—

"the local authority concerned" has the meaning given by section 12 (8);
"operator" includes a prospective operator.   **[80]**

COMMENCEMENT
See s. 70 (5), *post*, and the note "Orders under this section" thereto.

SUB-S. (2): DISTRICT COUNCIL
See the note "County council; district council" to s. 5, *ante*.

PRESCRIBED
I.e., prescribed by regulations made under the Road Traffic Act 1960, s. 160, A.L.S. Vol. 124; see, by virtue of s. 1 (3), *ante*, s. 160 (2) of that Act. At the time of going to press no regulations had been made for the purposes of sub-ss. (2) and (3) above.

SUB-S. (6): PERSON
See the note to s. 2, *ante*.

SHALL BE LIABLE
See the first and third paragraphs of the note to s. 4, *ante*, and the note to s. 7, *ante*.

SUMMARY CONVICTION
See the note to s. 4, *ante*.

PARTNERSHIPS
See the note to s. 5, *ante*.

EXPERIMENTAL AREAS
This section is unaffected by the Passenger Vehicles (Experimental Areas) Act 1977, s. 2 (8),

A.L.S. Vol. 254, as amended by s. 43 (1) and Sch. 5, Part II, *post* (as to which, see the note to s. 2 (3), *ante*); see s. 2 (8A) of that Act, as inserted by Sch. 5, Part II, *post*.

EXCLUSION

A person acting under and in accordance with a general or special authority granted by the Secretary of State under the Energy Act 1976, s. 4 (2), 46, Halsbury's Statutes (3rd edn.), p. 2066, is not obliged to comply with the requirements of this section; see Sch. 1, para. 1, to that Act, as amended by s. 43 (1) and Sch. 5, Part II, *post*.

DEFINITIONS

For "trial area", see s. 12 (1), *ante*; for "the local authority concerned", see s. 12 (8), *ante*, as applied by sub-s. (8) above; or "road service licence" and "stage carriage service", see s. 44 (1), *post*; for "operator", see s. 44 (2), (3), *post*. Note also as to "operator", sub-s. (8) above.

15. Relaxation in trial areas of operators' duties to co-operate and exchange information

(1) Subject to subsection (3) the duties of public passenger transport operators under the provisions mentioned in subsection (2), being duties to co-operate with and afford information to one another, shall not apply in relation to a service so far as it is provided within a trial area.

(2) The provisions referred to in subsection (1) are —

    (*a*) section 24 (2) and (3) of the Transport Act 1968 (services in passenger transport areas);

    (*b*) section 1 (1) (*c*) of the Transport Act 1978 (services in England and Wales outside passenger transport areas); and

    (*c*) (*applies to Scotland*).

(3) Subsection (1) shall not affect the duties of public passenger transport operators to co-operate with or afford information to —

    (*a*) a Passenger Transport Executive;

    (*b*) a county council; or

    (*c*) (*applies to Scotland*),

for the purpose of the discharge by any such Executive or council of its function of co-ordinating passenger transport services.

(4) In this section "public passenger transport operators" means persons providing public passenger transport services within the meaning of section 1 (2) of the Transport Act 1978. **[81]**

COMMENCEMENT

See s. 70 (5), *post*, and the note "Orders under this section" thereto.

COUNTY COUNCIL

See the note "County council; district council" to s. 5, *ante*.

PERSONS

See the note "Person" to s. 2, *ante*.

DEFINITIONS

For "trial area", see s. 12 (1), *ante*. Note as to "public passenger transport operators", sub-s. (4) above.

TRANSPORT ACT 1968, S. 24 (2), (3)

See A.L.S. Vol. 178.

TRANSPORT ACT 1978, S. 1 (1) (*c*), 1 (2)

See A.L.S. Vol. 265.

Fitness of public service vehicles

16. Powers of, and facilities for, inspection of public service vehicles

(1) A certifying officer or public service vehicle examiner, on production if so required of his authority —

> (a) may at any time inspect any public service vehicle, and for that purpose —
>
>> (i) may enter the vehicle; and
>> (ii) may detain the vehicle during such time as is required for the inspection;
>
> (b) may at any time which is reasonable having regard to the circumstances of the case enter any premises on which he has reason to believe that there is a public service vehicle.

(2) A person who intentionally obstructs a certifying officer or public service vehicle examiner acting in the exercise of his powers under subsection (1) shall be liable on summary conviction to a fine not exceeding £200.

(3) The Minister may —

> (a) provide and maintain stations where inspections of public service vehicles for the purposes of this Part may be carried out;
> (b) designate premises as stations where such inspections may be carried out; and
> (c) provide and maintain apparatus for the carrying out of such inspections;

and in this Part "official PSV testing station" means a station provided, or any premises for the time being designated, under this subsection.   [82]

COMMENCEMENT
    See s. 70 (5), *post*, and the note "Orders under this section" thereto.

PUBLIC SERVICE VEHICLE EXAMINER
    These examiners are appointed under the Road Traffic Act 1960, s. 128 (2), A.L.S. Vol. 124, as amended by s. 43 (1) and Sch. 5, Part I, para. 1 (3), *post*.

ON PRODUCTION IF SO REQUIRED OF HIS AUTHORITY
    This does not mean that the right of entry can only be exercised if there is someone to whom the authority can be produced; see *Grove* v. *Eastern Gas Board*, [1952] 1 K.B. 77; [1951] 2 All E.R. 1051, C.A.

INSPECT
    For the power to prohibit the driving of unfit public service vehicles based on the discoveries made during these inspections, see s. 18, *post*.

PREMISES
    The term "premises", though originally possessing a very limited meaning, *i.e.*, the parts of a deed which precede the habendum, is widely used in the popular sense as including land, houses, buildings, etc.; see, *e.g.*, *Metropolitan Water Board* v. *Paine*, [1907] 1 K.B. 285; *Whitley* v. *Stumbles*, [1930] A.C. 544, H.L.; *Bracey* v. *Read*, [1963] Ch. 88; [1962] 3 All E.R. 472; and *Maunsell* v. *Olins*, [1975] A.C. 373; [1975] 1 All E.R. 16, H.L. In general "premises" would seem to have been construed as meaning a whole property in either one occupation or one ownership according to the context in which it is used; see, *e.g.*, *Cadbury Brothers, Ltd.* v. *Sinclair*, [1934] 2 K.B. 389, at p. 393 (reversed on other grounds (1933) 103 L.J.K.B. 29), and *Brickwood & Co.*, v. *Reynolds*, [1898] 1 Q.B. 95.

REASON TO BELIEVE
    It is submitted that these words require not only that the person in question has reason to believe but also that he does actually believe; see *R.* v. *Banks*, [1916] 2 K.B. 621; [1916–17] All E.R. Rep. 356, and *R.* v. *Harrison*, [1938] 3 All E.R. 134; and see also *Nakkuda Ali* v. *Jayaratne* [1951] A.C. 66, P.C.

PERSON
See the note to s. 2, *ante*.

INTENTIONALLY OBSTRUCTS

Obstruction need not involve physical violence; see, especially, *Borrow* v. *Howland* (1896), 74 L.T. 787, and *Hinchliffe* v. *Sheldon*, [1955] 3 All E.R. 406. In fact there is authority for saying that anything which makes it more difficult for a person to carry out his duty amounts to obstruction; see *Hinchliffe* v. *Sheldon, supra*. Yet standing by and doing nothing is not obstruction unless there is a legal duty to act; see *Swallow* v. *London County Council,* [1916] 1 K.B. 224; [1914 – 15] All E.R. Rep. 403, and cf. *Rice* v. *Connolly,* [1966] 2 Q.B. 414; [1966] 2 All E.R. 649, and contrast *Baker* v. *Ellison,* [1914] 2 K.B. 762. However, a positive act does not cease to be obstructive just because it is lawful in itself, see *Dibble* v. *Ingleton,* [1972] 1 Q.B. 480; *sub nom. Ingleton* v. *Dibble,* [1972] 1 All E.R. 275.

Obstruction must, however, to be an offence under this section, be intentional; and an act is done intentionally if it is deliberate and wilful, not accidental or inadvertent, but so that the mind of the person who does the act goes with it; cf. *R.* v. *Senior,* [1899] 1 Q.B. 283; [1895 – 9] All E.R. Rep. 511, *per* Lord Russell of Killowen, at pp. 290, 291, and p. 514, respectively. It is therefore necessary for the prosecution to prove that the act in question was done with the intention of obstructing and intervention with the intention of assisting the person obstructed is not an offence; see *Willmott* v. *Atack,* [1976] 3 All E.R. 794. See also *R.* v. *Walker* (1934), 24 Cr. App. Rep. 117; *Eaton* v. *Cobb,* [1950] 1 All E.R. 1016; Arrowsmith v. *Jenkins,* [1963] 2 Q.B. 561; [1963] 2 All E.R. 210; *Rice* v. *Connolly, supra; Dibble* v. *Ingleton;* and *Wershof* v. *Commissioner of Police for the Metropolis,* [1978] 3 All E.R. 540.

SHALL BE LIABLE
See the first and third paragraphs to s. 4, *ante*.

SUMMARY CONVICTION
See the note to s. 4, *ante*.

THIS PART
I.e., Part I (ss. 1 – 44) of this Act.

FOREIGN VEHICLES
An examiner exercising his functions under sub-s. (1) above may, in certain cases, prohibit the driving of a foreign public service vehicle; see the Road Traffic (Foreign Vehicles) Act 1972, s. 1, Sch. 1, A.L.S. Vol. 208, as amended, in the case of Sch. 1, by s. 43 (1) and Sch. 5, Part II, *post*.

EXCLUSIONS
This section and ss. 17, 18 and 19 (1), *post,* do not apply to a school bus belonging to a local education authority which is used to carry fare-paying passengers, etc.; see s. 32 (1), *post.*

DEFINITIONS
For "public service vehicle", see s. 2, *ante;* for "the Minister", see s. 70 (2), *ante;* by virtue of s. 1 (3), *ante,* for "certifying officer", see the Road Traffic Act 1960, s. 128 (1), A.L.S. Vol. 124, as amended by s. 43 (1) and Sch. 5, Part I, para. 1 (2), *post.*

17. Certificate of initial fitness (or equivalent) required for use of public service vehicle

(1) A public service vehicle adapted to carry more than eight passengers shall not be used on a road unless—

    (*a*) a certifying officer has issued a certificate (in this section referred to as a "certificate of initial fitness") that the prescribed conditions as to fitness are fulfilled in respect of the vehicle; or

    (*b*) a certificate under section 130 of the 1960 Act (type approval) was in force immediately before this section came into force or has since been issued in respect of the vehicle; or

    (*c*) there has been issued in respect of the vehicle a certificate under section 47 of the Road Traffic Act 1972 (type approval) of a kind which by virtue of regulations is to be treated as the equivalent of a certificate of initial fitness.

(2) For the purposes of this Part and Part III of the 1960 Act a certificate of fitness issued in respect of a vehicle under section 129 of that Act which is in force immediately before the date on which this section comes into force shall have effect on and after that date as if it were a certificate of initial fitness issued in respect of the vehicle on that date.

(3) If a vehicle is used in contravention of subsection (1), the operator of the vehicle shall be liable on summary conviction to a fine not exceeding £500.   **[83]**

COMMENCEMENT
See s. 70 (5), *post*, and the note "Orders under this section" thereto.

ADAPTED
See the note to s. 2, *ante*.

CERTIFICATE OF INITIAL FITNESS
As to whether the issue of a certificate of initial fitness provides any defence in an action based on a defect in the vehicle, cf. *Donnelly* v. *Glasgow Corporation,* [1953] S.C. 107.

PRESCRIBED
I.e., by regulations made under the Road Traffic Act 1960, s. 160, A.L.S. Vol. 124; see by virtue of s. 1 (3), *ante*, s. 160 (2) of that Act. By virtue of s. 1 (3), *ante*, the Public Service Vehicles (Conditions of Fitness, Equipment and Use) Regulations 1972. S.I. 1972 No. 751, regs. 1 – 3, Parts II, III, as amended by S.I. 1976 No. 726 and S.I. 1980 No. 141, and as construed in accordance with the Interpretation 1978, ss. 17 (2) (*a*), 23 (2), A.L.S. Vol. 258, will, if still in force at the commencement of this section, have effect as if made for the purposes of sub-s. (1) (*a*) above.

CERTIFICATE UNDER S. 130 OF THE 1960 ACT
The Minister's withdrawal of his approval under the Road Traffic Act 1960, s. 130 (3), A.L.S. Vol. 124, as amended by s. 43 (1) and Sch. 5, Part I, para. 2, *post*, does not affect the operation of any certificate previously issued for the purposes of sub-s. 1 (*b*) above; see the final limb of that subsection as so amended. See, further, the note on the 1960 Act below.

THIS PART
I.e., Part I (ss. 1 – 44) of this Act.

SHALL BE LIABLE; SUMMARY CONVICTION
See the notes to s. 4, *ante*.

EXPERIMENTAL VEHICLES
For the modification of this section in relation to experimental vehicles, see the Road Traffic Act 1960, s. 131, A.L.S. Vol. 124, as amended by s. 43 (1) and Sch. 5, Part I, para. 3, *post*.

FORGERY AND MISUSE OF DOCUMENTS, ETC
A certificate of initial fitness under this section, an operator's disc under s. 24, *post*, and a certificate under s. 27, *post*, as to the repute, financial standing or professional competence of any person, are documents to which the Road Traffic Act 1960, s. 233, A.L.S. Vol. 124 applies; see s. 43 (1) and Sch. 5, Part I, para. 12 (*a* – (*c*), *post*.

FALSE STATEMENTS TO OBTAIN CERTIFICATE, ETC
A person who knowingly makes a false statement for the purpose of obtaining the issue of a certificate under this section, an operator's disc under s. 24, *post*, or a certificate under s. 27, *post*, as to the repute, financial standing or professional competence of any person, is guilty of an offence under the Road Traffic Act 1960, s. 235 (1), A.L.S. Vol. 124 as affected by s. 43 (1) and Sch. 5, Part I, para. 12, *post*.

APPEAL
A person applying for a certificate of initial fitness may appeal to the Minister against the refusal of a certifying officer to issue such a certificate; see s. 28 (6), (9), (10), *post*.

PROSPECTIVE REPEAL
Sub-s. (1) (*b*) above, s. 28 (6) (*b*), *post*, and Sch. 5, Part I, paras. 2 and 12 (*d*), *post*, may be repealed by the Road Traffic Act 1974, s. 24 (3), Sch. 7, A.L.S. Vol. 226, on a day to be appointed under s. 24 (4) of that Act; see s. 43 (1) and Sch. 5, Part II, *post*.

EXCLUSIONS
This section and ss. 18 and 19 (1), *post*, do not apply to the driving or use of a vehicle in the course of a community bus service or in the course of its use as a contract carriage or express carriage in accordance with any provision mentioned in the Transport Act 1978, s. 5 (3), as substituted by s. 43 (1) and Sch. 5, Part II, *post*; see s. 5 (4) of that Act, as so substituted. See also the note to s. 16, *ante*.

FEES; PARTNERSHIPS
See the notes to s. 5, *ante*.

DEFINITIONS
For "public service vehicle", see s. 2, *ante*; for "contravention", see s. 44 (1), *post*; for "operator", see s. 44 (2), (3), *post*; by virtue of s. 1 (3), *ante*, for "certifying officer", see the Road Traffic Act 1960, s. 128 (1), A.L.S. Vol. 124, as amended by s. 43 (1) and Sch. 5, Part I, para. 1 (2), *post*, for "prescribed" and "regulations", see s. 160 (2) of that Act, and for "road", see s. 257 (1) of that Act. Note as to "certificate of initial fitness", sub-s. (1) (*a*) above.

1960 ACT
I.e., the Road Traffic Act 1960; see s. 44 (1), *post*. For Part III and ss. 129 and 130 of that Act, see A.L.S. Vol. 124. S. 129 is repealed by s. 1 (1), (2), *ante*, and s. 69 and Sch. 9, Part I, *post*. S. 130 is amended by s. 43 (1) and Sch. 5, Part I, para. 2, *post*, and is partly repealed by s. 69 and Sch. 9, Part I, *post*; it is wholly repealed by the Road Traffic Act 1974 ss. 10 (7), 24 (3), Sch. 2, Part I, para. 2, Sch. 7, A.L.S. Vol. 226, as from a day to be appointed under s. 24 (4) of the Act of 1974.

ROAD TRAFFIC ACT 1972, S. 47
See A.L.S. Vol. 208.

REGULATIONS UNDER THIS SECTION
At the time of going to press no regulations had been made for the purposes of sub-s. (1) (*c*) above. By virtue of s. 1 (3), *ante*, for general provisions as to regulations, see the Road Traffic Act 1960, ss. 160, 260, A.L.S. Vol. 124, as amended by s. 43 (1) and Sch. 5, Part I, paras. 11 and 15, respectively, *post*, and as partly repealed, in the case of s. 160, by s. 69 and Sch. 9, Part I, *post*.

18. Power to prohibit driving of unfit public service vehicles

(1) If on any inspection of a public service vehicle it appears to a certifying officer or public service vehicle examiner that owing to any defects therein the vehicle is, or is likely to become, unfit for service, he may prohibit the driving of the vehicle on a road either —

    (*a*) absolutely; or
    (*b*) for one or more specified purposes; or
    (*c*) except for one or more specified purposes.

(2) A prohibition under subsection (1) may be imposed with a direction making it irremovable unless and until the vehicle has been inspected at an official PSV testing station.

(3) Where a certifying officer or examiner prohibits the driving of a vehicle under subsection (1), he shall forthwith give notice in writing of the prohibition to the person in charge of the vehicle at the time of the inspection —

    (*a*) specifying the defects which occasioned the prohibition;
    (*b*) stating whether the prohibition is on all driving of the vehicle or driving it for one or more specified purposes or driving it except for one or more specified purposes (and, where applicable, specifying the purpose or purposes in question); and
    (*c*) stating whether the prohibition is to come into force immediately or at the end of a specified period.

(4) If the person to whom written notice of a prohibition is given under subsection (3) as being the person in charge of the vehicle at the time of the inspection is not —

(*a*) the operator of the vehicle; or

(*b*) if there is no operator at that time, the owner of the vehicle,

the officer or examiner shall as soon as practicable take steps to bring the contents of the notice to the attention of the said operator or owner.

(5) If, in the opinion of the certifying officer or examiner concerned, the defects in the vehicle in question are such that driving it, or driving it for any purpose prohibited by the notice given to the person in charge of it, would involve danger to the driver or to passengers or other members of the public, the prohibition under subsection (1) with respect to the vehicle shall come into force as soon as that notice has been given.

(6) In any other case a prohibition under subsection (1) shall come into force at such time not later than ten days from the date of the inspection as seems appropriate to the certifying officer or examiner having regard to all the circumstances.

(7) Where a notice has been given under subsection (3), any certifying officer or public service vehicle examiner may—

(*a*) grant an exemption in writing for the use of the vehicle in such manner, subject to such conditions and for such purpose or purposes as may be specified in the exemption;

(*b*) by endorsement on the notice vary its terms and, in particular—

(i) alter the time at which the prohibition is to come into force, or suspend it if it has come into force; or

(ii) cancel a direction under subsection (2) with which the prohibition was imposed.

(8) Subject to any subsisting direction under subsection (2), a prohibition under subsection (1) with respect to any vehicle may be removed by any certifying officer or public service vehicle examiner if he is satisfied that the vehicle is fit for service; and a person aggrieved by the refusal of a public service vehicle examiner to remove a prohibition may make an application to the traffic commissioners for any area to have the vehicle inspected by a certifying officer and, where such an application is made, the certifying officer to whom the matter is referred by the commissioners shall, if he considers that the vehicle is fit for service, remove the prohibition.

(9) Except in such cases as may be prescribed, a person who—

(*a*) knowingly drives a vehicle in contravention of a prohibition under subsection (1); or

(*b*) causes or permits a vehicle to be driven in contravention of such a prohibition,

shall be liable on summary conviction to a fine not exceeding £1,000.   **[84]**

COMMENCEMENT
　　See s. 70 (5), *post*, and the note "Orders under this section" thereto.

SUB-S. (1): INSPECTION OF A PUBLIC SERVICE VEHICLE
　　See s. 16, *ante*.

APPEARS
　　See the note "Satisfied" to s. 5, *ante*.

PUBLIC SERVICE VEHICLE EXAMINER
　　See the note to s. 16, *ante*.

LIKELY
　　"Likely" has been construed so as to mean a "reasonable prospect" of something happening; see

Dunning v. *Board of Governers of the United Liverpool Hospitals,* [1973] 2 All E.R. 454, C.A., at p. 460, *per* James, L.J.

PROHIBIT THE DRIVING OF THE VEHICLE
For the duty of a certifying officer or a public service vehicle examiner to give notice of the imposition or removal or a prohibition on the driving of a public service vehicle to traffic commissioners, see s. 26 (6), *post*.

SUB-S. (3); FORTHWITH
A provision to the effect that a thing must be done "forthwith" or "immediately" means that it must be done as soon as possible in the circumstances, the nature of the act to be done being taken into account; see *Re Southam, Ex parte Lamb* (1818), 19 Ch. D. 169, C.A.; [1881–5] All E.R. Rep. 391; *Re Muscovitch, Ex parte Muscovitch,* [1939] Ch. 694; [1939] 1 All E.R. 135, C.A.; and *Sameem* v. *Abeyewickrema,* [1963] A.C. 597; [1963] 3 All E.R. 382, P.C. Provided, however, that no harm is done, "forthwith" means "at any reasonable time thereafter", and in the absence of some detriment suffered by the person affected, failure to act "forthwith" does not invalidate the action taken; see *London Borough of Hillingdon* v. *Cutler,* [1968] 1 Q.B. 124; [1967] 2 All E.R. 361, C.A. See further, on the meaning of "forthwith", 37 Halsbury's Laws (3rd Edn.), p. 103 and 2 Words and Phrases (2nd Edn.) 273–275.

WRITING
Expressions referring to writing are, unless the contrary intention appears, to be construed as including references to other modes of representing or reproducing words in a visible form; see the Interpretation Act 1978, s. 5, Sch. 1, A.L.S. Vol. 258.

PERSON
See the note to s. 2, *ante*.

SUB-S. (5): OPINION
See the note "Satisfied" to s. 5, *ante*.

MEMBERS OF THE PUBLIC
See the note "Against the interests of the public" to s. 5, *ante*.

SUB-S. (8): PROHIBITION . . . MAY BE REMOVED
See the note "Prohibit the driving of the vehicle" to sub-s. (1) above.

SATISFIED
See the note to s. 5, *ante*.

PERSON AGGRIEVED
The meaning of a "person aggrieved" may vary substantially according to the context and where, as in this instance, the statute does not define the classes of persons falling into the category of persons aggrieved the court will have to consider the purpose for which the right of challenge has been granted. There have been decisions on the meaning of "person aggrieved" in a number of statutes and the effect of these is summarised in 1 Halsbury's Laws (4th Edn.), para. 49; see also 4 Words and Phrases (2nd Edn.) 114–116.

TRAFFIC COMMISSIONERS
See the note to s. 3, *ante*.

SUB-S. (9): PRESCRIBED
I.e., prescribed by regulations made under the Road Traffic Act 1960, s. 160, A.L.S. Vol. 124; see, by virtue of s. 1 (3), *ante*, s. 160 (2) of that Act. At the time of going to press no regulations had been made for the purposes of sub-s. (9) above.

KNOWINGLY
Knowledge is an essential ingredient of the offence and must be proved by the prosecution; see, in particular, *Gaumont British Distributors, Ltd.* v. *Henry,* [1939] 2 K.B. 711; [1939] 2 All E.R. 808. Knowledge includes the state of mind of a person who shuts his eyes to the obvious; see *James & Son, Ltd.* v. *Smea,* [1955] 1 Q.B. 78, at p. 91; [1954] 3 All E.R. 273 at p. 278, *per* Parker, J. Moreover, there is authority for saying that where a person deliberately refrains from making inquiries the results of which he might not care to have, this constitutes in law actual knowledge of the facts in question; see *Knox* v. *Boyd,* 1941 J.C. 82, at p. 86, and *Taylor's Central Garages (Exeter), Ltd.* v. *Roper* (1951), 115 J.P. 445, at pp. 449, 450, *per* Devlin, J.; and see also, in particular, *Mallon* v. *Allon,* [1964] 1 Q.B. 385; [1963] 3 All E.R. 843, at p. 394 and p. 847, respectively. Yet mere neglect to ascertain what could have been found out by making reasonable

inquiries is not tantamount to knowledge; *Taylor's Central Garages (Exeter), Ltd.* v. *Roper, ubi supra, per* Devlin, J.; and cf. *London Computator, Ltd.* v. *Seymour,* [1944] 2 All E.R. 11; but see also *Mallon* v. *Allon, ubi supra.*

CAUSES OR PERMITS

To "cause" involves some degree of dominance or control, or some express or positive mandate from the person "causing": (*McLeod (or Houston)* v. *Buchanan,* [1940] 2 All E.R. 179, at p. 187, H.L., *per* Lord Wright; *Shave* v. *Rosner* [1954] 2 Q.B. 113; [1954] 2 All E.R. 280; *Lovelace* v. *Director of Public Prosecutions,* [1954] 3 All E.R. 481; *Shulton (Great Britain), Ltd.* v. *Slough Borough Council,* [1967] 2 Q.B. 471; [1967] 2 All E.R. 137). A person cannot be said to have "caused" another to do or omit to do something unless he either knows or deliberately chooses not to know what it is that the other is doing or failing to do (*James & Son, Ltd.* v. *Smee,* [1955] 1 Q.B. 78; [1954] 3 All E.R. 273; *Ross Hillman, Ltd.* v. *Bond,* [1974] Q.B. 435; [1974] 2 All E.R. 287.

To "permit" involves a general or particular permission; the permission may be express or implied (*McLeod (or Houston)* v. *Buchanan, supra.*). To "permit" involves a knowledge of the facts constituting the user; but shutting one's eyes to the obvious, or allowing a person to do something in circumstances where a contravention is likely, not caring whether a contravention takes place or not, is sufficient (*James & Son, Ltd.* v. *Smee, supra; Gray's Haulage Co., Ltd.* v. *Arnold,* [1966] 1 All E.R. 896; *Ross Hillman, Ltd.* v. *Bond, supra*). Reasonable grounds for suspicion that the offence will be committed may be sufficient but suspicion itself is not enough (*Sweet* v. *Parsley,* [1970] A.C. 132; [1969] 1 All E.R. 347, H.L.; *R.* v. *Souter,* [1971] 2 All E.R. 1151, C.A.). But a person cannot permit unless he is in a position to forbid (*Goodbarne* v. *Buck,* [1940] 1 K.B. 771; [1940] 1 All E.R. 613, C.A.; *Lloyd* v. *Singleton,* [1953] 1 Q.B. 357; [1953] 1 All E.R. 291) and no one can permit what he cannot control (*Tophams, Ltd.* v. *Earl of Sefton,* [1967] 1 A.C. 50; [1961] 1 All E.R. 1039, H.L.).

For a corporation to be liable for "causing" or "permitting" it must be shown that some person for whose criminal acts the corporation would be liable caused or permitted the commission of the offence, knowledge on the part of an ordinary employee is not sufficient; it has to be that of someone exercising a directing mind over the company's affairs (*James & Son, Ltd., supra; Ross Hillman, Ltd.* v. *Bond, supra; Tesco Supermarkets, Ltd.* v. *Nattrass,* [1972] A.C. 153; [1971] 2 All E.R. 127, H.L.).

SHALL BE LIABLE; SUMMARY CONVICTION

See the notes to s. 4, *ante;* and see the next note.

GROUNDS FOR REVOKING, SUSPENDING, ETC., PSV OPERATORS' LICENCES

The imposition of a prohibition under this section with respect to a vehicle owned or operated by the holder of a PSV operator's licence and the conviction of the holder of a PSV operator's licence under sub-s. (9) above are both grounds upon which traffic commissioners may revoke, suspend (or otherwise tamper with) an existing PSV operator's licence under s. 23 (2), *post;* see s. 23 (3) (*c*), *post.*

EXCLUSIONS

See the notes to ss. 16 and 17, *ante.*

PARTNERSHIPS

See the note to s. 5, *ante.*

DEFINITIONS

For "public service vehicle", see s. 2, *ante;* for "official PSV testing station", see s. 16 (3), *ante;* for "contravention" and "owner", see s. 44 (1), *post;* for "operator", see s. 44 (2), (3), *post;* by virtue of s. 1 (3), *ante,* for "the traffic commissioners", see the Road Traffic Act 1960, s. 120 (4), A.L.S. Vol. 124, for "certifying officer", see s. 128 (1) of that Act, as amended by s. 43 (1) and Sch. 5, Part I, para. 1 (2), *post,* for "prescribed", see s. 160 (2) of that Act, and for "drive", "driver" and "road", see s. 257 (1) of that Act.

Public service vehicle operator's licences

19. PSV operators' licences

(1) A vehicle shall not be used on a road as a stage, express or contract carriage except under a PSV operator's licence granted in accordance with the following provisions of this Part.

(2) The authority having power to grant a PSV operator's licence is the traffic commissioners for any traffic area in which, if the licence is granted, there will be

one or more operating centres of vehicles used under the licence; and, subject to the provisions of this Part, a PSV operator's licence authorises the holder to use anywhere in Great Britain vehicles which have their operating centre in the area of the traffic commissioners by whom the licence was granted.

(3) A person may hold two or more PSV operators' licences each granted by the traffic commissioners for different areas, but shall not at the same time hold more than one such licence granted by the commissioners for the same area.

(4) An application for a PSV operator's licence shall be made in such form as the traffic commissioners may require, and an applicant shall give the commissioners such information as they may reasonably require for disposing of the application.

(5) If a vehicle is used in contravention of subsection (1) the operator of the vehicle shall be liable on summary conviction to a fine not exceeding £500. **[85]**

COMMENCEMENT
See s. 70 (5), *post*, and the note "Orders under this section" thereto.

SUB-S. (1): THIS PART
I.e., Part I (ss. 1–44) of this Act.

SUB-S. (2): TRAFFIC COMMISSIONERS
See the note to s. 3, *ante*.

TRAFFIC AREA
See the note to s. 4, *ante*.

GREAT BRITAIN
See the note to s. 12, *ante*.

SUB-S. (3): PERSON
See the note to s. 2, *ante*.

SUB-S. (5): SHALL BE LIABLE; SUMMARY CONVICTION
See the notes to s. 4, *ante*.

FOREIGN VEHICLES
As to the production of certain documents by foreign public service vehicles registered outside Great Britain, see the Road Traffic (Foreign Vehicles) Act 1972, s. 4 (2) (*b*), A.L.S. Vol. 208, as amended by s. 43 (1) and Sch. 5, Part II, *post*.

STANDS FOR HACKNEY CARRIAGES; PUBLIC SERVICE VEHICLES PROVIDING INTERNATIONAL PASSENGER SERVICES
See the notes to s. 4, *ante*.

SPEED LIMITS
For speed limits for certain vehicles being used under a PSV operator's licence, see the Road Traffic Regulation Act 1967, s. 78 (1), Sch. 5, para. 1 (1), 1 (5) (*a*), as amended in the case of Sch. 5, para. 1 (1), 1 (5) (*a*), by s. 43 (1) and Sch. 5, Part II, *post*. For s. 78 (1) of that Act, see A.L.S. Vol. 165.

FURTHER PROVISIONS
See, further, in connection with PSV operator's licences, s. 20, *post* (classification of licences); s. 21, *post* (grant and duration of licences); s. 22, *post* (conditions attached to licences); s. 23, *post* (revocation, suspension, etc. of licences); s. 24, *post* (duty to exhibit operator's disc); s. 25, *post* (duty to inform traffic commissioners of relevant convictions, etc.); s. 26, *post* (duty to give traffic commissioners information about vehicles); and s. 31, *post* (death, bankruptcy, etc., of licence-holder).

EXCLUSIONS
See the notes to ss. 4, 16 and 17, *ante*.

DEFINITIONS
For "stage carriage", see s. 3 (1) (*a*), *ante*; for "express carriage", see s. 3 (1) (*b*), *ante*; for

"contract carriage", see s. 3 (1) (c), *ante*; for "contravention", "operating centre" and "PSV operator's licence", see s. 44 (1), *post*; for "operator", see s. 44 (2), (3), *post*; by virtue of s. 1 (3), *ante*; for "the traffic commissioners", see the Road Traffic Act 1960, s. 120 (4), A.L.S. Vol. 124, and for "road", see s. 257 (1) of that Act.

20. Classification of licences

(1) A PSV operator's licence may be either a standard licence or a restricted licence.

(2) A standard licence authorises the use of any description of public service vehicle and may authorise use either—

(*a*) on both national and international operations; or

(*b*) on national operations only.

(3) A restricted licence authorises the use (whether on national or international operations) of—

(*a*) public service vehicles not adapted to carry more than eight passengers; and

(*b*) public service vehicles not adapted to carry more than sixteen passengers when used—

(i) otherwise than in the course of a business of carrying passengers; or

(ii) by a person whose main occupation is not the operation of public service vehicles adapted to carry more than eight passengers.

(4) For the purposes of subsection (3) (*b*) (i), a vehicle used for carrying passengers by a local or public authority shall not be regarded as used in the course of a business of carrying passengers unless it is used by the public service vehicle undertaking of that authority. **[86]**

COMMENCEMENT
See s. 70 (5), *post*, and the note "Orders under this section" thereto.

PSV OPERATOR'S LICENCE
As to these generally, see s. 19, *ante*.

ADAPTED; PERSON; IN THE COURSE OF A BUSINESS OF CARRYING PASSENGERS
See the notes to s. 2, *ante*.

DEFINITIONS
For "public service vehicle", see s. 2, *ante*; for "international operation", "national operation", "PSV operator's licence", "restricted licence" and "standard licence", see s. 44 (1), *post*.

21. Grant and duration of licences

(1) An application for a standard licence shall not be granted unless the traffic commissioners are satisfied that the applicant meets the following requirements, namely—

(*a*) the requirement to be of good repute;

(*b*) the requirement to be of appropriate financial standing; and

(*c*) the requirement as to professional competence;

and an application for a restricted licence shall not be granted unless the traffic commissioners are satisfied that the applicant meets the requirements to be of good repute and of appropriate financial standing.

(2) The provisions of Schedule 3 shall have effect for supplementing the provisions of subsection (1), and for modifying the operation of that subsection in the case of persons engaged in road passenger transport before 1st January 1978.

(3) Notwithstanding that it appears to the traffic commissioners on an application for a standard or restricted licence that the requirements mentioned in subsection (1) are met, the application shall not be granted unless the commissioners are further satisfied —

(*a*) that there will be adequate facilities or arrangements for maintaining in a fit and serviceable condition the vehicles proposed to be used under the licence; and

(*b*) that there will be adequate arrangements for securing compliance with the requirements of the law relating to the driving and operation of those vehicles.

(4) If on an application for a PSV operator's licence the traffic commissioners determine that the relevant requirements mentioned in subsection (1) and the further requirements mentioned in subsection (3) are satisfied they shall, subject to the following provisions of this section and to section 22, grant the licence in accordance with the application.

(5) There shall be specified in every PSV operator's licence the date on which the licence is to come into force and the date with which it is to expire; and, subject to subsection (6), the last-mentioned date shall be such as will make the duration of the licence such period not exceeding five years as the traffic commissioners on granting the licence consider appropriate in the circumstances.

(6) Traffic commissioners on granting a PSV operator's licence may direct that the duration of the licence shall be such period not exceeding five years as is in the opinion of the commissioners desirable in order to arrange a reasonably convenient programme of work for the commissioners.

(7) If, immediately before a PSV operator's licence is due to expire, proceedings are pending before the traffic commissioners on an application by the holder of that licence for the grant to him of a new licence in substitution for it, the existing licence shall continue in force until the application is disposed of, but without prejudice to the exercise in the meantime of the powers conferred by section 23.

(8) Where an application is made to the traffic commissioners by the holder of a PSV operator's licence for the grant to him of a new licence to take effect on the expiry of the existing licence and the traffic commissioners decide not to grant the new licence, they may direct that the existing licence continue in force for such period as appears to them reasonably required to enable the business carried on under the licence to be transferred to another person duly licensed to carry it on. **[87]**

COMMENCEMENT
See s. 70 (5), *post*, and the note "Orders under this section" thereto.

SUB-S. (1): **TRAFFIC COMMISSIONERS**
As to the appropriate traffic commissioners, see s. 19 (2), *ante*, and see the note to s. 3, *ante*.

SATISFIED
See the note to s. 5, *ante*.

REQUIREMENTS
If any of the requirements mentioned in sub-s. (1) above were at one time met, but are no longer satisfied, the licence in question may be revoked or suspended, etc.; see s. 23 (1), (2) and (3) (*d*), *post*.

SUB-S. (2): **PERSONS ENGAGED IN ROAD PASSENGER TRANSPORT**
As to persons wishing to carry on a road passenger transport business in another member state or in Northern Ireland, see s. 27, *post*.

1ST JANUARY 1978
 It is thought that this is an arbitrary date chosen to give persons who have been in business before that date certain privileges.

SUB-S. (3): FIT AND SERVICEABLE CONDITION
 As to the fitness of public service vehicles generally, see ss. 16 – 18, *ante*.

SUB-S. (4): SHALL . . . GRANT THE LICENCE
 As to the granting of road service licences, see s. 5, *ante*, and for the duty of traffic commissioners on granting a PSV operator's licence to supply the applicant with operators discs, see s. 24 (2), *post*.
 A PSV operator's licence is not to be granted to an unincorporated body as such or to more than one person jointly except in cases permitted by regulations under s. 30, *post*; see s. 30 (2), *post*.

SUB-SS. (5), (6): DURATION
 Traffic commissioners may, on any of the grounds specified in s. 23 (3), *post*, curtail the period of validity of the licence; see s. 24 (2) (*c*), *post*. Note also sub-s. (7) above.

OPINION
 See the note "Satisfied" to s. 5, *ante*.

APPEALS; PARTNERSHIPS; FEES
 See the corresponding notes to s. 5, *ante*.

DEFINITIONS
 For "restricted licence" and "standard licence", see s. 44 (1), *post*; by virtue of s. 1 (3), *ante*, for "the traffic commissioners", see the Road Traffic Act 1960, s. 120 (4), A.L.S. Vol. 124.

22. Conditions attached to licences

(1) Traffic commissioners on granting a PSV operator's licence shall attach to it one or more conditions specifying the maximum number of vehicles (being vehicles having their operating centre in the area of those commissioners) which the holder of the licence may at any one time use under the licence.

(2) Conditions attached under subsection (1) to a PSV operator's licence may specify different maximum numbers for different descriptions of vehicle.

(3) Traffic commissioners may (whether at the time when the licence is granted or at any time thereafter) attach to a PSV operator's licence granted by them such conditions or additional conditions as they think fit for restricting or regulating the use of vehicles under the licence, being conditions of any prescribed description.

(4) Without prejudice to the generality of the power to prescribe descriptions of conditions for the purposes of subsection (3), the descriptions which may be so prescribed include conditions for regulating the places at which vehicles being used under a PSV operator's licence may stop to take up or set down passengers.

(5) The traffic commissioners by whom a PSV operator's licence was granted may at any time while it is in force vary the licence by —

  (*a*) altering in such manner as they think fit any condition attached under subsection (3) of the licence; or

  (*b*) removing any condition so attached to the licence.

(6) On the application of the holder of a PSV operator's licence, the traffic commissioners by whom the licence was granted may at any time while it is in force —

  (*a*) vary the conditions attached under subsection (1) to the licence; or

  (*b*) exercise their powers (whether of alteration or removal) under subsection (5);

and a person making an application under this subsection shall give to the traffic commissioners such information as they may reasonably require for the discharge of their duties in relation to the application.

(7) If a condition attached to a PSV operator's licence is contravened, the holder of the licence shall be liable on summary conviction to a fine not exceeding £200.

(8) Compliance with any condition attached to a PSV operator's licence under this section may be temporarily dispensed with by the traffic commissioners by whom the licence was granted if they are satisfied that compliance with the condition would be unduly onerous by reason of circumstances not foreseen when the condition was attached or, if the condition has been altered, when it was last altered.

(9) It is hereby declared that the conditions attached under subsection (1) to a PSV operator's licence granted by the traffic commissioners for any area do not affect the use by the holder of the licence of a vehicle —

(a) under a PSV operator's licence granted to him by the traffic commissioners for another area; or

(b) in circumstances such that another person falls to be treated as the operator of the vehicle (for example, by virtue of regulations under section 44 (2) (a)). **[88]**

COMMENCEMENT
See s. 70 (5), *post*, and the note "Orders under this section" thereto.

SUB-S. (1): TRAFFIC COMMISSIONERS ON GRANTING A PSV OPERATOR'S LICENCE
See s. 20 (4), *ante*.

CONDITIONS
Traffic commissioners may, on any of the grounds specified in s. 23 (3), *post*, vary any condition attached under sub-s. (1) above to the PSV operator's licence, or may attach to the licence any condition as is mentioned in sub-s. (1) above; see s. 22 (2) (*d*), *post*.

MAXIMUM NUMBER OF VEHICLES
Traffic commissioners must supply the person to whom the licence is granted with a number of operator's discs equal to the maximum number of vehicles which he may use under the licence; see s. 24 (2), *post*. Note also s. 24 (3) (*d*), *post*.

SUB-S. (3): THINK FIT
See the note "Satisfied" to s. 5, *ante*.

PRESCRIBED
I.e., prescribed by regulations made under the Road Traffic Act 1960, s. 160, A.L.S. Vol. 124; see, by virtue of s. 1 (3), *ante*, s. 160 (2) of that Act. At the time of going to press no regulations had been made for the purposes of sub-s. (4) above; and note sub-s. (4) above.

SUB-SS. (5), (6): TRAFFIC COMMISSIONERS BY WHOM A PSV OPERATOR'S LICENCE (THE LICENCE) WAS GRANTED
As to the appropriate traffic commissioners, see s. 19 (2), *ante*.

PERSON
See the note to s. 2, *ante*.

SUB-S. (7): IF A CONDITION . . . IS CONTRAVENED
Contravention of any condition attached to a PSV operator's licence is one of the gounds upon which traffic commissioners may revoke, suspend, etc., an existing PSV operator's licence under s. 23 (2), *post*; see s. 23 (3) (*b*), *post*.

SHALL BE LIABLE; SUMMARY CONVICTION
See the notes to s. 4, *ante*.

SUB-S. (8): SATISFIED
See the note to s. 5, *ante*.

PERMISSIBLE RELAXATION OF ROAD TRAFFIC AND TRANSPORT LAW
   See the note to s. 6, *ante.*

APPEALS; PARTNERSHIPS
   See the notes to s. 5, *ante.*

DEFINITIONS
   For "contravene", "operating centre" and "PSV operator's licence", see s. 44 (1), *post*; for
   "operator", see s. 44 (2), (3), *post*; by virtue of s. 1 (3), *ante*, for "the traffic commissioners", see
   the Road Traffic Act 1960, s. 120 (4), A.L.S. Vol. 124, and for "prescibed", see s. 160 (2) of that
   Act.

23. Revocation, suspension, etc. of licences

(1) The traffic commissioners by whom a standard licence was granted shall revoke the licence if it appears to them at any time that the holder no longer satisfies the requirement to be of good repute, the requirement to be of appropriate financial standing or the requirement as to professional competence.

(2) Without prejudice to subsection (1), the traffic commissioners by whom a PSV operator's licence was granted may, on any of the grounds specified in subsection (3), at any time —

  (a) revoke the licence;
  (b) suspend the licence for such period as the commissioners direct (during which time it shall be of no effect);
  (c) curtail the period of validity of the licence;
  (d) vary any condition attached under subsection (1) of section 22 to the licence, or attach to the licence (whether in addition to or in place of any existing condition so attached to it) any such condition as is mentioned in that subsection.

(3) The grounds for action under subsection (2) are —

  (a) that the holder of the licence made or procured to be made for the purposes of his application for the licence, or for the purposes of an application for a variation of the licence, a statement of fact which (whether to his knowledge or not) was false, or a statement of intention or expectation which has not been fulfilled;
  (b) that there has been a contravention of any condition attached to the licence;
  (c) that a prohibition under section 18 has been imposed with respect to a vehicle owned or operated by the holder of the licence, or that the holder of the licence has been convicted of an offence under subsection (9) of that section;
  (d) in the case of a restricted licence, that the holder no longer satisfies the requirements to be of good repute or the requirement to be of appropriate financial standing;
  (e) that there has been since the licence was granted or varied a material change in any of the circumstances of the holder of the licence which were relevant to the grant or variation of his licence.

(4) Traffic commissioners shall not take any action under subsection (1) or (2) in respect of any licence without first holding a public sitting if the holder of the licence requests them to do so.

(5) Where traffic commissioners decide to revoke a licence under this section, they may direct that the revocation shall not take effect for such period as appears to them reasonably required to enable the business carried on under the licence to be transferred to another person duly licensed to carry it on.

(6) The provisions of Schedule 3 shall apply for the purposes of subsections (1) and (3) (*d*) as they apply for the purposes of section 21 (1).   **[89]**

COMMENCEMENT
See s. 70 (5), *post*, and the note "Orders under this section" thereto.

SUB-S. (1): TRAFFIC COMMISSIONERS BY WHOM A STANDARD LICENCE WAS GRANTED
Standard licences are granted under s. 21, *ante*. For the appropriate traffic commissioners, see s. 19 (2), *ante*.

APPEARS
Se the note "Satisfied" to s. 5, *ante*.

SUB-S. (2): TRAFFIC COMMISSIONERS BY WHOM A PSV OPERATOR'S LICENCE WAS GRANTED
PSV operator's licences (*i.e.*, standard or restricted licences; see s. 20 (1), *ante*) are granted under s. 21, *ante*. For the appropriate traffic commissioners, see s. 19 (2), *ante*.

PERIOD OF VALIDITY OF THE LICENCE
See s. 21 (5), *ante*.

SUB-S. (3): FALSE
See the note to s. 7, *ante*.

CONDITION ATTACHED TO THE LICENCE
I.e., under s. 22, *ante*.

SUB-S. (5): PERSON
See the note to s. 2, *ante*.

APPEALS; PARTNERSHIPS
See the notes to s. 5, *ante*.

APPLICATION TO EXPIRED LICENCES
This section applies to PSV operator's licences which continue in force after their date of expiry in the cases specified in s. 21 (7), *ante*, and s. 28 (2), *post*.

DEFINITIONS
For "contravention", "PSV operator's licence", "restricted licence" and "standard licence", see s. 44 (1), *post*; by virtue of s. 1 (3), *ante*, for "the traffic commissioners", see the Road Traffic Act 1960, s. 120 (4), A.L.S. Vol. 124.

24. Duty to exhibit operator's disc

(1) Where a vehicle is being used in circumstances such that a PSV operator's licence is required, there shall be fixed and exhibited on the vehicle in the prescribed manner an operator's disc issued under this section showing particulars of the operator of the vehicle and of the PSV operator's licence under which the vehicle is being used.

(2) Traffic commissioners on granting a PSV operator's licence shall supply the person to whom the licence is granted with a number of operator's discs equal to the maximum number of vehicles which he may use under the licence in accordance with the condition or conditions attached to the licence under section 22 (1); and if that maximum number is later increased on the variation of one or more of those conditions, the traffic commissioners on making the variation shall supply him with further operator's discs accordingly.

(3) Regulations may make provisions —

    (*a*) as to the form of operator's discs and the particulars to be shown on them;

    (*b*) with respect to the custody and production of operator's discs;

    (*c*) for the issue of new operator's discs in place of those lost, destroyed, or defaced;

    (*d*) for the return of operator's discs on the revocation or expiration of a PSV operator's licence or in the event of a variation of one or more conditions attached to a licence under section 22 (1) having the effect of reducing the maximum number of vehicles which may be used under the licence.

(4) If a vehicle is used in contravention of subsection (1), the operator of the vehicle shall be liable on summary conviction to a fine not exceeding £200.   **[90]**

COMMENCEMENT
See s. 70 (5), *post*, and the note "Orders under this section" thereto.

PRESCRIBED
I.e., prescribed by regulations made under the Road Traffic Act 1960, s. 160, A.L.S. Vol. 124; see, by virtue of s. 1 (3), *ante*, s. 160 (2) of that Act. At the time of going to press no regulations had been made for the purposes of sub-s. (1) above.

TRAFFIC COMMISSIONERS ON GRANTING A PSV OPERATOR'S LICENCE
I.e., pursuant to s. 20 (4), *ante*.

PERSON
See the note to s. 2, *ante*.

SHALL BE LIABLE; SUMMARY CONVICTION
See the notes to s. 4, *ante*.

FORGERY AND MISUSE OF DOCUMENTS, ETC.; FALSE STATEMENTS TO OBTAIN CERTIFICATES, ETC
See the notes to s. 17, *ante*.

FEES
As to the fees which are to be charged by the traffic commissioners in respect of the issue of operator's discs under this section and in respect of applications for, and the issue of, certificates under s. 27, *post*, as to repute, professional competence or financial standing, see the Road Traffic Act 1960, s. 159 (1) (*a*) (iii) (iv), as substituted by s. 38, *post*. At the time of going to press no fees had been prescribed for the purposes of this section or s. 27, *post*, by regulations made by virtue of s. 159 of the Act of 1960.

    If the relevant fees have not been paid, the traffic commissioners may decline to proceed with the application in question; see s. 159 (1A) of the Act of 1960 as substituted by s. 38, *post*.

DEFINITIONS
For "contravention" and "PSV operator's licence", see s. 44 (1), *post*; for "operator", see s. 44 (2), (3), *post*; by virtue of s. 1 (3), *ante*, for "the traffic commissioners", the Road Traffic Act 1960, s. 120 (4), A.L.S. Vol. 124, for "prescribed" and "regulations", see s. 160 (2) of that Act, and for "road", see s. 257 (1) of that Act.

REGULATIONS UNDER THIS SECTION
At the time of going to press no regulations had been made for the purposes of sub-s. (3) above.

    By virtue of s. 1 (3), *ante*, for general provisions as to regulations, see the Road Traffic Act 1960, ss. 160, 260, A.L.S. Vol. 124, as amended by s. 43 (1) and Sch. 5, Part I, paras. 11 and 15, respectively, *post*, and as partly repealed, in the case of s. 160, by s. 69 and Sch. 9, Part I, *post*.

25. Duty to inform traffic commissioners of relevant convictions, etc

(1) A person who has applied for a PSV operator's licence shall forthwith notify the traffic commissioners to whom the application was made if, in the interval between the making of the application and the date on which it is disposed of, a relevant conviction occurs of the applicant, or any employee or agent of his, or of any person proposed to be engaged as transport manager whose repute and competence are relied on in connection with the application.

(2) It shall be the duty of the holder of a PSV operator's licence to give notice

in writing to the traffic commissioners by whom the licence was granted of—

(a) any relevant conviction of the holder; and

(b) any relevant conviction of any officer, employee or agent of the holder for an offence committed in the course of the holder's road passenger transport business,

and to do so within 28 days of the conviction in the case of a conviction of the holder or his transport manager and within 28 days of the conviction coming to the holder's knowledge in any other case.

(3) It shall be the duty of the holder of a PSV operator's licence within 28 days of the occurrence of—

(a) the bankruptcy or liquidation of the holder, or the sequestration of his estate or the appointment of a receiver, manager or trustee of his road passenger transport business; or

(b) any change in the identity of the transport manager of the holder's road passenger transport business,

to give notice in writing of that event to the traffic commissioners by whom the licence was granted.

(4) Traffic commissioners on granting or varying a PSV operator's licence, or at any time thereafter, may require the holder of the licence to inform them forthwith or within a time specified by them of any material change specified by them in any of his circumstances which were relevant to the grant or variation of the licence.

(5) A person who fails to comply with subsection (1), (2) or (3) or with any requirement under subsection (4) shall be liable on summary conviction to a fine not exceeding £200. **[91]**

COMMENCEMENT
See s. 70 (5), *post*, and the note "Orders under this section" thereto.

SUB-S. (1): PERSON
See the note to s. 2, *ante*.

FORTHWITH
See the note to s. 18, *ante*.

TRAFFIC COMMISSIONERS TO WHOM THE APPLICATION WAS MADE
See s. 19 (2), *ante*.

SUB-S. (2): WRITING
See the note to s. 18, *ante*.

TRAFFIC COMMISSIONERS BY WHOM THE LICENCE WAS GRANTED
See s. 19 (2), *ante*.

WITHIN 28 DAYS OF, ETC
The general rule in cases where an act is to be done within a specified time from a certain date is that the day of that date is to be excluded; see *Goldsmiths' Co.* v. *West Metropolitan Rail. Co.*, [1904] 1 K.B. 1; [1900–3] All E.R. Rep. 667, C.A.; *Stewart* v. *Chapman*, [1951] 2 K.B. 792; [1952] 2 All E.R. 613; and the cases cited in 37 Halsbury's Laws (3rd Edn.), p. 95, para. 168.

SUB-S. (4): TRAFFIC COMMISSIONERS ON GRANTING OR VARYING A PSV OPERATOR'S LICENCE
I.e., pursuant to s. 21 (4), 22 (5) or (6) or s. 23 (2) (d), *ante*.

SUB-S. (5): SHALL BE LIABLE
See the first and third paragraphs of the note to s. 4, *ante*, and the note to s. 7, *ante*.

SUMMARY CONVICTION
See the note to s. 4, *ante*.

DEFINITIONS
     For "PSV operator's licence", "relevant conviction" and "transport manager", see s. 44 (1), *post*;
     by virtue of s. 1 (3), *ante*, for "the traffic commissioners"; see the Road Traffic Act 1960, s. 120
     (4), A.L.S. Vol. 124.

26. Duty to give traffic commissioners information about vehicles

(1) It shall be the duty of the holder of a PSV operator's licence, on the happening
to any public service vehicle owned by him of any failure or damage of a nature
calculated to affect the safety of occupants of the public service vehicle or of
persons using the road, to report the matter as soon as is practicable to the traffic
commissioners who granted the licence.

(2) It shall be the duty of the holder of a PSV operator's licence, on any alteration otherwise than by replacement of parts being made in the structure of fixed
equipment of any public service vehicle owned by him, to give notice of the alteration as soon as is practicable to the traffic commissioners who granted the licence.

(3) The traffic commissioners by whom a PSV operator's licence was granted
may—

    (*a*) require the holder of the licence to supply them forthwith or within a
         specified time with such information as they may reasonably require
         about the public service vehicles owned by him and normally kept at an
         operating centre within the area of those commissioners, and to keep up
         to date information supplied by him under this paragraph; or

    (*b*) require the holder or former holder of the licence to supply them forth-
         with or within a specified time with such information as they may
         reasonably require about the public service vehicles owned by him at
         any material time specified by them which were at that time normally
         kept at an operating centre within the area of those commissioners.

In this subsection "material time" means a time when the PSV operator's
licence in question was in force.

(4) A person who fails to comply with the provisions of subsection (1) or (2) or
with any requirement under subsection (3) shall be liable on summary conviction
to a fine not exceeding £200.

(5) A person who in purporting to comply with any requirement under subsection (3) supplies any information which he knows to be false or does not believe
to be true shall be liable on summary conviction to a fine not exceeding £500.

(6) Where a certifying officer or public service vehicle examiner imposes or
removes a prohibition on the driving of a public service vehicle, he shall forthwith
give notice of that fact to the traffic commissioners who granted the PSV
operator's licence under which the vehicle was last used before the prohibition was
imposed. **[92]**

COMMENCEMENT
     See s. 70 (5), *post*, and the note "Orders under this section" thereto.

SUB-S. (1): TRAFFIC COMMISSIONERS WHO GRANTED THE LICENCE
     See s. 19 (2), *ante*.

FORTHWITH
     See the note to s. 18, *ante*.

SUB-S. (4): PERSON
     See the note to s. 2, *ante*.

SUMMARY CONVICTION
See the note to s. 4, *ante*.

SUB-S. (5): FALSE
See the note to s. 7, *ante*.

SUB-S. (6): WHERE A CERTIFYING OFFICER . . . IMPOSES OR REMOVES . . . PUBLIC SERVICE VEHICLE
See s. 18, *ante*.

PARTNERSHIP
See the note to s. 5, *ante*.

DEFINITIONS
For "public service vehicle", see s. 2, *ante*; for "operating centre", "owned" and "PSV operator's licence", see s. 44 (1), *post*; by virtue of s. 1 (3), *ante*, for "the traffic commissioners", see the Road Traffic Act 1960, s. 120 (4), A.L.S. Vol. 124, for "certifying", see s. 128 (1) of that Act, as amended by s. 43 (1) and Sch. 5, Part I, para. 1 (2), *post*, and for "road", see s. 257 (1) of that Act.

27. Certificates of qualification

(1) A person who wishes to do either of the following things in another member State or in Northern Ireland, namely to carry on a road passenger transport business or to be the transport manager of such a business, may apply—

    (*a*) if he holds a standard licence, to the traffic commissioners by whom that licence was granted or, if he holds more than one, by whom the last such licence was granted;

    (*b*) in any other case, to the traffic commissioners for any traffic area,

for a certificate as to his repute and professional competence and, where relevant, his financial standing.

(2) A person applying for a certificate under subsection (1) shall give to the traffic commissioners such information as they may reasonably require for the discharge of their duties in relation to the application.

(3) The traffic commissioners to whom an application under subsection (1) is made shall certify such matters relating to the applicant as—

    (*a*) they are satisfied they may properly certify, and

    (*b*) appear to them to be of assistance to the applicant in satisfying the requirements of the law of the other member State in which he wishes to carry on business or to work or, as the case may be, the requirements of the law of Northern Ireland. **[93]**

COMMENCEMENT
See s. 70 (5), *post*, and the note "Orders under this section" thereto.

PERSON
See the note to s. 2, *ante*.

MEMBER STATE
I.e., a state which is a member of the European Communities; see the European Communities Act 1972, s. 1 (2), Sch. 1, Part II, A.L.S. Vol. 205, as applied by the Interpretation Act 1978, s. 5, Sch. 1, A.L.S. Vol. 258.

TRAFFIC COMMISSIONERS BY WHOM THAT LICENCE WAS GRANTED, ETC
See s. 19 (2), *ante*.

TRAFFIC COMMISSIONERS
See the note to s. 3, *ante*.

TRAFFIC AREA
    See the note to s. 4, *ante*.

SATISFIED; APPEAR
    See the note "Satisfied" to s. 5, *ante*.

FORGERY AND MISUSE OF DOCUMENTS, ETC.; FALSE STATEMENTS TO OBTAIN CERTIFICATES, ETC
    See the notes to s. 17, *ante*.

FEES
    See the note to s. 24, *ante*.

DEFINITIONS
    For "standard licence" and "transport manager", see s. 44 (1), *post*; by virtue of s. 1 (3), *ante*, for
    "the traffic commissioners", see the Road Traffic Act 1960, s. 120 (4), A.L.S. Vol. 124.

Supplementary provisions relating to licences

28. Appeals to the Minister

(1) A person who has applied for the grant of a licence under this Part may appeal
to the Minister against any decision of the traffic commissioners —

  (a) to refuse to grant the licence in accordance with the application; or
  (b) to attach any condition to the licence otherwise than in accordance with
        the application.

(2) Where a person who has applied for a new licence under this Part in substitution for a licence held by him and in force at the date of his application
appeals to the Minister under subsection (1) against any such decision of the traffic
commissioners as is mentioned in paragraph (a) or (b) of that subsection, the existing licence shall continue in force until the appeal is disposed of, but without prejudice to the exercise in the meantime of the powers conferred by section 10 or 23.

(3) The holder of a licence granted under this Part may appeal to the Minister
against any decision of the traffic commissioners —

  (a) to refuse an application by the holder for the variation or removal of any
        condition attached to the licence;
  (b) to vary any such condition, or to attach any new condition to the
        licence, otherwise than on an application by the holder; or
  (c) to revoke or suspend the licence or to curtail its period of validity.

(4) Traffic commissioners making any such decision with respect to a licence
as is mentioned in paragraph (b) or (c) of subsection (3) may, if the holder of the
licence so requests, direct that their decision shall not have effect until the expiration of the period within which an appeal against it may be made to the Minister
under that subsection and, if such an appeal is made, until the appeal is disposed
of; and if they refuse to give such a direction, the holder of the licence may apply to
the Minister for such a direction, and the Minister shall give his decision on the
application within 14 days.

(5) A person who has applied for the grant of a licence under this Part, or for
the variation or removal of any conditions attached to such a licence, shall, if the
traffic commissioners to whom the application was made fail to come to a decision
on the application within a reasonable time, have the same right to appeal to the
Minister as if the commissioners had decided to refuse the application.

(6) A person applying for —

  (a) a certificate of initial fitness; or
  (b) a certificate under section 130 of the 1960 Act (type approval),

may appeal to the Minister against the refusal of a certifying officer to issue such a certificate.

(7) A person other than the applicant for, or holder of, a road service licence may, if he has standing in the matter in accordance with subsection (8), appeal to the Minister against any decision of the traffic commissioners with respect to—

(*a*) the grant, revocation or suspension of a road service licence; or

(*b*) the attachment of any condition to the road service licence or the variation or removal of any condition attached to such a licence.

(8) The persons having standing to appeal under subsection (7) against a decision of the traffic commissioners with respect to a road service licence are—

(*a*) any local authority in whose area the service, or any part of the service, is being or is to be provided under the licence; and

(*b*) any person providing transport facilities along or near the route, or part of the route, of the service which is being or is to be provided under the licence,

being an authority or person who has made objections or other representations to the traffic commissioners in the course of the proceedings resulting in that decision.

In this subsection "local authority" means—

(i) in relation to England and Wales, any local authority within the meaning of the Local Government Act 1972;

(ii) (*applies to Scotland*).

(9) An appeal under this section must be made within the prescribed time and in the prescribed manner, and provision may be made by regulations as to the procedure to be followed in connection with appeals under this section.

(10) On the determination of an appeal under this section, the Minister may confirm, vary or reverse the decision appealed against, and may give such directions as he thinks fit to the traffic commissioners or, as the case may be, to the certifying officer for giving effect to his decision; and it shall be the duty of the traffic commissioners or certifying officer to comply with any such directions.

[94]

COMMENCEMENT
See s. 70 (5), *post*, and the note "Orders under this section" thereto.

SUB-S. (1): PERSON WHO HAS APPLIED FOR THE GRANT OF A LICENCE UNDER THIS PART
I.e., under s. 5 or 21, *ante*.

APPEAL TO THE MINISTER
In the case of the decisions with respect to road service licences mentioned in the Road Traffic Regulation Act 1967, ss. 6 (8), 9 (8), A.L.S. Vol. 165, as amended by s. 43 (1) and Sch. 5, Part II, *post* (which sections relate to traffic regulations in Greater London and to experimental traffic orders respectively), no appeal lies under this section if and so far as the traffic commissioners certify as mentioned in those provisions.

No appeal lies under this section from a decision of the traffic commissioners to refuse to grant a road service licence in pursuance of s. 8 or 9; see ss. 8 (3) and 9 (4), *ante*.

ATTACH ANY CONDITION TO THE LICENCE OTHERWISE THAN IN ACCORDANCE WITH THE APPLICATION
I.e., under s. 6, 7 or 22, *ante*.

SUB-S. (3): APPLICATION . . . FOR THE VARIATION OR REMOVAL OF ANY CONDITION
See ss. 6 (4), 7 (4) and 22 (6), *ante*.

VARY ANY SUCH CONDITION . . . OTHERWISE THAN ON AN APPLICATION BY THE HOLDER
I.e., under s. 6, 7 or 22, *ante*.

REVOKE OR SUSPEND . . . PERIOD OF VALIDITY
I.e., under s. 10 or 23, *ante*.

SUB-S. (5): PERSON WHO HAS APPLIED . . . FOR THE VARIATION OR REMOVAL OF ANY CONDITIONS ATTACHED TO SUCH A LICENCE
I.e., under s. 6 (4), 7 (4) or 22 (6), *ante*.

WITHIN A REASONABLE TIME
Where anything is to be done within a "reasonable time", the question what is a reasonable time depends on the circumstances of the particular case and is therefore a question of fact; see *Burton* v. *Griffiths* (1843), 11 M. & W. 817.

SUB-S. (6): PERSON APPLYING FOR A CERTIFICATE OF INITIAL FITNESS
See s. 17, *ante*.

SUB-S. (7): PERSON
See the note to s. 2, *ante*.

ROAD SERVICE LICENCE
As to these generally, see s. 4, *ante*.

GRANT, REVOCATION OR SUSPENSION OF A ROAD SERVICE LICENCE
For the granting of a road service licence, see s. 5, *ante*; and for its revocation or suspension, see s. 10, *ante*.

ATTACHMENT OF ANY CONDITION . . . VARIATION OR REMOVAL . . . LICENCE
I.e., under s. 6 or 7, *ante*.

SUB-S. (8): AUTHORITY OR PERSON WHO HAS MADE OBJECTIONS, ETC
See s. 5 (3) (*c*), *ante*.

ENGLAND; WALES
For meaning see the Interpretation Act 1978, s. 5, Sch. 1, A.L.S. Vol. 258.

SUB-S. (9): PRESCRIBED TIME; PRESCRIBED MANNER
See The Public Service Vehicles (Road Service Licences and Express Services) Regulations 1980, S.I. 1980 No. 1354, reg. 20, which prescribes both the time for appeals and the form in which it must be made.

SUB-S. (10): THE MINISTER MAY CONFIRM, VARY OR REVERSE, ETC
In deciding the appeal the Minister of Transport must not usurp the powers of the traffic commissioners under s. 10, *ante*, and accordingly may neither direct them to revoke the licence on the happening of a certain event nor do so himself; see *R.* v. *Minister of Transport, ex parte upminster Services Ltd*, [1934] 1 K.B. 277; [1933] All E.R. Rep. 604. On the other hand, he may in making his decision have regard to decisions of his in other cases; see *Alexander & Son.* v. *Minister of Transport*, 1936 S.L.T. 553.

THINKS FIT
See the note "Satisfied" to s. 5, *ante*.

FURTHER APPEALS ON POINTS OF LAW
See s. 29, *post*.

LONDON
See the note to s. 5, *ante*.

PROSPECTIVE REPEAL
See the note to s. 17, *ante*.

DEFINITIONS
For "road service licence", see s. 44 (1), *post*, for "the Minister", see s. 70 (2), *post*; by virtue of s. 1 (3), *ante*, for "the traffic commissioners", see the Road Traffic Act 1960, s. 120 (4), A.L.S. Vol. 124, for "certifying officer", see s. 128 (1) of that Act, as amended by s. 43 (1) and Sch. 5, Part I, para. 1 (2), *post*, and for "prescribed" and "regulations", see s. 160 (2) of that Act. Note as to "local authority", sub-s. (8) above.

1960 ACT
   I.e., the Road Traffic Act 1960; see s. 44 (1), *post*. For s. 130 of that Act, see A.L.S. Vol. 124, and
as to its prospective repeal, see the note on the 1960 Act to s. 17, *ante*.

LOCAL GOVERNMENT ACT 1972
   For the meaning of "local authority" in that Act, see s. 270 (1), thereof, A.L.S. Vol. 209.

REGULATIONS UNDER THIS SECTION
   At the time of going to press no regulations had been made for the purposes of sub-s. (9) above but
by virtue of the Road Traffic Act 1960, s. 267 (2), Sch. 19, para. 1, A.L.S. Vol. 124, as construed
in accordance with s. 1 (3), *ante*, the Public Service Vehicles (Licences and Certificates) Regulations 1952, S.I. 1952 No. 900, reg. 13, as substituted by S.I. 1957 No. 123; 22 Halsbury's
Statutory Instruments, title Transport (Part 2c), with, if still in force at the commencement of this
section, have effect for the purposes of sub-s. (9). See also the note "Prescribed time; prescribed
manner" to sub-s. (9) above.
   By virtue of s. 1 (3), *ante*, for general provisions as to regulations, see the Road Traffic Act
1960, ss. 160, 260, as amended by s. 43 (1) and Sch. 5, Part I, para. 11 and 15, respectively, *post*,
and see partly repealed, in the case of s. 160, by s. 69 and Sch. 9, Part I, *post*.

29. Further appeals on points of law

(1) An appeal lies at the instance of any of the persons mentioned in subsection (2)
on any point of law arising from a decision of the Minister on an appeal from a
decision of the traffic commissioners for any area—

   (*a*) to the High Court where the proceedings before the traffic commis-
         sioners were in England or Wales; and

   (*b*) (*applies to Scotland*).

(2) The persons who may appeal against any such decision of the Minister
are—

   (*a*) the person who appealed to the Minister;

   (*b*) any person who had a right to appeal to the Minister against the relevant
         decision of the traffic commissioners but did not exercise that right; and

   (*c*) the traffic commissioners whose decision was appealed against.

(3) If on an appeal under this section the High Court or Court of Session is of
opinion that the decision appealed against was erroneous in point of law, it shall
remit the matter to the Minister with the opinion of the court for rehearing and
determination by him.

(4) No appeal to the Court of Appeal may be brought from a decision of the
High Court under this section except with the leave of the High Court or the Court
of Appeal.

(5) (*Applies to Scotland.*)   **[95]**

COMMENCEMENT
   See s. 70 (5), *post*, and the note "Orders under this section" thereto.

SUB-S. (1): PERSONS
   See the note "Person" to s. 2, *ante*.

POINT OF LAW
   On whether a point (or question) is one of fact or law, see in particular *Bracegirdle* v. *Oxley*, [1947]
K.B. 349; [1947] 1 All E.R. 126; *Hemns* v. *Wheeler*, [1948] 2 K.B. 61, C.A., *Edwards* v. *Bairstow*
[1956] A.C. 14; [1955] 3 All E.R. 48, H.L., *Re Helbert Wagg & Co. Ltd.*, [1956] 1 Ch. 323; [1956]
1 All E.R. 129, *Chivers & Sons, Ltd.*, v. *Cambridge County Council*, [1957] 2 Q.B. 68, [1957] 1 All
E.R. 882, C.A., and *Golbal Plant Ltd.* v. *Secretary of State for Health and Social Security* [1972] 1
Q.B. 139; [1971] 3 All E.R. 385. Many of the cases on this question are irreconcilable; see, *e.g.*, the
review of the decisions in 62 L.Q.R. 248. The court may, however, treat as a question of fact what
is described as a question of law (*Metropolitan Water Board* v. *Kingston Union Assessment*

Committee, [1925] 2 K.B. 509, C.A.; affirmed *sub nom. Kingston Union Assessment Committee* v. *Metropolitan Water Board,* [1926] A.C. 331; [1926] All E.R. Rep. 1). A mixed question of law and fact is open to review by the court (*Great Western Rail. Co.* v. *Bater,* [1922] 2 A.C. 1). See, further, the note to the Taxes Management Act 1970, s. 56, A.L.S. Vol. 188.

DECISION OF THE MINISTER ON AN APPEAL, ETC
See s. 28, *ante.*

TRAFFIC COMMISSIONERS
See the note to s. 3, *ante.*

HIGH COURT
I.e., Her Majesty's High Court of Justice in England; see the Interpretation Act 1978, s. 5, Sch. 1, A.L.S. Vol. 258. For the constitution of the court, see the Supreme Court of Judicature (Consolidation) Act 1925, s. 2, 7, Halsbury's Statutes (3rd edn.), p. 576, and for its divisions, see ss. 4 and 5 of that Act.

ENGLAND; WALES
For meanings see the Interpretation Act 1978, s. 5, Sch. 1, A.L.S. Vol. 258.

SUB-S. (4): COURT OF APPEAL
I.e., Her Majesty's Court of Appeal in England; see the Interpretation Act 1978, s. 5, Sch. 1, A.L.S. Vol. 258. For the constitution of the court, see the Supreme Court of Judicature (Consolidation) Act 1925, s. 6, 7, Halsbury's Statutes (3rd edn.), p. 578, and for its two divisions, see the Criminal Appeal Act 1966, s. 1 (2), A.L.S. Vol. 158.

DEFINITIONS
For "the Minister", see s. 70 (2), *post;* by virtue of s. 1 (3), *ante,* for "the traffic commissioners", see the Road Traffic Act 1960, s. 120 (4), A.L.S. Vol. 124.

Partnerships and related matters

(1) Provision may be made by regulations for modifying the provisions of this Part, and any other statutory provisions relating to public service vehicles, in their application to the operation of vehicles and the provision of services by persons in partnership.

(2) A road service licence or PSV operator's licence shall not be granted to an unincorporated body as such or to more than one person jointly except in cases permitted by regulations under this section.   **[96]**

COMMENCEMENT
See s. 70 (5), *post,* and the note "Orders under this section" thereto.

THIS PART
I.e., Part I (ss. 1 – 44) of this Act.

PERSONS
See the note "Person" to s. 2, *ante.*

ROAD SERVICE LICENCE OR PSV OPERATOR'S LICENCE SHALL NOT BE GRANTED
I.e., under s. 5 or 21, *ante.*

DEFINITIONS
For "public service vehicle", see s. 2, *ante;* for "PSV operator's licence" and "road service licence", see s. 44 (1), *post;* for "statutory provision", see s. 70 (2), *post;* by virtue of s. 1 (3), *ante,* for "regulations", see the Road Traffic Act 1960, s. 160 (2), A.L.S. Vol. 124.

REGULATIONS UNDER THIS SECTION
At the time of going to press no regulations had been made for the purposes of sub-s. (1) or (2) above.
      By virtue of s. 1 (3), *ante,* for general provisions as to regulations, see the Road Traffic Act 1960, ss. 160, 260, A.L.S. Vol. 124, as amended by s. 43 (1) and Sch. 5, Part I, paras. 11 and 15, respectively, *post,* and as partly repealed, in the case of s. 160, by s. 69 and Sch. 9, Part I, *post.*

31. Death, bankruptcy, etc., of licence-holder

(1) A road service licence or PSV operator's licence is not assignable or, subject to the following provisions of this section, transmissible on death or in any other way.

(2) A road service licence or PSV operator's licence held by an individual terminates if he —

(a) dies; or

(b) is adjudged bankrupt or, in Scotland, has his estate sequestrated; or

(c) becomes a patient within the meaning of Part VIII of the Mental Health Act 1959 or, in Scotland, becomes incapable of managing his own affairs.

(3) In relation to a road service licence or PSV operator's licence held by an individual or by a company regulations may specify other events relating to the licence-holder on the occurrence of which the licence is to terminate.

(4) The traffic commissioners by whom a road service licence or PSV operator's licence was granted may —

(a) direct that the termination of the licence by subsection (2), or under subsection (3), be deferred for a period not exceeding 12 months or, if it appears to the commissioners that there are special circumstances, 18 months; and

(b) authorise the business of the licence-holder to be carried on under the licence by some other person during the period of deferment, subject to such conditions as the commissioners may impose. **[97]**

COMMENCEMENT
See s. 70 (5), *post*, and the note "Orders under this section" thereto.

INDIVIDUAL
This word is used instead of the word "person" in order, presumably, to exclude bodies of persons corporate or unincorporate; cf. the Interpretation Act 1978, s. 5, Sch. 1 A.L.S. Vol. 258, and *Whitney* v. *Inland Revenue Comrs.*, [1926] A.C. 37, at p. 43, *per* Viscount Cave, L.C.

ADJUDGED BANKRUPT
As to how a person can be made a bankrupt, see the Bankruptcy Act 1914, ss. 1, 2, 4 (1) (a), 107 (4), 3, Halsbury's Statutes (3rd edn.), pp. 38, 42, 44, 133.

TRAFFIC COMMISSIONERS BY WHOM A ROAD SERVICE LICENCE OR PSV OPERATOR'S LICENCE WAS GRANTED
See s. 4 (2) or 19 (2), *ante*.

MONTHS
I.e., calendar months; see the Interpretation Act 1978, s. 5, Sch. 1, A.L.S. Vol. 258.

APPEARS
See the note "satisfied" to s. 5, *ante*.

PERSON
See the note to s. 2, *ante*.

PARTNERSHIPS
See the note to s. 5, *ante*.

PERMISSIBLE RELAXATIONS OF ROAD TRAFFIC AND TRANSPORT LAW
See the note to s. 6, *ante*.

DEFINITIONS
For "company", "PSV operator's licence" and "road service licence", see s. 44 (1), *post*; by virtue of s. 1 (3), *ante*, for "the traffic commissioners", see the Road Traffic Act 1960, s. 120 (4), A.L.S. Vol. 124 and for "regulations", see s. 180 (2) of that Act.

REGULATIONS UNDER THIS SECTION
At the time of going to press no regulations had been made for the purposes of sub-s. (3) above.

By virtue of s. 1 (3), *ante*, for general provisions as to regulations, see the Road Traffic Act 1960, ss. 160, 260, A.L.S. Vol. 124, as amended by s. 43 (1) and Sch. 5, Part I, paras. 11 and 15 respectively, *post* and as partly repealed, in the case of s. 160, by s. 69 and Sch. 9, Part I, *post*.

Other matters

32. Fare-paying passengers on school buses

(1) Subject to subsection (2), a local education authority may—

(*a*) use a school bus, when it is being used to provide free school transport, to carry as fare-paying passengers persons other than those for whom the free school transport is provided; and

(*b*) use a school bus belonging to the authority, when it is not being used to provide free school transport, to provide a local bus service;

and the following provisions, that is to say section 144 of the 1960 Act (public service vehicle drivers' licences) and sections 16, 17, 18 and 19 (1) of this Act, shall not apply to a school bus belonging to a local education authority in the course of its use by the authority in accordance with this subsection.

(2) Subsection (1) does not affect the duties of a local education authority in relation to the provision of free school transport or authorise a local education authority to make any charge for the carriage of a pupil on a journey which he is required to make in the course of his education at a school maintained by such an authority.

(3) In this section—

"free school transport" means transport provided by a local education authority in pursuance of arrangements under section 55 (1) of the Education Act 1944 for the purpose of facilitating the attendance of pupils at a place of education;

"local bus service" means a stage carriage service other than a service as regards which the condition specified in section 3 (3) (*a*) is satisfied;

"school bus", in relation to a local education authority, means a motor vehicle which is used by that authority to provide free school transport.

(4) (*Applies to Scotland.*)

(5) The repeal by this Act of section 12 of the Education (Miscellaneous Provisions) Act 1953 and section 118 (4) of the 1960 Act shall not affect the operation of those provisions in relation to any consent given under the said section 12 which is in force immediately before that repeal takes effect.　　**[98]**

COMMENCEMENT
See s. 70 (5), *post*, and the note "Orders under this section" thereto.

SUB-S. (1): LOCAL EDUCATION AUTHORITY
See the note to s. 4, *ante*.

BELONGING
This word, which is not a term of art, is clearly used here in a sense which it bears in ordinary language; cf. *Re Miller, Ex parte Official Receiver*, [1893] 1 Q.B. 327, C.A., at pp. 334, 335, *per* Lord Esher, M.R.

SUB-S. (3): MOTOR VEHICLE
As to the treatment of articulated vehicles for the purposes of this Part of this Act, see the Road Traffic Act 1972, s. 191, as substituted by s. 63, *post*.

SUB-S. (5): THAT REPEAL TAKES EFFECT
    See s. 70 (5.), *post*, and the note "Orders under this section" thereto.

DEFINITIONS
    For "stage carriage service", see s. 44 (1), *post*; by virtue of s. 1 (3), *ante*, for "motor vehicle", see the Road Traffic Act 1960, s. 253 (2), A.L.S. Vol. 124. Note as to "free school transport", "local bus service" and "school bus", sub-s. (3) above.

1960 ACT
    I.e., the Road Traffic Act 1960; see s. 44 (1), *post*. For ss. 118 (4) and 144 of that Act, see A.L.S. Vol. 124. S. 118 is repealed by s. 1 (1), (2), *ante*, and s. 69 and Sch. 9, Part I, *post*, and s. 144 is amended by ss. 36, 37 (1), 40 and 43 (1), Sch. 4 and Sch. 5, Part I, para. 4, *post*, and is partly repealed by s. 69 and Sch. 9, Part I, *post*.

EDUCATION ACT 1944, S. 55 (1)
    See 11, Halsbury's Statutes (3rd edn.), p. 217.

EDUCATION (MISCELLANEOUS PROVISIONS) ACT 1953, S. 12
    See 28, Halsbury's Statutes (3rd edn.), p. 310. That section is repealed by s. 69 and Sch. 9, Part I, *post*.

33. Use of certain vehicles by educational and other bodies

(1) In subsection (1) of section 1 of the Minibus Act 1977 (exemption of certain vehicles from requirements applicable to public service vehicles) for "vehicle which is adapted to carry more than seven but not more than sixteen passengers" there shall be substituted "small passenger-carrying vehicle", and after that sub-section there shall be inserted the following subsection —

"(1A) If a large passenger-carrying vehicle is used for carrying passengers for hire or reward, then, if and so long as the conditions set out in paragraphs (*a*) to (*c*) of subsection (1) above are satisfied, the following provisions shall not apply to the driving or use of the vehicle, namely —

(*a*) section 144 of the Road Traffic Act 1960 (public service vehicle drivers' licences);

(*b*) section 23 (2) of the Transport (London) Act 1969 and section 4 of the Transport Act 1980 (licensing of stage carriage services); and

(*c*) section 19 (1) of the Transport Act 1980 (PSV operators' licences).".

(2) In section 1 (2) of that Act (persons authorised to grant permits) —

(*a*) at the beginning of paragraph (*a*) (powers of traffic commissioners) there shall be inserted "in the case of small passenger-carrying vehicles,"; and

(*b*) at the beginning of paragraph (*b*) (power of designated bodies) there shall be inserted "in the case of small or large passenger-carrying vehicles,".

(3) After section 1 (3) of that Act (designation orders) there shall be inserted the following subsection —

"(3A) Different provision may be made by orders under subsection (3) above in relation to large passenger-carrying vehicles from that made in relation to small passenger-carrying vehicles.";

and a designation order made under the said section 1 (3) before the commencement of this section shall not apply in relation to large passenger-carrying vehicles.

(4) In section 3 (1) of that Act (power to make regulations), in paragraph (*e*) (power to prescribe conditions of fitness) for "vehicles" there shall be substituted "small passenger-carrying vehicles".

(5) After section 3 (1) of that Act there shall be inserted the following subsection —

"(1A) Regulations made by virtue of any of paragraphs (*a*) to (*d*) of subsection (1) above may make different provision in relation to large passenger-carrying vehicles from that made in relation to small passenger-carrying vehicles.".

(6) In section 3 (2) of that Act (consequences of breach of regulations) for "Section 1 (1)" substitute "Subsection (1) or, as the case may be, subsection (1A) of section 1".

(7) In section 4 (2) of that Act (interpretation) after paragraph (*b*) there shall be inserted the following paragraph —

"(*bb*) "small passenger-carrying vehicle" means a vehicle which is adapted to carry more than eight but not more than sixteen passengers, and "large passenger-carrying vehicle" means a vehicle which is adapted to carry more than sixteen passengers;"   **[99]**

COMMENCEMENT
See s. 70 (5), *post*, and the note "Orders under this section" thereto.

ADAPTED
See the note to s. 2, *ante*.

MINIBUS ACT 1977, SS. 1 (3), 4 (2) (*b*)
See A.L.S. Vol. 254.

ROAD TRAFFIC ACT 1960, S. 144
See A.L.S. Vol. 124. That section is amended by ss. 36, 37 (1), 40 and 43 (1) and Sch. 4 and Sch. 5, Part I, para. 4, *post*, and partly repealed by s. 69 and Sch. 9, Part I, *post*.

TRANSPORT (LONDON) ACT 1969, S. 23 (2)
See A.L.S. Vol. 185.

34. Obligatory test certificates for passenger-carrying vehicles

In section 44 of the Road Traffic Act 1972 (obligatory test certificates), in subsection (4) (excluded classes of vehicles) the following words (which relate to the exclusion of large public service vehicles) shall be omitted —

(*a*) the words from "to public service vehicles" to "passengers or"; and

(*b*) the words from "but shall apply" onwards.   **[100]**

COMMENCEMENT
See s. 70 (5), *post*, and the note "Orders under this section" thereto.

ROAD TRAFFIC ACT 1972, S. 44 (4)
See A.L.S. Vol. 208. The words to be omitted are also repealed by s. 69 and Sch. 9, Part I, *post*, and s. 44 (4) is also amended by s. 43 (1) and Sch. 5, Part II, *post*.

35. Amendment of Transport (London) Act 1969

After section 23 of the Transport (London) Act 1969 (restrictions on provision of London bus services otherwise than by the London Transport Executive and their subsidiaries) there shall be inserted: —

"23A. Right of appeal where Executive refuse to make or vary an agreement authorising a London bus service
(1) Where a person other than the Executive or a subsidiary of theirs seeks —

    (*a*) an agreement with the Executive under subsection (2) of section 23 of this Act to enable him to provide a London bus service; or

    (*b*) an agreement with the Executive to vary the terms of an agreement under that subsection (whenever made) which for the time being subsists between himself and the Executive,

then, if the Executive refuse to enter into the agreement sought or fail to enter into it within a reasonable period, that person may appeal to the Minister on the ground of the refusal or failure.

(2) A person appealing under this section shall give notice of the appeal —

    (*a*) to the Council;

    (*b*) to the commissioner or commissioners of police concerned; and

    (*c*) to any of the councils of the London boroughs or the Common Council within whose area it is proposed to provide a service under the agreement sought by the appellant;

and the Minister shall not proceed with the appeal unless he is satisfied that such notice has been given.

(3) In determining an appeal under this section the Minister shall take into account —

    (*a*) any representations made by the Council; and

    (*b*) any representations with respect to relevant road traffic matters made by any of the persons notified as mentioned in paragraph (*b*) or (*c*) of subsection (2) of this section.

(4) An appeal under this section must be made within the prescribed time and in the prescribed manner; and provision may be made by regulations as to the procedure to be followed in connection with appeals under this section.

(5) On such an appeal the Minister may make such order, if any, as he thinks fit requiring the Executive to enter into an agreement with the appellant on such terms as may be specified in the order; and it shall be the duty of the Executive to comply with any such order.

(6) For the purposes of any reference in this or any other Act to an agreement under subsection (2) of section 23 of this Act any agreement entered into or varied by the Executive in compliance with an order under subsection (5) above shall be taken to be such an agreement.

(7) In this section —

    "commissioner of police" and "London bus service" have the same meaning as in section 23 of this Act;

    "prescribed" means prescribed by regulations made by the Minister;

    "relevant road traffic matters", in relation to an appeal, means the following matters relating to the service proposed to be provided under the agreement sought by the appellant —

        (*a*) the route of the service and its terminal points;

        (*b*) the points at which passengers may or may not be taken up or set down;

        (*c*) the places at which, and streets by the use of which, vehicles used for the service may turn at a terminal point.

23B. Further appeals on points of law

(1) An appeal lies to the High Court at the instance of any of the persons mentioned in subsection (2) of this section on any point of law arising from a

decision of the Minister on an appeal under section 23A of this Act.

(2) The persons who may appeal against any such decision of the Minister are —

    (*a*) the person who appealed to the Minister;

    (*b*) any person required to be notified of that appeal under subsection (2) of section 23A of this Act; and

    (*c*) the Executive.

(3) If on an appeal under this section the High Court is of opinion that the decision appealed against was erroneous in point of law, it shall remit the matter to the Minister with the opinion of the court for rehearing and determination by him.

(4) No appeal to the Court of Appeal may be brought from a decision of the High Court under this section except with the leave of the High Court or the Court of Appeal.".   **[101]**

COMMENCEMENT
See s. 70 (5), *post*, and the note "Orders under this section" thereto.

PERSON
See the note to s. 2, *ante*.

WITHIN A REASONABLE PERIOD
Cf. the note "Within a reasonable time" to s. 28, *ante*.

COUNCILS OF THE LONDON BOROUGHS
See the note "London borough council" to s. 5, *ante*.

SATISFIED; THINKS FIT
See the note "Satisfied" to s. 5, *ante*.

PRESCRIBED TIME; PRESCRIBED MANNER
"Prescribed" means prescribed by regulations made by the Minister; see the Transport (London) Act 1969, s. 23A (7), as inserted by this section. At the time of going to press no regulations had been made for the purposes of s. 23A (4) of that Act as so inserted.

HIGH COURT; POINT OF LAW; COURT OF APPEAL
See the corresponding notes to s. 29, *ante*.

INQUIRIES
The Minister or the Secretary of State may hold inquiries for the purposes of the Transport (London) Act 1969, s. 23A, as inserted by this section; see the Road Traffic Act 1960, s. 248, A.L.S. Vol. 124 as amended by s. 43 (1) and Sch. 5, Part I, para. 13, *post*.

DEFINITIONS
For "commissioner of police" and "London bus service", see the Transport (London) Act 1969, s. 23 (7), A.L.S. Vol. 185, as applied by s. 23A (7) of that Act as inserted by this section; for "the Common Council", "the Council", "the Executive", "the Minister", "subsidiary" and "vehicle", see s. 45 (1) of that Act. Note as to "prescribed" and "relevant road traffic matters", s. 23A (7) of that Act as inserted by this section.

TRANSPORT (LONDON) ACT 1969, S. 23
See A.L.S. Vol. 185. That section is amended by s. 43 (1) and Sch. 5, Part II, *post*, and partly repealed by s. 69 and Sch. 9, Part I, *post*.

REGULATIONS UNDER THIS SECTION
At the time of going to press no regulations had been made under the Transport (London) Act 1969, s. 23A (4) or (7), as inserted by this section.
For general provisions as to regulations, see s. 43 of the Act of 1969, A.L.S. Vol. 185.

36. Abolition of licensing of conductors of public service vehicles

Subsection (1) of section 144 of the 1960 Act (drivers' and conductors' licences) shall cease to have effect so far as it requires a person acting as conductor of a public service vehicle on a road to be licensed for the purpose under that section or prohibits the employment for that purpose of a person not so licensed.   [102]

COMMENCEMENT
> See s. 70 (5), *post*, and the note "Orders under this section" thereto.

DEFINITIONS
> For "public service vehicle", see s. 2, *ante*; by virtue of s. 1 (3), *ante*, for "road", see the Road Traffic Act 1960, s. 257 (1), A.L.S. Vol. 124.

1960 ACT
> *I.e.*, Road Traffic Act 1960; see s. 44 (1), *post*. For s. 144 (1) of that Act, see A.L.S. Vol. 124. That subsection is also partly repealed by s. 69 and Sch. 9, Part I, *post*.

37. Reduction of minimum age for drivers of public service vehicles

(1) In subsection (3) of section 144 of the 1960 Act (PSV drivers' licences: minimum age and other conditions) for the words from "unless", in the first place where it occurs, to the end of the subsection there shall be substituted "unless he fulfils such conditions as may be prescribed".

(2) Subsection (1) of section 96 of the Road Traffic Act 1972 (minimum ages at which licences may be held for different classes of vehicles) shall have effect as if in the Table in that subsection, in item 6, the age of 18 were substituted for the age of 21 in relation to a large passenger vehicle where —

(*a*) the driver is not engaged in the carriage of passengers and either holds a PSV driver's licence or is acting under the supervision of a person who holds a PSV driver's licence; or

(*b*) the driver holds a PSV driver's licence and is engaged in the carriage of passengers —

    (i) on a regular service over a route which does not exceed 50 kilometres; or

    (ii) on a national transport operation when the vehicle used is constructed and equipped to carry not more than 15 persons including the driver,

and in either case the operator of the vehicle holds a PSV operator's licence granted by the traffic commissioners for any area, not being a licence which is of no effect by reason of its suspension.

(3) In subsection (2) —

"large passenger vehicle" means a motor vehicle which is constructed solely to carry passengers and their effects and is adapted to carry more than nine persons inclusive of the driver;

"PSV driver's licence" means a licence to drive a public service vehicle granted under section 144 of the 1960 Act.

(4) The provisions of subsections (2) and (3) may be amended or repealed by regulations under section 96 (2) of the Road Traffic Act 1972.   [103]

COMMENCEMENT
> See s. 70 (5), *post*, and the note "Orders under this section" thereto.

SUCH CONDITIONS AS MAY BE PRESCRIBED
> See the note "Such other conditions as may be prescribed" to the Road Traffic Act 1960, s. 144, A.L.S. Vol. 124.

    See the note to s. 3, *ante*.

MOTOR VEHICLE; ADAPTED
    See the notes to s. 2, *ante*.

CONSTRUCTED SOLELY, ETC
    It is thought that in the definition of large passenger vehicle "constructed" does not mean "originally constructed", but means "constructed at the material time" and accordingly includes "reconstructed" (cf. *Keeble* v. *Miller*, [1950] 1 K.B. 601; [1950] 1 All E.R. 261). Note the word "solely" (cf. *Flower Freight Co., Ltd.* v. *Hammond*, [1963] 1 Q.B. 275; [1962] 3 All E.R. 950, at p. 282 and p. 952, respectively).

DEFINITIONS
    For "PSV operator's licence", see s. 44 (1), *post*; by virtue of s. 1 (3), *ante*, for "the traffic commissioners", see the Road Traffic Act 1960, s. 120 (4), A.L.S. Vol. 124, and for "motor vehicle", see s. 253 (1) of that Act. Note as to "large passenger vehicle" and "PSV driver's licence", sub-s. (3) above.

1960 ACT
    I.e., the Road Traffic Act 1960; see s. 44 (1), *post*. For s. 144 (3) of that Act, see A.L.S. Vol. 124. That subsection is also amended by s. 43 (1) and Sch. 5, Part I, para. 4 (*a*), *post*, and it is partly repealed by s. 69 and Sch. 9, Part I, *post*.

ROAD TRAFFIC ACT 1972, S. 96
    For that section as substituted, see the Road Traffic (Drivers' Ages and Hours of Work) Act 1976, s. 1, A.L.S. Vol. 244.

38. Fees for grant of licences, etc.

For section 159 (1) of the 1960 Act (fees for grant or issue of licences) there shall be substituted —

> "(1) Such fees, payable at such times, and whether in one sum or by instalments, as may be prescribed shall be charged —
>
> > (*a*) by the traffic commissioners for each traffic area in respect of —
> >
> > > (i) applications for, and the grant of, road service licences and PSV operators' licences;
> > >
> > > (ii) applications for, and the issue of, certificates of initial fitness under section 17 of the Transport Act 1980;
> > >
> > > (iii) the issue of operator's discs under section 24 of that Act;
> > >
> > > (iv) applications for, and the issue of, certificates under section 27 of that Act as to repute, professional competence or financial standing; and
> > >
> > > (v) applications for, and the issue of, documents required in relation to public service vehicles registered in Great Britain while making journeys to or from places outside Great Britain or in relation to public service vehicles registered outside Great Britain;
> >
> > (*b*) by the traffic commissioners for each traffic area and by the commissioner of police for the metropolis in respect of —
> >
> > > (i) applications for, and the issue of, licences to drive public service vehicles; and
> > >
> > > (ii) the provision by the traffic commissioners or the said commissioner of police of facilities for a person to undergo a test of his competence as a driver in connection with an application by him for a licence to drive a public service vehicle, being a test

which he is by virtue of regulations required to undergo in that connection.

(1A) The traffic commissioners or the said commissioner may, if any fee or instalment of a fee due in respect thereof has not been paid, decline to proceed with —

(a) any such application as is mentioned in subsection (1) above,

(b) the grant of any licence or issue of any certificate, disc or other document referred to in that subsection, or

(c) the provision of any such facilities as are mentioned in paragraph (b) (ii) of that subsection,

until the fee or instalment in question has been paid.".   **[104]**

COMMENCEMENT
See s. 70 (5), *post*, and the note "Orders under this section" thereto.

AS MAY BE PRESCRIBED
If the regulations listed in the note "As may be prescribed' to the Road Traffic Act 1960, s. 159, A.L.S. Vol. 124 are still in force at the commencement of this section, that note will still be applicable except that the last limb of that note referring to the Transport Act 1968, s. 30, will have been made obsolete by the repeal of s. 30 of the Act of 1968 by s. 1 (1), (2), (b), *ante*, and s. 69 and Sch. 9, Part I, *post*.

TRAFFIC COMMISSIONERS
See the note to s. 3, *ante*.

TRAFFIC AREA
See the note to s. 4, *ante*.

APPLICATIONS FOR . . . ROAD SERVICE LICENCES AND PSV OPERATORS' LICENCES
See ss. 5 and 21, respectively, *ante*.

GREAT BRITAIN
See the note to s. 12, *ante*.

COMMISSIONER OF POLICE FOR THE METROPOLIS
This Commissioner is appointed under the Metropolitan Police Act 1829, s. 1, 25, Halsbury's Statutes (3rd edn.), p. 240, in conjunction with the Metropolitan Police Act 1856, s. 1, 25, Halsbury's Statutes (3rd edn.), p. 262.

APPLICATION FOR . . . LICENCES TO DRIVE PUBLIC SERVICE VEHICLES
See the Road Traffic Act 1960, s. 144, A.L.S. Vol. 124, as amended by ss. 36, 37 (1), 40 and 43 (1) and Sch. 4 and Sch. 5, Part I, para. 4, *post*, and as partly by s. 69 and Sch. 9, Part I, *post*.

DEFINITIONS
For "the traffic commissioners", see the Road Traffic Act 1960, s. 120 (4), A.L.S. Vol. 124: for "prescribed" and "regulations", see s. 160 (2) of that Act; for "drive" and "driver", see s. 257 (1) of that Act; by virtue of s. 1 (3), *ante*, for "public service vehicle", see s. 2, *ante*, and for "PSV operator's licence" and "road service licence", see s. 44 (1), *post*.

1960 ACT
I.e., the Road Traffic Act 1960; see s. 44 (1), *post*. For s. 159 (1) of that Act, see A.L.S. Vol. 124.

REGULATIONS
At the time of going to press no regulations had been made for the purposes of the Road Traffic Act 1960, s. 159 (1) (b) (ii), as substituted by this section.

For general provisions as to regulations, see the Road Traffic Act 1960, ss. 160, 260, A.L.S. Vol. 124, as amended by s. 43 (1) and Sch. 5, Part I, paras. 11 and 15 respectively, *post*, and as partly repealed in the case of s. 160, by s. 69 and Sch. 9, Part I, *post*.

39. Arrangements for appointment of traffic commissioners

In section 121 of the 1960 Act (appointment etc. of traffic commissioners), for subsections (4) and (5) (appointments, and constitution of panels of nominees for appointment) there shall be substituted —

"(4) Of the three commissioners —

(a) one shall be such person as the Minister thinks fit to appoint to be chairman of the commissioners;

(b) one shall be appointed by the Minister from a panel of persons nominated by such of the following councils, namely in England and Wales county councils and the Greater London Council and in Scotland regional or islands councils, as are councils whose area is wholly or partly comprised in the traffic area; and

(c) the third shall be appointed by the Minister from a panel of persons nominated by such of the following councils, namely in England and Wales district councils, London borough councils and the Common Council of the City of London and in Scotland district councils, as are councils whose area is wholly or partly comprised in the traffic area.

(5) Provision shall be made by regulations as to the arrangements for constituting the panels mentioned in subsection (4) above.".   **[105]**

COMMENCEMENT
See s. 70 (5) *post*, and the note "Orders under this section" thereto.

THINKS FIT
See the note "satisfied" to s. 5, *ante*.

ENGLAND; WALES
For meaning's, see the Interpretation Act 1978, s. 5, Sch. 1, A.L.S. Vol. 258.

COUNTY COUNCILS; DISTRICT COUNCILS
See the note "County council; district council" to s. 5, *ante*.

GREATER LONDON COUNCIL; COMMON COUNCIL OF THE CITY OF LONDON
See the corresponding notes to s. 5, *ante*.

LONDON BOROUGH COUNCILS
See the note "London borough council" to s. 5, *ante*.

DEFINITIONS
For "the traffic commissioners", see the Road Traffic Act 1960, s. 120 (4), A.L.S. Vol. 124; for "regulations", see s. 160 (2) of that Act; by virtue of s. 1 (3), *ante*; for "the Minister", see s. 70 (2), *post*.

1960 ACT
I.e., the Road Traffic Act 1960; see s. 44 (1), *post*. For s. 121 (4) and (5) of that Act, see A.L.S. Vol. 124.

REGULATIONS
Regulations made for the purposes of the Road Traffic Act 1960, s. 121 (5), as substituted by this section will be noted to that section, A.L.S. Vol. 124, in the Service to this work.

40. Increase of penalties

In the case of an offence against any provision of the 1960 Act specified in column 1 of Schedule 4 (of which the general nature is indicated in column 2) the maximum punishment is increased from that now in force (which is indicated in column 3) to that specified in column 4; and for that purpose the provisions of that

Act specified in column 1 shall have effect subject to the amendments specified in column 5. **[106]**

COMMENCEMENT
See s. 70 (5), *post*, and the note "Orders under this section" thereto.

1960 ACT
I.e., the Road Traffic Act 1960 A.L.S. Vol. 124; see s. 44 (1), *post*.

41. Offences by bodies corporate

(1) Where an offence under this Part or Part III of the 1960 Act committed by a company is proved to have been committed with the consent or connivance of, or to be attributable to any neglect on the part of, any director, manager, secretary or other similar officer of the company, or any person who was purporting to act in any such capacity, he, as well as the company, shall be guilty of that offence and be liable to be proceeded against and punished accordingly.

(2) Where the affairs of a company are managed by its members, subsection (1) shall apply in relation to the acts and defaults of a member in connection with his functions of management as if he were a director of the company. **[107]**

COMMENCEMENT
See s. 70 (5), *post*, and the note "Order under this section" thereto.

THIS PART
I.e., Part I (ss. 1–44) of this Act.

CONSENT
This implies knowledge; see *Re Caughey, Ex parte Ford* (1876) 1 Ch. D. 521, C.A., at p. 528, *per* Jessel, M.R., and *Lamb* v. *Wright & Co.*, [1924] 1 K.B. 857, at p. 864: [1924] All E.R. Rep. 220, at p. 223. It is thought, however, that actual knowledge is not necessary; cf. *Knox* v. *Boyd*, 1941 J.C. 82, at p. 86, and *Taylor's Central Garages (Exeter), Ltd.* v. *Roper* (1951), 115 J.P. 445, at pp. 440, 450, *per* Devlin, J.; and see also, in particular, *Mallon* v. *Allon*, [1964] 1 Q.B. 385, at p. 394; [1963] 3 All E.R. 843, at p. 847.

CONNIVANCE
There are many decisions on the meaning of this word in matrimonial law; see *Godfrey* v. *Godfrey*, [1965] A.C. 444; [1964] 3 All E.R. 154, H.L., especially the speech of Lord Guest, in which earlier decisions are reviewed. It would seem that an element of encouragement is essential. The word has been used in many statutes in the same context as in this section, but there is little authority as to its meaning in this context; see Glanville Williams, *Criminal Law: The General Part*, para. 222, and *Gregory* v. *Walker* (1912), 77 J.P. 55; 29 T.L.R. 51.

NEGLECT
This word implies failure to perform a duty of which the person knows or ought to know; see *Re Hughes, Rea* v. *Black*, [1943] Ch. 296, at p. 298; [1943] 2 All E.R. 269, at p. 271, *per* Simonds, J. For circumstances in which an offence was held to be attributable to neglect on the part of a director, see *Crickitt* v. *Kursaal Casino, Ltd. (No. 2)*, [1968] 1 All E.R. 139, H.L., at pp. 146, 147, and for circumstances in which the opposite was held, see *Huckerby* v. *Elliott*, [1970] 1 All E.R. 189.

ANY PERSON WHO WAS PURPORTING TO ACT
The reference to any person who was purporting to act in any such capacity is introduced in view of *Dean* v. *Hiesler*, [1942] 2 All E.R. 340, where a director who had not been duly appointed was held not liable for an offence committed by the company.

SHALL BE GUILTY, ETC
See the first paragraph of the note "Shall be liable" to s. 4, *ante*.

DEFINITIONS
For "company" and "director", see s. 44 (1), *post*.

1960 ACT
  I.e., the Road Traffic Act 1960; see s. 44 (1), *post*. For Part III of that Act, see A.L.S. Vol. 124.

42. Defences available to persons charged with certain offences

(1) It shall be a defence for a person charge with an offence under any of the provisions mentioned in subsection (2) to prove that there was a reasonable excuse for the act or omission in respect of which he is charged.

(2) The provisions referred to in subsection (1) are —

> (*a*) sections 7 (7), 14 (6), 25 (5) and 26 (4);
>
> (*b*) in the 1960 Act —
>
>> (i) so much of section 144 (8) as relates to contravention of section 144 (1) (*a*);
>>
>> (ii) sections 146 (2) and (3), 147 (2) and 148 (2);
>>
>> (iii) so much of section 232 (3) as relates to failure to comply with the requirement of section 232 (2) (*b*); and
>>
>> (iv) section 239.

(3) It shall be a defence for a person charged with an offence under any of the provisions mentioned in subsection (4) to prove that he took all reasonable precautions and exercised all due diligence to avoid the commission of any offence under that provision.

(4) The provisions referred to in subsection (3) are —

> (*a*) sections 4 (6) and (7), 17 (3), 18 (9) (*b*), 19 (5), 22 (7) and 24 (4);
>
> (*b*) in the 1960 Act —
>
>> (i) so much of section 144 (8) as relates to contravention of section 144 (1) (*b*); and
>>
>> (ii) sections 148 (2) and 157 (2).   **[108]**

COMMENCEMENT
See s. 70 (5), *post*, and the note "Orders under this section" thereto.

IT SHALL BE A DEFENCE, ETC
The burden of proof resting on the accused is not so onerous as that which is, in general, laid on the prosecutor as regards proving an offence and may be discharged by satisfying the court of the probability, or rather the preponderance of probability, of what the accused is called on to prove; see *R.* v. *Carr-Briant*, [1943] K.B. 607; [1943] 2 All E.R. 156; *R.* v. *Dunbar*, [1958] 1 Q.B. 1; [1957] 2 All E.R. 737; and *R.* v. *Hudson*, [1966] 1 Q.B. 448; [1965] 1 All E.R. 721.

PERSON
See the note to s. 2, *ante*.

REASONABLE EXCUSE
What is a reasonable excuse is largely a question of fact; cf. *Leck* v. *Epsom Rural District Council*, [1922] 1 K.B. 383; [1922] All E.R. Rep. 784. Yet it is clear that ignorance of the statutory provisions provides no reasonable excuse (cf. *Aldridge* v. *Warwickshire Coal Co., Ltd.* (1925). 133 L.T. 439, C.A.), nor does a mistaken view of the effect of those provisions (*R.* v. *Reid (Philip)*, [1973] 3 All E.R. 1020, C.A. *Quaere* whether reliance on the advice of an expert can amount to a reasonable excuse; see *Saddleworth Urban District Council* v. *Aggregate and Sand. Ltd.* (1970), 69 L.G.R. 103.
    Once evidence of a reasonable excuse emerges, it is for the prosecution to eliminate the existence of that defence to the satisfaction of the court; see *R.* v. *Clarke*, [1969] 2 All E.R. 1008, C.A.

EXERCISED ALL DUE DILIGENCE
Whether or not the accused has exercised all due diligence is a question of fact, but on a case stated the High Court will interfere if there was no evidence to support a finding on this point; see *R. C. Hammett, Ltd.* v. *Crabb* (1931), 145 L.T. 638; [1931] All E.R. Rep. 70.
    The failure of the directors of a limited company to exercise due diligence is the failure of the

company; see *Pearce* v. *Cullen* (1952), 96 Sol. J. 132. But the failure of subordinate managers and similar employees in a company with large-scale business to exercise due diligence is not necessarily the failure of the company; see *Tesco Supermarkets, Ltd.* v. *Nattrass,* [1972] A.C. 153; [1971] 2 All E.R. 127, H.L.

It has been said that a contractual obligation to exercise due diligence is indistinguishable from an obligation to exercise reasonable care; see *Riverstone Meat Co., Pty., Ltd.* v. *Lancashire Shipping Co., Ltd.,* [1960] 1 Q.B. 536; [1960] 1 All E.R. 193, C.A., at p. 581 and p. 219, respectively, *per* Willmer, L.J. (reversed on other grounds, [1961] A.C. 807; [1961] 1 All E.R. 495).

1960 ACT
   I.e., the Road Traffic Act 1960; see s. 44 (1), *post.* For ss. 144 (1), (8), 146 (2), (3), 147 (2), 148 (2), 157 (2), 232 (2) (*b*), (3) and 239 of that Act, see A.L.S. Vol. 124. S. 144 (1) is partly repealed by s. 36, *ante,* and s. 69 and Sch. 9, Part I, *post;* ss. 146 and 147 are amended and otherwise affected by s. 43 (1) and Sch. 5, Part I, paras. 5, 6, *post;* and ss. 144 (8), 146 (2), (3), 147 (2) and 157 (2) are amended by s. 40, *ante,* and Sch. 4, *post.*

43. Amendments of other Acts

(1) The provisions of the 1960 Act mentioned in Part I of Schedule 5, and the enactments specified in Part II of that Schedule, shall have effect subject to the amendments there specified, being minor amendments and amendments consequential on the provisions of this Part.

(2) Where the running of public service vehicles is restricted or prohibited by any provision contained in—

   (*a*) a local Act (including an Act confirming a provisional order) passed before the commencement of this subsection; or
   (*b*) an instrument made before the commencement of this subsection under any such local Act,

the Minister may, on the application of any person affected by the restriction or prohibition, by order made by statutory instrument modify or revoke the restriction or prohibition.   **[109]**

COMMENCEMENT
   See s. 70 (5), *post,* and the note "Orders under this section" thereto.

THIS PART
   I.e., Part I (ss. 1–44) of this Act.

PERSON
   See the note to s. 2, *ante.*

STATUTORY INSTRUMENT
   For general provisions as to statutory instruments, see the Statutory Instruments Act 1946, A.L.S. Vol. 36.

DEFINITIONS
   For "public service vehicle", see s. 2, *ante;* for "the Minister", see s. 70 (2), *post.*

ORDERS UNDER THIS SECTION
   At the time of going to press no order had been made under sub-s. (2) above.

1960 ACT
   I.e., the Road Traffic Act 1960 A.L.S. Vol. 124; see s. 44 (1), *post.*

44. Interpretation of Part I

(1) In this Part, unless the context otherwise requires—

   "the 1960 Act" means the Road Traffic Act 1960;
   "company" means a body corporate;

"contract carriage" has the meaning given by section 3;

"contravention", in relation to any condition or provision, includes a failure to comply with the condition or provision and "contravene" shall be construed accordingly;

"director", in relation to a company, includes any person who occupies the position of a director, by whatever name called;

"excursion or tour" means a stage or express carriage service on which the passengers travel together on a journey, with or without breaks, from one or more places to one or more other places and back;

"express carriage" has the meaning given by section 3, and "express carriage service" means a service provided by means of one or more express carriages;

"international operation" means a passenger transport operation starting or terminating in the United Kingdom and involving an international journey by the vehicle concerned, whether or not any driver leaves or enters the United Kingdom with that vehicle;

"national operation" means a passenger transport operation wholly within the United Kingdom;

"official PSV testing station" has the meaning given by section 16 (3);

"operating centre", in relation to a vehicle, means the base or centre at which the vehicle is normally kept;

"operator" has the meaning given by subsections (2) and (3);

"owner", in relation to a vehicle which is the subject of an agreement for hire, hire-purchase, conditional sale or loan, means the person in possession of the vehicle under that agreement, and references to owning a vehicle shall be construed accordingly;

"PSV operator's licence" means a PSV operator's licence granted under the provisions of this Part;

"public service vehicle" has the meaning given by section 2;

"relevant conviction" means a conviction (other than a spent conviction) of any offence prescribed for the purposes of this Part, or of an offence under the law of Northern Ireland, or of a country or territory outside the United Kingdom, corresponding to an offence so prescribed;

"restricted licence" means such a PSV operator's licence as is mentioned in section 20 (3);

"road service licence" means a road service licence granted under the provisions of this Part;

"stage carriage" has the meaning given by section 3, and "stage carriage service" means a service provided by means of one or more stage carriages;

"standard licence" means a PSV operator's licence which is not a restricted licence;

"transport manager", in relation to a business, means an individual who, either alone or jointly with one or more other persons, has continuous and effective responsibility for the management of the road passenger transport operations of the business;

"trial area" has the meaning given by section 12 (1).

(2) For the purposes of this Part—

    (*a*) regulations may make provision as to the person who is to be regarded as the operator of a vehicle which is made available by one holder of a PSV operator's licence to another under a hiring arrangement; and

    (*b*) where regulations under paragraph (*a*) do not apply, the operator of a vehicle is—

        (i) the driver, if he owns the vehicle; and

(ii) in any other case, the person for whom the driver works (whether under a contract of employment or any other description of contract personally to do work).

(3) For the purposes of this Part the operator of a stage or express carriage service is the person, or each of the persons, providing the service; and for those purposes the operator of a vehicle being used as a stage or express carriage shall be taken to be providing the service thereby provided unless he proves that the service is or forms part of a service provided not by himself but by one or more other persons.

(4) Any reference in this Part to a Community instrument or to a particular provision of such an instrument —

(*a*) is a reference to that instrument or provision as amended from time to time, and

(*b*) if that instrument or provision is replaced, with or without modification, shall be construed as a reference to the instrument or provision replacing it. **[110]**

COMMENCEMENT
See s. 70 (5), *post*, and the note "Orders under this section" thereto.

THIS PART
I.e., Part I (ss. 1 – 44) of this Act.

BODY CORPORATE
For the general law relating to corporations, see 9 Halsbury's Laws (4th Edn.), paras. 1201 *et seq*.

UNITED KINGDOM
I.e., Great Britain (as to which see the note to s. 12, *ante*) and Northern Ireland; see the Interpretation Act 1978, s. 5, Sch. 1, A.L.S. Vol. 258.

PRESCRIBED
I.e., prescribed by regulations made under the Road Traffic Act 1960, s. 160 A.L.S. Vol. 124; see, by virtue of s. 1 (3), *ante*, s. 160 (2) of that Act. At the time of going to press no regulation had been made prescribing offences for the purposes of the definition of "relevant conditon".

INDIVIDUAL
See the note to s. 31, *ante*.

PERSONS
See the note "Person" to s. 2, *ante*.

COMMUNITY INSTRUMENT
I.e., an instrument issued by a Community institution; see the European Communities Act 1972, s. 1 (2), Sch. 1, Part II, A.L.S. Vol. 205 (which Part also defines "Community institution"), as applied by the Interpretation Act 1978, s. 5, Sch. 1, A.L.S. Vol. 258.

DEFINITIONS
For "modification", see s. 70 (2), *post*; by virtue of s. 1 (3), *ante*, for "regulations" and "prescribed", see the Road Traffic Act 1960, s. 160 (2), A.L.S. Vol. 124, and for "driver", see s. 257 (1) of that Act.

ROAD TRAFFIC ACT 1960
See A.L.S. Vol. 124.

REGULATIONS UNDER THIS SECTION
At the time of going to press no regulations had been made for the purposes of sub-s. (2)(*a*) above.
By virtue of s. 1 (3), *ante*, for general provisions as to regulations, see the Road Traffic Act 1960, ss. 160, 260, A.L.S. Vol. 124, as amended by s. 43 (1) and Sch. 5, Part I, paras. 11 and 15, respectively, *post*, and as partly repealed, in the case of s. 160, but s. 69 and Sch. 9, Part I, *post*.

PART II

TRANSFER OF UNDERTAKING OF NATIONAL FREIGHT CORPORATION

Transfer of undertaking of National Freight Corporation to a company limited by shares

45. Transfer of undertaking of National Freight Corporation

(1) On the appointed day the whole of the undertaking of the National Freight Corporation (in this Part referred to as "the Corporation") shall, subject to subsection (4), be transferred by virtue of this section and without further assurance to a company formed for the purposes of this section and nominated under subsection (5) (in this Part referred to as "the successor company").

(2) In this Part "the appointed day" means such day as the Minister, with the consent of the Treasury, may appoint for the purposes of this section by order made by statutory instrument.

(3) References in this Part to the undertaking of the Corporation are references to all the property, rights, liabilities and obligations of the Corporation, whether or not of such a nature that they could be assigned by the Corporation.

(4) Any entitlement of the Minister and any liability of the Corporation in respect of—

    (*a*) the commencing capital debt of the Corporation; and

    (*b*) outstanding loans to the Corporation from the Minister, shall be extinguished immediately before the appointed day.

(5) The Minister may by order made by statutory instrument nominate for the purposes of this section a company formed and registered under the Companies Act 1948 which on the appointed day satisfies the following requirements, that is to say—

    (*a*) it is a company limited by shares; and

    (*b*) all the issued shares of the company are held by the Minister or by nominees for him.

(6) This section shall have effect subject to the provisions of Schedule 6, being supplementary provisions with respect to the transfer by virtue of this section of the undertaking of the Corporation to the successor company; but nothing in those provisions shall be taken as prejudicing the general effect of subsection (1).

[111]

COMMENCEMENT

This Part (ss. 45–51 and Sch. 6 and 7) of this Act, except s. 51 (2) and Sch. 7, *post*, came into force on the passing of the Act on 30th June 1980 (s. 70 (3), *post*), but in the main it does not become effective until "the appointed day" as defined by sub-s. (2) above. At the time of going to press no day had been appointed under that subsection.

NATIONAL FREIGHT CORPORATION

This public authority was established under the Transport Act 1968, s. 1, Sch. 1, A.L.S. Vol. 178. For consequential repeals in that Act, see s. 69 and Sch. 9. Part III, *post*.

THIS PART

I.e., Part II (ss. 45–51) of this Act.

TREASURY

I.e., the Commissioners of Her Majesty's Treasury; see the Interpretation Act 1978, s. 5, Sch. 1, A.L.S. Vol. 258.

STATUTORY INSTRUMENT

See the note to s. 43, *ante*.

46. Initial government holding in successor company

(1) In consideration of the transfer of the undertaking of the Corporation to the successor company by virtue of section 45, the successor company shall issue to the Minister or, if the Minister so directs, to nominees for him such securities of the company as the Minister may direct.

(2) Any shares issued in pursuance of subsection (1)—

    (*a*) shall be of such nominal value as the Minister may direct; and

    (*b*) shall be credited as fully paid up.

(3) The Minister shall not give any directions for the purposes of this section without the consent of the Treasury.

(4) Securities of the successor company held by the Minister or by nominees for him shall not be disposed of except with the consent of the Treasury and in such manner and on such terms as the Treasury may direct.

(5) Subject to section 49 (5), any dividends or other sums received by the Minister, or by nominees for him, in right of, on the disposal of, or otherwise in connection with, any securities of the successor company shall be paid into the Consolidated Fund.

(6) Stamp duty shall not be chargeable under section 47 of the Finance Act 1973 in respect of any increase in the capital of the successor company which is certified by the Treasury as having been—

    (*a*) effected for the purpose of complying with the requirements of this section; or

    (*b*) where any convertible securities were issued in pursuance of this section, effected in consequence of the exercise of the conversion rights attached to those securities. **[112]**

DEFINITIONS
    For "the Corporation" and "the successor company", see s. 45 (1), *ante*; for "the undertaking of
    the Corporation", see s. 45 (3), *ante*; for "securities" and "shares", see s. 51 (1), *post*; for "the
    Minister", see s. 70 (2), *post*.

FINANCE ACT 1973, S. 47
    See A.L.S. Vol. 213.

47. Transitional provisions with respect to reserves etc.

(1) An amount corresponding to any reserves of the Corporation immediately before the appointed day which represent accumulated profits shall be treated by the successor company as reserves of that company applicable for the same purposes as the corresponding reserves of the Corporation.

(2) Nothing in section 56 of the Companies Act 1948 (which requires premiums received on the issue of shares to be transferred to a share premium account) shall affect the operation of subsection (1).

(3) The successor company shall treat the reserves of any company in which the Corporation held shares which were available for distribution immediately before the appointed day as if they had arisen immediately after the appointed day.

(4) Where any dividend is paid to the successor company in respect of shares transferred to the company by virtue of section 45, that dividend shall be available for distribution as profits of the successor company notwithstanding that it is paid out of profits of the company paying the dividend attributable to a period falling wholly or partly before the appointed day.

(5) In ascertaining for the purposes of section 56 of the Companies Act 1948 what amount (if any) falls to be treated as a premium received on the issue of any shares in pursuance of section 46, the amount of the net assets transferred by virtue of section 45 shall be taken to be reduced by an amount corresponding to the amount of any reserve within subsection (1).   **[113]**

COMMENCEMENT
    See the note to s. 45, *ante*.

DEFINITIONS
    For "the Corporation" and "the successor company", see s. 45 (1), *ante*; for "the appointed day",
    see s. 45 (2), *ante*; for "shares", see s. 51 (1), *post*.

COMPANIES ACT 1948, S. 56
    See 5, Halsbury's Statutes (3rd edn.), p. 164.

48. Dissolution and final accounts of National Freight Corporation

(1) The Corporation shall cease to exist on the appointed day.

(2) The successor company shall prepare a statement of the Corporation's accounts for the period from the end of that dealt with in the last annual statement of accounts published by the Corporation down to the appointed day (in the following provisions of this section referred to as "the final period").

(3) The statement shall be in such form and contain such particulars, compiled in such manner, as the Minister may direct with the approval of the Treasury.

(4) The successor company shall arrange for the accounts of the Corporation for the final period to be audited by auditors appointed by the Minister; and a

person shall not be qualified to be so appointed unless he is a member of, or is a Scottish firm in which all the partners are members of, one or more bodies of accountants established in the United Kingdom and for the time being recognised by the Secretary of State for the purposes of section 161 (1) (*a*) of the Companies Act 1948.

(5) As soon as the accounts for the final period have been audited, the successor company shall send to the Minister a copy of the statement of accounts for that period together with a copy of the auditors' report on that statement; and the Minister shall lay a copy of the statement and report before each House of Parliament. **[114]**

COMMENCEMENT
See the note to s. 45, *ante*.

SUB-S. (3): TREASURY
See the note to s. 45, *ante*.

SUB-S. (4): UNITED KINGDOM
See the note to s. 44, *ante*.

SECRETARY OF STATE
I.e., one of Her Majesty's Principal Secretaries of State; see the Interpretation Act 1978, s. 5, Sch. 1, A.L.S. Vol. 258. The Secretary of State here concerned is the Secretary of State for Trade.

SUB-S. (5): LAY . . . BEFORE EACH HOUSE OF PARLIAMENT
For meaning, see the Laying of Documents before Parliament (Interpretation) Act 1948, s. 1 (1), A.L.S. Vol. 56.

DEFINITIONS
For "the Corporation" and "the successor company", see s. 45 (1), *ante*; for "the appointed day", see s. 45 (2), *ante*; for "the Minister", see s. 70 (2), *post*. Note as to "the final period", sub-s. (2) above.

COMPANIES ACT 1948,S. 161 (1) (a)
See 5, Halsbury's Statutes (3rd edn.), p. 240.

Funding of certain pension obligations

49. Funding of relevant pension obligations

(1) If it appears to the Minister, having determined that all or any of the securities of the successor company held by him or by nominees for him should be offered for sale, that on the date on which those securities are to be so offered the relevant pension obligations will not be completely funded, he may, with the consent of the Treasury, undertake to make to the persons administering the relevant pension schemes such payments towards the funding of those obligations as he may specify in the undertaking.

(2) An undertaking under subsection (1)—

    (*a*) shall specify the aggregate amount of the payments which the Minister proposes to make in pursuance of the undertaking; and

    (*b*) shall be conditional on the amount received by the Minister in consideration for the disposal of the securities being not less than that amount.

(3) If the Minister gives an undertaking under subsection (1) but the condition mentioned in subsection (2) if not fulfilled, he may nevertheless, with the consent of the Treasury, make to the persons administering the relevant pension schemes

such payments towards the funding of the relevant pension obligations as he thinks fit.

(4) If no undertaking is given under subsection (1) but it appears to the Minister that, on the date on which all or any of the securities of the successor company held by him or by nominees for him are offered for sale, the relevant pension obligations are not completely funded, he may, with the consent of the Treasury, make to the persons administering the relevant pension schemes such payments towards the funding of those obligations as he thinks fit.

(5) The aggregate amount of any payments made under subsection (3) or (4) shall not exceed the amount received in consideration for the disposal of the securities of the successor company; and the sums required for making any such payments or any payments in pursuance of an undertaking under subsection (1) shall be paid out of that amount.

(6) In this section —

"the relevant pension obligations" has the meaning given by section 50;
"the relevant pension schemes" means the National Freight Corporation (Salaried Staff) Pension Fund, the National Freight Corporation (Wages Grades) Pension Fund and the N.F.C. (1978) Pension Fund;

and for the purposes of this section the N.F.C. (1978) Pension Fund shall be taken to comprise the pension schemes specified or described in the Schedule to the Central Trust deed within the meaning of the National Freight Corporation (Central Trust) Order 1978. **[115]**

COMMENCEMENT
> See the note to s. 45, *ante*.

APPEARS; THINKS FIT
> See the note "satisfied" to s. 5, *ante*.

TREASURY
> See the note to s. 45, *ante*.

PERSONS
> See the note "Person" to s. 2, *ante*.

NATIONAL FREIGHT CORPORATION (SALARIED STAFF) PENSION FUND
> *I.e.*, a funded pension scheme established by the National Freight Corporation, with the consent of the Secretary of State, under the terms of an Interim Trust Deed executed by the National Freight Corporation and N.F.C. Trustees Limited on the 12th January 1971. The National Freight Corporation (Alteration of Pension Schemes) (No. 2) Order 1971, S.I. 1971 No. 117 (made under the Transport Act 1962, s. 74, 26, Halsbury's Statutes (3rd edn.), p. 987 as read with the Transport Act 1968, s. 136, A.L.S. Vol. 178), affects this Pension Fund.

NATIONAL FREIGHT CORPORATION (WAGES GRADES) PENSION FUND
> *I.e.*, a funded pension scheme established by the National Freight Corporation, with the consent of the Secretary of State, under the terms of an Interim Trust Deed executed by the National Freight Corporation and N.F.C. Trustees Limited on the 12th January 1971. The National Freight Corporation (Alteration of Pension Schemes) (No. 1) Order 1971, S.I. 1971 No. 116 (made under the Transport Act 1962, s. 74, 26, Halsbury's Statutes (3rd edn.), p. 987, as read with the Transport Act 1968, s. 136, A.L.S. Vol. 178), affects this Pension Fund.

DEFINITIONS
> For "the successor company", see s. 45 (1), *ante*; for "the relevant pension obligations", see s. 50, *post*; for "securities", see s. 51 (1), *post*; for "the Minister", see s. 70 (2), *post*. Note as to "the relevant pension schemes", sub-s. (6) above.

NATIONAL FREIGHT CORPORATION (CENTRAL TRUST) ORDER 1978
> S.I. 1978 No. 1290. That order was made under the Transport Act 1962, s. 74, 26, Halsbury's Statutes (3rd end.), p. 987.

50. Meaning of "the relevant pension obligations"

(1) In section 49 "the relevant pension obligations" means, subject to subsection (2)—

> (*a*) any obligations of the successor company or a relevant subsidiary which were owed on 1st April 1975 ("the operative date") in connection with any of the relevant pension schemes; and
>
> (*b*) where any such obligation is one to pay or secure the payment of pensions, any obligation of the successor company or a relevant subsidiary arising after the operative date to pay or secure the payment of increases of those pensions; and
>
> (*c*) any obligation of the successor company or a relevant subsidiary arising after the operative date to pay or secure the payment of increases payable under any of the relevant pension schemes, being increases of pensions payable under any other pension scheme established before that date (whether one of the relevant pension schemes or not); and
>
> (*d*) any obligation of the successor company or a relevant subsidiary which results from an amendment made to any of the relevant pension schemes by virtue of section 74 of the Transport Act 1962 after the operative date and before 1st January 1980.

(2) The definition in subsection (1) does not include—

> (*a*) any obligation which, in relation to one of the relevant pension schemes, is a relevant pension obligation for the purposes of Part III;
>
> (*b*) any obligation to pay or secure the payment of increases of pensions in excess of increases payable on official pensions under the Pensions (Increase) Act 1971 and section 59 of the Social Security Pensions Act 1975;
>
> (*c*) any obligation to pay contributions in respect of current periods of employment of a member of a scheme;
>
> (*d*) any obligation to pay expenses incurred in connection with a scheme which is specifically imposed on the body by which it is owed;
>
> (*e*) any obligation owed by a body in their capacity as the trustees of a scheme or the persons administering a scheme; and
>
> (*f*) any obligation in respect of which the body by which it is owed have a right to be indemnified by any other body.

(3) In this section—

> "pension", in relation to any of the relevant pension schemes, has the same meaning as in Part III;
> "the relevant pension schemes" has the same meaning as in section 49;
> "relevant subsidiary" means any subsidiary of the successor company other than National Carriers Limited and any subsidiary of National Carriers Limited;
> "subsidiary" has the same meaning as in the Transport Act 1962.

(4) For the purposes of this section—

> (*a*) any increase in an obligation which results from an amendment made to a scheme after the operative date shall be treated as a separate obligation; and
>
> (*b*) where at any time, whether before or after the operative date, any pensions or increases payable under any of the relevant pension schemes are or have been paid by any person, that person shall be treated as being or having been under an obligation at that time to make those payments.

[116]

COMMENCEMENT
See the note to s. 45, *ante*.

PART III
I.e., ss. 52 – 60, *post*. For the meanings of "the relevant pension obligation" and "pension" in that Part, see ss. 53 and 60 (1), respectively, *post*.

DEFINITIONS
For "the successor company", see s. 45 (1), *ante*; for "the relevant pension schemes", see, by virtue of sub-s. (3) above, s. 49 (6), *ante*. Note as to "pension", "relevant subsidiary" and "subsidiary", sub-s. (3) above.

TRANSPORT ACT 1962
For s. 74 of that Act, see 26, Halsbury's Statutes (3rd edn.), p. 987; and for the meaning of "subsidiary" in that Act, see s. 92 (1) thereof.

PENSIONS (INCREASE) ACT 1971
See 41, Halsbury's Statutes (3rd edn.), p. 1065.

SOCIAL SECURITY PENSIONS ACT 1975, S. 59
See 45, Halsbury's Statutes (3rd edn.), p. 1451.

Supplementary

51. Interpretation of Part II and consequential amendments

(1) In this Part —

"the appointed day" has the meaning given by section 45 (2);

"the Corporation" has the meaning given by section 45 (1);

"securities" of the successor company includes shares, debentures, debenture stock, bonds and other securities of the company, whether or not constituting a charge on the assets of the company;

"shares" includes stock;

"the successor company" has the meaning given by section 45 (1);

and references to the undertaking of the Corporation shall be construed in accordance with section 45 (3).

(2) The enactments mentioned in Schedule 7 shall have effect subject to the amendments there specified, being amendments consequential on the provisions of this Part.   **[117]**

COMMENCEMENT
Sub-s. (1) above came into force on the passing of this Act (s. 70 (3), *post*) and sub-s. (2) is to come into force on the appointed day "as defined by s. 45 (2), *ante* (s. 70 (4), *post*). At the time of going to press no day had been appointed under that subsection.

THIS PART
I.e., Part II (ss. 45 – 51) of this Act.

PART III

RAILWAY ETC. PENSIONS

52. Payments by Minister in respect of B.R. and N.F.C. pension schemes

(1) Subject to the provisions of this section and section 58, the Minister shall, in relation to each B.R. or N.F.C. pension scheme and for each financial year, make to the persons administering the scheme payments equal in aggregate to the product of —

(a) the proportion determined under section 54 (1) as the proportion of the relevant pension obligations which has not been funded;

(b) the proportion determined in relation to that year under section 55 (1) as the proportion of the pensions, increases and expenses payable under or incurred in connection with the scheme which corresponds to those obligations; and

(c) the aggregate amount of the pensions, increases and expenses payable under or incurred in connection with the scheme for that year.

(2) Where in the case of any such scheme the funding of the relevant pension obligations has, by virtue of subsection (3) of section 54, been left out of account in making a determination under subsection (1) of that section, the aggregate amount of the payments made under subsection (1) to the persons administering the scheme shall be reduced for each financial year —

(a) by the amount of any income accruing to the scheme for that year which may be applied towards the payment of such of the pensions, increases and expenses payable under or incurred in connection with the scheme as correspond to the obligations; and

(b) in the case of the first financial year, by an amount equal to the value of the assets by which the obligations are funded.

(3) Where, for any financial year, the aggregate amount of the payments made under subsection (1) to the persons administering any such scheme requires adjustment by reason of —

(a) any variation between the proportion finally determined under section 55 (1) in relation to that year and the proportion previously so determined; or

(b) any unforeseen increase or reduction in the aggregate amount of the pensions, increases and expenses payable under or incurred in connection with the scheme for that year,

that adjustment shall be made by increasing or, as the case may require, reducing the aggregate amount of the payments made under subsection (1) for the following financial year.

(4) Payments under subsection (1) shall be made, so far as practicable, not later than the day on which the pensions, increases and expenses to which they relate fall to be paid or incurred.

(5) The making of any payment under subsection (1) shall be subject to compliance with such conditions as to the keeping of records, the issue of certificates and the auditing of accounts as the Minister may with the approval of the Treasury determine.

(6) Any sums required for making payments under subsection (1) shall be paid out of money provided by Parliament.   **[118]**

COMMENCEMENT
   Part (ss. 52 – 60 and Sch. 8) of this Act came into force on the passing of this Act on 30th June 1980; see s. 70 (3), *post*.

SUB-S. (1): MAKE TO THE PERSONS ADMINISTERING THE SCHEME PAYMENTS, ETC
   As to certain payments which are deemed to be made under sub-s. (1) above, see s. 58 (2), (3), *post*. The making of any payment under sub-s. (1) above does not discharge any relevant pension obligation so far as it is an obligation to pay pensions or increases of pensions under a B.R. or N.F.C. pension scheme or is an obligation to receive the payment of those pensions or increases; see s. 59 (1), *post*. See, also, as to "persons", the note "Person" to s. 2, *ante*.

SUB-S. (5): TREASURY
   See the note to s. 45, *ante*.

DEFINITIONS
   For "B.R. pension scheme", "first financial plan", "financial year", "N.F.C. pension scheme" and
"pension", see s. 60 (1), *post*; for "the Minister", see s. 70 (2), *post*.

53. Meaning of "the relevant pension obligations"

(1) In this Part "the relevant pension obligations", in relation to a B.R. pension scheme, means subject to subsection (3) —

   (*a*) any obligations of the Board which were owed on 1st January 1975 ("the operative date") in connection with the scheme; and

   (*b*) where any such obligation is one to pay or secure the payment of pensions, any obligation of the Board arising after the operative date to pay or secure the payment of increases of or sums representing accrued rights in respect of those pensions; and

   (*c*) any obligation of the Board arising after the operative date to pay or secure the payment of increases payable under the scheme, being increases of pensions payable under any other pension scheme established before that date (whether a B.R. pension scheme or not).

(2) In this Part "the relevant pension obligations", in relation to an N.F.C. pension scheme, means subject to subsection (3) —

   (*a*) any obligations of the successor company or a relevant subsidiary which were owed on 1st April 1975 ("the operative date") in connection with the scheme; and

   (*b*) where any such obligation is one to pay or secure the payment of pensions, any obligation of the successor company or a relevant subsidiary arising after the operative date to pay or secure the payment of increases of or sums representing accrued rights in respect of those pensions; and

   (*c*) any obligation of the successor company or a relevant subsidiary arising after the operative date to pay or secure the payment of increases payable under the scheme, being increases of pensions payable under any other pension scheme established before that date (whether an N.F.C. pension scheme or not); and

   (*d*) any obligation of the successor company or a relevant subsidiary which results from an amendment made to the scheme by virtue of section 74 of the Transport Act 1962 after the operative date and before 1st January 1980,

being (in each case) obligations which relate to employees or former employees of a relevant subsidiary or employees or former employees of the successor company or the Corporation who are or were employed as directors or managers of a relevant subsidiary.

(3) The definitions in subsections (1) and (2) do not include —

   (*a*) any obligation to pay or secure the payment of increases of pensions in excess of increases payable on official pensions under the Pensions (Increase) Act 1971 and section 59 of the Social Security Pensions Act 1975;

   (*b*) any obligation to pay contributions in respect of current periods of employment of a member of a scheme;

   (*c*) any obligation to pay expenses incurred in connection with the management of a scheme which is specifically imposed on the body by which it is owed;

   (*d*) any obligation owed by a body in their capacity as the trustees of a scheme or the persons administering a scheme; and

(e) subject to subsection (4), any obligation in respect of which the body by which it is owed have a right to be indemnified by any other body.

(4) Subsection (3) (e) does not apply —

(a) in the case of an obligation owed by the Board, where the Board has a right to be indemnified by the successor company;

(b) in the case of an obligation owed by the successor company, where the successor company has a right to be indemnified by a relevant subsidiary;

(c) in the case of an obligation owed by the successor company, where the successor company has a right to be indemnified by the Board and the obligation relates to employees or former employees of Freightliners Limited or employees or former employees of the successor company or the Corporation who are or were employed as directors or managers of Freightliners Limited;

(d) in the case of an obligation owed by a relevant subsidiary, where that subsidiary has a right to be indemnified by the successor company or by another relevant subsidiary; and

(e) in the case of an obligation owed by Freightliners Limited, where Freightliners Limited has a right to be indemnified by the Board.

(5) In this section "relevant subsidiary" means National Carriers Limited, Freightliners Limited and any subsidiary of National Carriers Limited.

(6) For the purposes of this section —

(a) any increase in an obligation which results from an amendment made to a scheme after the operative date shall be treated as a separate obligation; and

(b) where at any time, whether before or after the operative date, any pensions or increases payable under a B.R. or N.F.C. pension scheme are or have been paid by any person, that person shall be treated as being or as having been under an obligation at that time to make those payments.

[119]

COMMENCEMENT
See the note to s. 52, *ante.*

SUB-S. (1): THIS PART
I.e., Part III (ss. 52–60) of this Act.

SUB-S. (3): PERSONS
See the note "Person" to s. 2, *ante.*

SUB-S. (6): AMENDMENT
For supplementary provisions relating to amendment of pension schemes, see s. 59 (2), *post.*

DEFINITIONS
For "the successor company", see by virtue of s. 60 (1), *post,* s. 45 (1), *ante* (and see also s. 60 (4), *post*); for "the Board", "B.R. pension scheme", "the Corporation", "N.F.C. pension scheme" and "pension", see s. 60)1), *post;* by virtue of s. 60 (1), *post,* for "subsidiary", see the Transport Act 1962, s. 92 (1), A.L.S. Vol. 124. Note as to "the operative date", sub-ss. (1) (*a*) and (2) (*a*) above, and as to "relevant subsidiary", sub-s. (5) above.

54. Unfunded proportion of relevant pension obligations

(1) The Minister shall, in relation to each B.R. or N.F.C. pension scheme —

(a) determine, as soon as practicable after the passing of this Act, what proportion of the relevant pension obligations has not been funded; and (*b*) after consulting with the persons administering the scheme and the Board or, as the case may be, the successor company, confirm or vary that determination, before the end of the first financial year, by a further determination of that proportion contained in an order.

(2) Where at the time when a determination under subsection (1) falls to be made any class of the relevant pension obligations appear to be completely funded, that class of obligations and their funding may, if the Minister thinks fit, be left out of account in making that determination.

(3) Where at the time when a determination under subsection (1) falls to be made the assets by which the relevant pension obligations are funded appear to be insufficient to meet such of the pensions, increases and expenses payable under or incurred in connection with the scheme for the first financial year as correspond to those obligations, that funding may, if the Minister thinks fit, be left out of account in making that determination.

(4) An order under subsection (1)—

(*a*) shall be made by statutory instrument which shall be subject to annulment in pursuance of a resolution of the Commons House of Parliament; and

(*b*) may be varied or revoked by a subsequent order made before the end of the first financial year.

(5) References in subsection (1) to a determination or further determination made by the Minister shall include references to a determination or further determination made by the actuary to the scheme and approved by the Minister.

[120]

COMMENCEMENT
See the note to s. 52, *ante*.

SUB-S. (1): MINISTER SHALL . . . DETERMINE, ETC
For amounts which are to be left out of account in making a determination under sub-s. (1) above, see s. 58 (2), (3), *post*.

PASSING OF THIS ACT
This Act was passed, *i.e.*, received the Royal Assent, on 30th June 1980.

CONSULTING
On what constitutes consultation, see, in particular, *Rollo* v. *Minister of Town and Country Planning*, [1948] 1 All E.R. 13, C.A.; *Re Union of Whippingham and East Cowes Benefices, Derham* v. *Church Comrs for England*, [1954] A.C. 245; [1954] 2 All E.R. 22, P.C.; and *Agricultural and Forestry Industry Training Board* v. *Aylesbury Mushrooms, Ltd.*, [1972] 1 All E.R. 280.

PERSONS
See the note "Person" to s. 2, *ante*.

SUB-S. (2): THAT CLASS OF OBLIGATION . . . MAY . . . BE LEFT OUT OF ACCOUNT
Where any class of the relevant pension obligations and their funding have been left out of account by virtue of sub-s. (2) above, that class of obligations is not to be regarded as relevant pension obligations for the purposes of any determination under s. 55 (1), *post*; see s. 55 (2), *post*.

THINKS FIT
See the note "Satisfied" to s. 5, *ante*.

SUB-S. (4): STATUTORY INSTRUMENT; SUBJECT TO ANNULMENT
See the note to s. 12, *ante*.

CONSEQUENTIAL CANCELLATION OF DEBTS
In the consequential cancellation of debts owed by the British Railways Board and the National Freight Corporation, see s. 58 (1), *post*.

DEFINITIONS
For "the successor company", see by virtue of s. 60 (1), *post*, s. 45 (1), *ante*, (and see also s. 60 (4), *post*) for "the relevant pension obligations", see s. 53, *ante*; for "the Board", "B.R. pension scheme", "first financial year", "N.F.C. pension scheme" and "pension", see s. 60 (1), *post*; for "the Minister", see s. 70 (2), *post*. Note as to "determination" and "further determination", sub-s. (5) above.

ORDERS UNDER THIS SECTION
At the time of going to press no order had been made under sub-s. (1) above.

55. Proportion of pensions etc. which corresponds to relevant pension obligations

(1) The Minister shall, in relation to each B.R. or N.F.C. pension scheme and for each financial year —

> (*a*) determine, before the beginning of the year or, in the case of the first financial year, as soon as practicable after the passing of this Act, what proportion of the pensions, increases and expenses payable under or incurred in connection with the scheme corresponds to the relevant pension obligations; and
>
> (*b*) confirm or vary that determination, from time to time during the year and as soon as practicable after the end of the year, by a further determination of that proportion.

(2) Where in the case of any such scheme any class of the relevant pension obligations and their funding have, by virtue of subsection (2) of section 54, been left out of account in making a determination under subsection (1) of that section, that class of obligations shall not be regarded as relevant pension obligations for the purposes of any determination under subsection (1).

(3) References in subsection (1) to a determination or further determination made by the Minister shall include references to a determination or further determination made by the actuary or auditor to the scheme and approved by the Minister. **[121]**

COMMENCEMENT
See the note to s. 52, *ante*.

MINISTER SHALL . . . DETERMINE
As to the exclusion of payments in respect of certain transfer values with respect to any determination under sub-s. (1) above, see s. 57, *post*.

PASSING OF THIS ACT
See the note to s. 54, *ante*.

CONSEQUENTIAL CANCELLATION OF DEBTS
See s. 58 (1), *post*.

DEFINITIONS
For "the relevant pension obligations", see s. 53, *ante*, and s. 56 (2), *post*; for "B.R. pension scheme", "first financial year", "financial year", "N.F.C. pension scheme" and "pension", see s. 60 (1), *post*; for "the Minister", see s. 70 (2), *post*. Note as to "determination" and "further determination", sub-s. (3) above.

56. Reduction of payments in respect of certain supplementation schemes

(1) This section applies where, in relation to a B.R. or N.F.C. pension scheme ("the supplementation scheme"), the relevant pension obligations include obligations arising after the passing of this Act to pay or secure the payment of increases

of pensions payable under any other pension scheme, being a scheme established by the Board or the Corporation ("the basis scheme").

(2) If the actuary to the basic scheme certifies that the assets of that scheme exceed its liabilities, then, in relation to the supplementation scheme, any obligation arising after the date of the actuary's certificate to pay or secure the payment of any increases of pensions payable under the basic scheme or, if less, the relevant proportion of any such increases shall not be regarded as a relevant pension obligation for the purposes of any determination under section 55 (1).

(3) In subsection (2) "the relevant proportion", in relation to any increases, means, subject to subsection (4), the proportion (if any) certified by the actuary to the basic scheme to be the proportion of those increases which, if payable under that scheme, could be funded by 75 per cent. of the amount by which the assets of that scheme exceed its liabilities.

(4) Where any obligation arising after the date of a certificate under subsection (3) is an obligation to pay or secure the payment of a proportion only of any increases to which the certificate relates, then, in relation to that obligation, the relevant proportion for the purposes of subsection (2) shall be given by the formula —

$$\frac{A + B - 1}{A}$$

where A is the first mentioned proportion and B is the proportion certified by the actuary.

(5) The Minister may direct the persons administering the basic scheme —

(*a*) to arrange for the actuary to the scheme to certify whether or not the assets of the scheme exceed its liabilities; and

(*b*) to send a copy of the actuary's certificate to the Minister;

but no direction shall be given under this subsection within the period of three years beginning with the giving by the actuary of such a certificate.

(6) References in this section to the assets and liabilities of the basic scheme are references to the assets and liabilities of that scheme so far as it relates to the payment of pensions increases of which are or are likely to become payable under the supplementation scheme.   **[122]**

COMMENCEMENT
See the note to s. 52, *ante.*

SUB-S. (1): PASSING OF THIS ACT
See the note to s. 54, *ante.*

SUB-S. (5): PERSONS
See the note "Person" to s. 2, *ante.*

THREE YEARS BEGINNING WITH, ETC
See the note "Five years beginning with, etc", to s. 12, *ante.*

SUB-S. (6): LIKELY
See the note to s. 18, *ante*

CONSEQUENTIAL CANCELLATION OF DEBTS
See s. 58 (1), *post.*

DEFINITIONS
For "the relevant pension obligations", see s. 53, *ante*; for "the Board", "B.R. pension scheme", "the Corporation", "N.F.C. pension scheme" and "pension" see s. 60 (1), *post*; as to "pension scheme established by the Board", see s. 60 (3), *post*; for "the Minister", see s. 70 (2), *post*. Note as

to "the supplementation scheme" and "the basic scheme", sub-s. (1) above; as to "the relevant proportion", sub-s. (3) above; and as to "assets and liabilities of the basic scheme", sub-s. (6) above.

57. Exclusion of payments in respect of certain transfer values

Where the whole or any part of a person's accrued pension rights under a B.R. or N.F.C. pension scheme are transferred to any other pension scheme, being a scheme established by the Board or the successor company or any subsidiary or either of those bodies, the Minister may direct that for the purposes of —

(*a*) any determination of the aggregate amount of the pensions, increases and expenses payable under or incurred in connection with the first-mentioned scheme; and

(*b*) any determination under section 55 (1) in relation to that scheme,

it shall be assumed that the said rights had not been transferred and that the payment of any sum representing those rights had not been made. **[123]**

COMMENCEMENT
See the note to s. 52, *ante*.

CONSEQUENTIAL CANCELLATION OF DEBTS
See s. 58 (1), *post*.

DEFINITIONS
For "the successor company", see by virtue of s. 60 (1), *post*, s. 45 (1), *ante*, (and see also s. 60 (4), *post*) for "the Board", "B.R. pension scheme" and "N.F.C. pension scheme", see s. 60 (1), *post*; as to "pension scheme established by the Board", see s. 60 (3), *post*; for "the Minister", see s. 70 (2), *post*; by virtue of s. 60 (1), *post*; for "subsidiary", see the Transport Act 1962, s. 92 (1), A.L.S. Vol. 124.

58. Consequential cancellation of debts owed by Board and Corporation

(1) In consequence of the foregoing provisions of this Part —

(*a*) the debts owed by the Board by virtue of sections 5 and 6 of the Railways Act 1974 (funding of the relevant pension obligations of the Board); and

(*b*) the debts owed by the Corporation by virtue of sections 19 and 20 of the Transport Act 1978 (funding of the relevant pension obligations of the Corporation),

are hereby cancelled and those sections are hereby repealed.

(2) Any payments in respect of the principal of or interest on any such debt —

(*a*) which are made on or after 1st April 1980 and before the passing of this Act to the persons administering a scheme to which this subsection applies; and

(*b*) in respect of which the Minister reimburses the Board or, as the case may be, the Corporation,

shall be deemed to be payments made to those persons in advance under section 52 (1), and any money which is deemed to be money so paid, and any investments representing any such money, shall be left out of account in making any determination under section 54 (1).

(3) Subsection (2) applies to any B.R. or N.F.C. pension scheme other than one in the case of which the relevant pension obligations have been completely funded.

(4) The Minister may discharge his liability to make any payment under section 52 (1) to the persons administering a scheme to which subsection (2) applies

by appropriating to that payment so much of any money which is deemed to be money paid to those persons in advance under section 52 (1) as, with the appropriate interest thereon, is equal to the amount of that payment.

(5) Any money which is deemed to be money paid in advance under section 52 (1) shall carry interest for the period beginning with the date on which it was paid to the persons administering the scheme and ending with the date on which it is appropriated by the Minister at such rate as the Minister may with the consent of the Treasury determine.   **[124]**

COMMENCEMENT
See the note to s. 52, *ante.*

SUB-S. (1): FOREGOING PROVISIONS OF THIS PART
I.e., ss. 52—57, *ante.*

SUB-S. (2): PASSING OF THIS ACT
See the note to s. 54, *ante.*

PERSONS
See the note "Person" to s. 2, *ante.*

SUB-S. (5): PERIOD BEGINNING WITH, ETC
See the note "Five years beginning with, etc." to s. 12, *ante.*

TREASURY
See the note to s. 45, *ante.*

DEFINITIONS
For "the relevant pension obligations", see s. 53, *ante*; for "the Board", "B.R. pension scheme", "the Corporation" and "N.F.C. pension scheme", see s. 60 (1), *post*; for "the Minister", see s. 70 (2), *post.*

RAILWAYS ACT 1974, SS. 5, 6
See 44, Halsbury's Statutes (3rd edn.), pp. 1297, 1299. Those sections are also repealed by s. 69 and Sch. 9, Part II, *post.*

TRANSPORT ACT 1978, SS. 19, 20
See A.L.S. Vol. 265. Those sections are also repealed by s. 69 and Sch. 9, Part II, *post.*

59. Supplemental provisions

(1) The making of any payment under section 52 (1) to the persons administering any B.R. or N.F.C. pension scheme shall not discharge any relevant pension obligation so far as it is an obligation to pay pensions or increases of pensions under the scheme or is an obligation to secure the payment of those pensions or increases.

(2) If the persons administering any such scheme or any other pension scheme established by the Board or the Corporation have no power to amend the scheme apart from this subsection, they may amend it by instrument in writing for the purpose of—

(*a*) enabling them to pay increases of any pensions payable under the scheme; or

(*b*) bringing the scheme into conformity with any provision of this Part;

and the power of amending any such scheme apart from this subsection may for either purpose be exercised without regard to any limitations on the exercise of the power and without compliance with any procedural provisions applicable to its exercise.   **[125]**

COMMENCEMENT
See the note to s. 52, *ante*.

PERSONS
See the note "Person" to s. 2, *ante*.

WRITING
See the note to s. 18, *ante*.

THIS PART
I.e., Part III (ss. 52–60) of this Act.

DEFINITIONS
For "the relevant pension obligations", see s. 53, *ante*; for "the Board", "B.R. pension scheme", "the Corporation", "N.F.C. pension scheme" and "pension", see s. 60 (1), *post*.

60. Interpretation of Part III

(1) In this Part—

"the Board" means the British Railways Board;

"B.R. pension scheme" means any section of the British Railways Super-annuation Fund specified in Schedule 8 or any other pension scheme so specified;

"the Corporation" means the National Freight Corporation;

"first financial year", in relation to a B.R. or N.F.C. pension scheme, means such period as—

(*a*) begins on 1st April 1980; and

(*b*) ends with the last day of an accounting year of the scheme,

and is a period of not less than twelve months and less than two years, and "financial year", in relation to any such scheme, means that period and each successive accounting year of the scheme;

"N.F.C. pension scheme" means the National Freight Corporation (Salaried Staff) Pension Fund, the National Freight Corporation (Wages Grades) Pension Fund or the N.F.C. (1978) Pension Fund;

"pension", in relation to a B.R. or N.F.C. pension scheme, means any pension, whether contributory or not, payable under the scheme to or in respect of any person and includes—

(*a*) a gratuity or lump sum so payable;

(*b*) a return of contributions to the scheme, with or without interest thereon or any other addition thereto;

(*c*) any sum payable under the scheme on or in respect of the death of any person; and

(*d*) any sum payable under the scheme in respect of any person and representing the whole or any part of his accrued pension rights under the scheme;

"the relevant pension obligations" has the meaning given by section 53;

"subsidiary" has the same meaning as in the Transport Act 1962;

"the successor company" has the same meaning as in Part II.

(2) For the purposes of this Part—

(*a*) the B.R. (1974) Pension Fund shall be taken to comprise the pension schemes specified or described in the Schedule to the Central Trust deed within the meaning of the British Railways (Central Trust) Order 1974; and (*b*) the N.F.C. (1978) Pension Fund shall be taken to comprise the pension schemes specified or described in the Schedule to the Central Trust deed within the meaning of the National Freight Corporation (Central Trust) Order 1978.

(3) References in this Part to any pension scheme established by the Board include references to any scheme in relation to which the rights, liabilities and functions of the British Transport Commission were transferred to the Board by the British Transport Reorganisation (Pensions of Employees) (No. 3) Order 1962.

(4) In relation to any time before the day appointed by the Minister for the purposes of Part II, references in this Part to the successor company shall be construed as references to the Corporation.   **[126]**

COMMENCEMENT
See the note to s. 52, *ante.*

THIS PART
I.e., Part III (ss. 52 – 60) of this Act.

BRITISH RAILWAYS BOARD
This body is constituted by the Transport Act 1962, s. 1, Sch. 1, Part II, 26, Halsbury's Statutes (3rd edn.), pp. 927, 1008.

NATIONAL FREIGHT CORPORATION
See the note to s. 45, *ante.*

MONTHS
See the note to s. 31, *ante.*

NATIONAL FREIGHT CORPORATION (SALARIED STAFF) PENSION FUND; NATIONAL FREIGHT CORPORATION (WAGES GRADES) PENSION FUND
See the notes to s. 40, *ante.*

N.F.C. (1978) PENSION FUND
For its composition, see sub-s. (2) (*b*) above.

SUCCESSOR COMPANY
For the meaning of "the successor company" in Part II of this Act, see s. 45 (1), *ante*; and note sub-s. (4) above.

DAY APPOINTED BY THE MINISTER FOR THE PURPOSES OF PART II
See s. 45 (2), *ante*, and the note "Orders under this section" thereto.

TRANSPORT ACT 1962
For the meaning of "subsidiary" in that Act, see s. 92 (1) thereof, 26, Halsbury's Statutes (3rd edn.), p. 1004.

BRITISH RAILWAYS (CENTRAL TRUST) ORDER 1974
S.I. 1974 No. 2001. That order was made under the Transport Act 1962, s. 74.

NATIONAL FREIGHT CORPORATION (CENTRAL TRUST) ORDER 1978
S.I. 1978 No. 1290. That order was made under the Transport Act 1962, s. 74.

BRITISH TRANSPORT REORGANISATION (PENSIONS OF EMPLOYEES) (NO. 3) ORDER 1962
S.I. 1962 No. 2758. That order was made under the Transport Act 1962, ss. 74, 75, Sch. 7, para. 14.

PART IV

MISCELLANEOUS AND GENERAL

61. Insurance or security in respect of private use of vehicle to cover use under car-sharing arrangements

At the end of section 148 of the Road Traffic Act 1972 (avoidance of certain exceptions to policies or securities, etc.) there shall be added the following subsections —

"(5) To the extent that a policy or security issued or given for the purposes of this Part of this Act —

(*a*) restricts, as the case may be, the insurance of the persons insured by the policy or the operation of the security to use of the vehicle for specified purposes (for example, social, domestic and pleasure purposes) of a non-commercial character; or

(*b*) excludes from, as the case may be, that insurance or the operation of the security —

(i) use of the vehicle for hire or reward; or

(i) business or commercial use of the vehicle; or

(iii) use of the vehicle for specified purposes of a business or commercial character,

then, for the purposes of that policy or security so far as it relates to such liabilities as are required to be covered by a policy under section 145 of this Act, the use of a vehicle on a journey in the course of which one or more passengers are carried at separate fares shall, if the conditions specified in subsection (6) below are satisfied, be treated as falling within that restriction or as not falling within that exclusion, as the case may be.

(6) The conditions referred to in subsection (5) above are —

(*a*) the vehicle is not adapted to carry more than eight passengers and is not a motor cycle;

(*b*) the fare or aggregate of the fares paid in respect of the journey does not exceed the amount of the running costs of the vehicle for the journey (which for the purposes of this paragraph shall be taken to include an appropriate amount in respect of depreciation and general wear); and

(*c*) the arrangements for the payment of fares by the passenger or passengers carried at separate fares were made before the journey began.

(7) Subsections (5) and (6) above apply however the restrictions or exclusions described in subsection (5) are framed or worded; and in those subsections "fare" and "separate fares" have the same meaning as in section 2 (4) of the Transport Act 1980.". **[127]**

COMMENCEMENT
See s. 70 (5), *post*, and the note "Orders under this section" thereto.

THIS PART OF THIS ACT
I.e., the Road Traffic Act 1972, Part VI (ss. 143 – 158), A.L.S. Vol. 208.

PERSONS
See the note "Person" to s. 2, *ante*.

ADAPTED
  See the note to s. 2, *ante*.

DEFINITIONS
  For "motor cycle", see the Road Traffic Act 1972, s. 190 (4), A.L.S. Vol. 208. Note as to "fare"
  and "separate fares", s. 148 (7) of that Act as added by this section.

ROAD TRAFFIC ACT 1972, SS. 145, 148
  See A.L.S. Vol. 208.

62. Grants towards duty charged on bus fuel, and new bus grants

(1) In subsection (8) of section 92 of the Finance Act 1965 (grants towards duty charged on bus fuel), for the definition of "bus service" there shall be substituted —

  " "bus service" means a stage carriage service within the meaning of Part I of the Transport Act 1980 which is available to the general public and is neither an excursion or tour within the meaning of that Part nor a service as regards which the condition specified in section 3 (3) (*a*) of that Act (long journeys only) is satisfied;".

(2) In section 32 of the Transport Act 1968 (new bus grants) —

  (*a*) in subsection (1), for the words "wholly or mainly as a stage carriage" there shall be substituted the words "wholly or mainly in the operation of bus services"; and

  (*b*) in subsection (2), after paragraph (*c*) there shall be inserted —

    "(*d*) "bus service" has the same meaning as in section 92 of the Finance Act 1965".   **[128]**

COMMENCEMENT
  See s. 70 (5), *post*, and the note "Orders under this section" thereto.

STAGE CARRIAGE SERVICE; EXCURSION OR TOUR
  For the purposes of Part I of this Act these expressions are defined by s. 44 (1), *ante*.

WHOLLY OR MAINLY
  See the note to Sch. 1, Part IV, *post*.

SAME MEANING AS IN S. 92 OF THE FINANCE ACT 1965
  I.e., the meaning set out in sub-s. (1) above.

FINANCE ACT 1965, S. 92 (8)
  For that subsection as substituted by the Transport (London) Act 1969, Sch. 3, para. 8, see
  A.L.S. Vol. 185.

TRANSPORT ACT 1968, S. 32
  See A.L.S. Vol. 178.

63. Articulated vehicles

For section 191 of the Road Traffic Act 1972 (certain articulated vehicles to be treated for the purposes of that Act as a motor vehicle with a trailer attached) there shall be substituted —

  "**191.**—(1) Unless it falls within subsection (2) below, a vehicle so constructed that it can be divided into two parts both of which are vehicles and one of which is a motor vehicle shall (when not so divided) be treated for the purposes of the enactments mentioned in subsection (3) below as that motor vehicle with the other part attached as a trailer.

(2) A passenger vehicle so constructed that —

> (*a*) it can be divided into two parts, both of which are vehicles and one of which is a motor vehicle, but cannot be so divided without the use of facilities normally available only at a workshop; and
>
> (*b*) passengers carried by it when not so divided can at all times pass from either part to the other,

shall (when not so divided) be treated for the purposes of the enactments mentioned in subsection (3) below as a single motor vehicle.

(3) The enactments referred to in subsections (1) and (2) above are the Road Traffic Act 1960, the Road Traffic Regulation Act 1967, this Act and Part I of the Transport Act 1980.

(4) In this section "passenger vehicle" means a vehicle constructed or adapted for use solely or principally for the carriage of passengers.".   **[129]**

COMMENCEMENT
See s. 70 (5), *post*, and the note "Orders under this section" thereto.

THIS ACT
I.e., the Road Traffic Act 1972, A.L.S. Vol. 208.

CONSTRUCTED OR ADAPTED
It is thought that this means originally constructed or subsequently altered so as to make apt; cf. *French* v. *Champkin*, [1920] 1 K.B. 76, and *Hubbard* v. *Messenger*, [1938] 1 K.B. 300; [1937] 4 All E.R. 48, at p. 307 and p. 50, respectively; and see also *Taylor* v. *Mead*, [1961] 1 All E.R. 626; *Maddox* v. *Storer*, [1963] 1 Q.B. 451; [1962] 1 All E.R. 831; *Flower Freight Co., Ltd.* v. *Hammond*, [1963] 1 Q.B. 275; [1962] 3 All E.R. 950; and *Propperwell* v. *Cockerton*, [1968] 1 All E.R. 1038.

SOLELY OR PRINCIPALLY
Cf. the note "Wholly or mainly" to Sch. 1, Part IV, *post*.

DEFINITIONS
For "motor vehicle", see the Road Traffic Act 1972; s. 190 (1), A.L.S. Vol. 208 and the notes thereto; for "trailer", see s. 190 (1) of that Act. Note as to "passenger vehicle", s. 191 (4) of the Act of 1972 as substituted by this section.

ROAD TRAFFIC ACT 1972, S. 191
See A.L.S. Vol. 208.

ROAD TRAFFIC ACT 1960
See A.L.S. Vol. 124.

ROAD TRAFFIC REGULATION ACT 1967
See A.L.S. Vol. 165. Consequent upon the present section, s. 100 of the Act of 1967 is repealed by s. 69 and Sch. 9, Part IV, *post*.

TRANSPORT ACT 1980, PART I
I.e., ss. 1–44, *ante*.

64. Roof-signs on vehicles other than taxis

(1) There shall not, in any part of England and Wales outside the metropolitan police district and the City of London, be displayed on or above the roof of any vehicle which is used for carrying passengers for hire or reward but which is not a taxi —

(*a*) any sign which consists of or includes the word "taxi" or "cab", whether in the singular or plural, or "hire", or any word of similar meaning or appearance to any of those words, whether alone or as part of another word; or

(*b*) any sign, notice, mark, illumination or other feature which may suggest that the vehicle is a taxi.

(2) Any person who knowingly—

(*a*) drives a vehicle in respect of which subsection (1) is contravened; or

(*b*) causes or permits that subsection to be contravened in respect of any vehicle,

shall be liable on summary conviction to a fine not exceeding £200.

(3) In this section "taxi" means a vehicle licensed under section 37 of the Town Police Clauses Act 1847, section 6 of the Metropolitan Carriage Act 1869, section 270 of the Burgh Police (Scotland) Act 1892 or any similar local enactment.

[130]

COMMENCEMENT
    See s. 70 (5), *post*, and the note "Orders under this section" thereto.

ENGLAND; WALES
    For meanings, see the Interpretation Act 1978, s. 5, Sch. 1, A.L.S. Vol. 258.

METROPOLITAN POLICE DISTRICT
    This district consists of the areas specified in the London Government Act 1963, s. 76 (1), A.L.S. Vol. 138A, as amended by the Local Authorities etc (Miscellaneous Provision) Order 1974, S.I. 1974, No. 482, art. 11.

PERSON
    See the note to s. 2, *ante*.

KNOWINGLY; CAUSES OR PERMITS
    See the notes to s. 18, *ante*.

SUMMARY CONVICTION
    See the note to s. 4, *ante*.

65. Repeal of s. 2 of 1954 c. 64

The provisions of section 2 of, and Schedule 1 to, the Transport Charges &c. (Miscellaneous Provisions) Act 1954 (which relate to charges on independent tramways, trolley vehicles and railways of the nature of a tramway), including those provisions as extended or applied by or under any other Act (including a local or private Act), shall cease to have effect.   [131]

COMMENCEMENT
    See s. 70 (5), *post*, and the note "Orders under this section" thereto.

TRANSPORT CHARGES &C. (MISCELLANEOUS PROVISIONS) ACT 1954, S. 2, SCH. 1
    See A.L.S. Vol. 88. Those provisions are also repealed by s. 69 and Sch. 9, Part I, *post*.

66. Abolition of Freight Integration Council and repeal of certain provisions about special authorisations for use of large goods vehicles

(1) The Freight Integration Council established under section 6 of the Transport Act 1968 is hereby abolished.

(2) The provisions of Part V of the Transport Act 1968 relating to special authorisations for the use of large goods vehicles (which have not been brought into force) are hereby repealed, and accordingly —

> (a) in section 82 (1) (b) of that Act, for "either of those sections" there shall be substituted "that section"; and
>
> (b) in section 91 (1) (a) of that Act, for "sections 69 and 79" there shall be substituted "section 69".   **[132]**

COMMENCEMENT
This section came into force on the passing of this Act on 30th June 1980; see s. 70 (3), *post*.

TRANSPORT ACT 1968, SS. 6, 82 (1) (*b*), 91 (1) (*a*), PART V
For s. 6, Part V and ss. 82 (1) (*b*) and 91 (1) (*a*), of that Act, see A.L.S. Vol. 178. S.6 of that Act is repealed and the provisions of Part V relating to special authorisations for the use of large goods vehicles (*i. e.*, ss. 72 – 80 with the exception of part of s. 71) are also repealed by s. 69 and Sch. 9, Part II, *post*. The provisions relating to special authorisations were never brought into force by order under s. 166 (2) of the Act of 1968.

67. Abolition of Railways and Coastal Shipping Committee

The Railways and Coastal Shipping Committee established under section 150 of the Transport Act 1968 is hereby abolished.   **[133]**

COMMENCEMENT
This section came into force on the passing of this Act on 30th June 1980; see s. 70 (3), *post*.

TRANSPORT ACT 1968, S. 150
See A.L.S. Vol. 178. That section is repealed by s. 69 and Sch. 9, Part II, *post*.

68. Expenses

There shall be paid out of money provided by Parliament —

> (a) any administrative expenses incurred by any government department in consequence of the provisions of this Act; and
>
> (b) any increase attributable to this Act in the sums payable out of money so provided under any other Act.   **[134]**

COMMENCEMENT
This section came into force on the passing of this Act on 30th June 1980; see s. 70 (3), *post*.

69. Repeals

The enactments mentioned in Schedule 9 (which include spent enactments) are hereby repealed to the extent specified in the third column of that Schedule.

[135]

COMMENCEMENT
This section comes into force on different dates in relation to the different parts of Sch. 9, *post*; see s. 70 (3), (5), *post*, and the notes "Orders under this section" to s. 45, *ante*, and to s. 70, *post*.

70. Citation, etc

(1) This Act may be cited as the Transport Act 1980.
  (2) In this Act —

"the Minister" means the Minister of Transport;

"modification" includes addition, omission and alteration, and related expressions shall be construed accordingly;

"statutory provision" means a provision contained in an Act or in subordinate legislation within the meaning of the Interpretation Act 1978.

(3) The following provisions of this Act, namely —

(*a*) Part II, except section 51 (2) and Schedule 7;

(*b*) Part III;

(*c*) sections 66 to 68 and this section;

(*d*) Part II of Schedule 9 (and section 69 so far as it relates to that Part),

shall come into force on the passing of this Act.

(4) The following provisions of this Act, namely —

(*a*) section 51 (2) and Schedule 7; and

(*b*) Part III of Schedule 9 (and section 69 so far as it relates to that Part),

shall come into force on the appointed day within the meaning of Part II of this Act.

(5) Subject to subsections (3) and (4), this Act shall come into force on such day as the Minister may by order made by statutory instrument appoint, and different days may be appointed under this subsection for different purposes.

(6) An order under subsection (5) may contain such transitional provisions and savings (whether or not involving the modification of any statutory provision) as appear to the Minister necessary or expedient in connection with the provisions thereby brought (wholly or partly) into force.

(7) The following provisions of this Act do not extend to Northern Ireland, namely, —

(*a*) Part I (which includes Schedules 1 to 5);

(*b*) sections 61 to 65 and 66 (2); and

(*c*) Parts I and IV of Schedule 9 (and section 69 so far as it relates to those Parts). **[136]**

COMMENCEMENT
This section came into force on the passing of this Act on 30th June 1980; see sub-s. (3) above.

SUB-S. (3): PART II
I.e., ss. 45 – 51, *ante*.

PART III
I.e., ss. 52 – 60, *ante*.

PASSING OF THIS ACT
This Act was passed, *i.e.*, received the Royal Assent, on 30th June 1980.

SUB-S. (4): APPOINTED DAY
For the meaning of "appointed day" in Part II of this Act, see s. 45 (2), *ante*. At the time of going to press no such day had been appointed.

SUB-S. (5): STATUTORY INSTRUMENT
See the note to s. 43, *ante*.

SUB-S. (6): APPEAR
See the note "Satisfied" to s. 5, *ante*.

SUB-S. (7): PART I
I.e., ss. 1 – 44, *ante*.

INTERPRETATION ACT 1978
For the meaning of "subordinate legislation" in that Act, see s. 21 (1) thereof, Vol. 48, p. 1309.

ORDERS UNDER THIS SECTION

The Transport Act 1980 (Commencement No. 1) Order 1980, S.I. 1980 No. 913 (bringing into operation on 31st July 1980 the following provisions of this Act: s. 1 (3), (4) so far as they relate to the other sections brought into force on 31st July 1980, ss. 27, 36, 39, s. 43 (1) in so far as it relates to the provisions of the Road Traffic Act 1960 mentioned in Sch. 5, Part I, specified below, s. 64 and s. 69 in so far as it relates to the enactments mentioned in Sch. 9, Part I, specified below; Sch. 5, Part I, para. 4, in so far as it relates to or consists of sub-para. (*a*), paras. 5, 6, para. 12 in so far as it relates to or consists of sub-paras. (*c*), (*d*) or (*e*), and paras. 14, 15; and the repeals specified in Sch. 9, Part I, relating to the Road Traffic Act 1960, ss. 144 (including sub-s. (3) thereof), 145 (1), 147 (1) (*d*), 154, 155, 158, 160 (1) (*f*), 163 (1), the Transport (London) Act 1969, s. 24 (2), (3), the Local Government (Scotland) Act 1973, Sch. 18, para. 30, the Road Taffic Act 1974, Sch. 6, para. 2, and the Energy Act 1976, (Sch. 1, para. 2).

The Transport Act 1980 (Commencement No. 2) Order 1980, S.I. 1980 No. 1353 brought the following provisions into operation on 6th October 1980: s. 1 (3), (4) so far as it relates to other sections listed, ss. 2, 3, Sch. 1, Pts. I – III, ss. 4 – 15, s. 25 (1) – (5), (7) – (9) and (10) in so far as it relates to road service licences, s. 29 in so far as it relates to road service licences, ss. 32, 33, 35, 37, s. 38 in so far as it amends the Act of 1960 in certain respects, s. 40, Sch. 4, s. 41 in so far as it relates to road service licences, s. 42 (1) in so far as it relates to the provisions specified in s. 42 (2) (except ss. 25 (5), 26 (4)), s. 42 (2) save in so far as it specifies ss. 25 (5), 26 (4), s. 42 (3) in so far as it relates to the provisions specified in s. 42 (4) (except ss. 17 (3), 18 (9) (*b*), 19 (5), 22 (7) and 24 (4)), s. 42 (4) save in so far as it specifies ss. 17 (3), 18 (9) (*b*), 19 (5), 22 (7) and 24 (4), s. 43 (1) so far as it relates to ss. 144, 149, 153, 160 and 248 of the Act of 1960 and to various other enactments specified in Part III to the Schedule of this Order, s. 43 (2), s. 44 in so far as it relates to any provision specified in this Order, ss. 61, 62, 65, 69 in so far as it relates to the repeals specified in Part IV of the Schedule to this Order.

The Transport Act 1980 (Commencement No. 3) Order 1980, S.I. 1980 No. 1424 brought Schs. 1 and 2 of the Act into operation on 6th October 1980.

Both Commencement No. 1 and 2 Orders contain certain transitional provisions made necessary by the appointing of different days for different sections or purposes.

SCHEDULES

SCHEDULE 1

Sections 2 and 3

PUBLIC SERVICE VEHICLES: CONDITIONS AFFECTING STATUS OR CLASSIFICATION

PART I

SHARING OF TAXIS AND HIRE-CARS

1. The making of the agreement for the payment of separate fares must not have been initiated by the driver or by the owner of the vehicle, by any person who has made the vehicle available under any arrangement, or by any person who receives any remuneration in respect of the arrangements for the journey.

2. — (1) The journey must be made without previous advertisement to the public of facilities for its being made by passengers to be carried at separate fares, except where the local authorities concerned have approved the arrangements under which the journey is made as designed to meet the social and welfare needs of one or more communities, and their approvals remain in force.

(2) In relation to a journey the local authorities concerned for the purposes of this paragraph are those in whose area any part of the journey is to be made; and in this sub-paragraph "local authority" means —

    (*a*) in relation to England and Wales, the Greater London Council or a county council;

    (*b*) (*applies to Scotland*).

3. The journey must not be made in conjunction with, or in extension of, a service

provided under a road service licence if the vehicle is owned by, or made available under any arrangement with, the holder of the licence or any person who receives any remuneration in respect of the service provided under it or in respect of arrangements for that service.   **[137]**

COMMENCEMENT
　　See s. 70 (5), *ante*, and the note "Orders under this section" thereto.

PERSON
　　See the note to s. 2, *ante*.

ADVERTISEMENT
　　Para. 2 must be read in conjunction with para. 9 of this Schedule, *post*.

THE PUBLIC
　　See the note "Against the interests of the public" to s. 5, *ante*.

ENGLAND; WALES
　　For meanings, see the Interpretation Act 1978, s. 5, Sch. 1, A.L.S. Vol. 258.

GREATER LONDON COUNCIL
　　See the note to s. 5, *ante*.

COUNTY COUNCIL
　　See the note "County council; district council" to s. 5, *ante*.

ROAD SERVICE LICENCE
　　As to these generally, see ss. 4, *et seq.*, *ante*.

DEFINITION
　　For "owned", "owner" and "road service licence", see s. 44 (1), *ante*; by virtue of s. 1 (3), *ante*, for "driver" and "fares", see the Road Traffic Act 1960, s. 257 (1), A.L.S. Vol. 124. Note as to "the local authorities concerned", para. 2 (2) above, and see also as to "fares", s. 2 (5) (*b*), *ante*.

PART II

PARTIES OF OVERSEAS VISITORS

　　4. Each of the passengers making the journey must have been outside Great Britain at the time of concluding his arrangements to make the journey.   **[138]**

PART III

ALTERNATIVE CONDITIONS AFFECTING STATUS OR CLASSIFICATION

　　5. Arrangements for the bringing together of all the passengers for the purpose of making the journey must have been made otherwise than by, or by a person acting on behalf of —

　　　　(*a*) the holder of the operator's licence under which the vehicle is to be used, if such a licence is in force,
　　　　(*b*) the driver or the owner of the vehicle or any person who has made the vehicle available under any arrangement, if no such licence is in force,

and otherwise than by any person who receives any remuneration in respect of the arrangements.
　　6. The journey must be made without previous advertisement to the public of the arrangements therefor.
　　7. All the passengers must, in the case of a journey to a particular destination, be carried to, or to the vicinity of, that destination, or, in the case of a tour, be carried for the greater part of the journey.
　　8. No differentiation of fares for the journey on the basis of distance or of time must be made.   **[139]**

COMMENCEMENT
See s. 70 (5), *ante*, and the note "Orders under this section" thereto.

PERSON
See the note to s. 2, *ante*.

OPERATOR'S LICENCE
I.e., It is thought that this refers to a PSV operator's licence granted under ss. 19 *et seq.*, *ante*.

ADVERTISEMENT
Para. 6 must be read in conjunction with para. 9 of this Schedule, *post*.

THE PUBLIC
See the note "Against the interests of the public" to s. 5, *ante*.

ALL THE PASSENGERS, ETC
For a case where the conditions laid down in what is now para. 7 above were held not to have been complied with, see *Clarke* v. *Dundee Town Council*, 1957, S.C.(J.) 63.

DEFINITIONS
For "owner", see s. 44 (1), *ante*; by virtue of s. 1 (3), *ante*, for "driver" and "fares", see the Road Traffic Act 1960, s. 257 (1), A.L.S. Vol. 124. See also as to "fares", s. 2 (5) (*b*), *ante*.

PART IV

SUPPLEMENTARY

9. For the purposes of paragraphs 2 and 6 no account shall be taken of any such advertisement as follows, that is to say—

(*a*) a notice displayed or announcement made—

(i) at or in any place of worship for the information of persons attending that place of worship;

(ii) at or in any place of work for the information of persons who work there; or

(iii) by any club or other voluntary association at or in any premises occupied or used by the club or association;

(*b*) a notice or announcement contained in any periodical published for the information of, and circulating wholly or mainly among—

(i) persons who attend or might reasonably be expected to attend a particular place of worship or a place of worship in a particular place; or

(ii) persons who work at a particular place of work or at any of two or more particular places of work; or

(iii) the members of a club or other voluntary association. **[140]**

COMMENCEMENT
See s. 70 (5), *ante*, and the note "Orders under this section" thereto.

CLUB
This expression is not defined in this Act, but see 3, Halsbury's Statutes (3rd edn.), p. 672, and 6 Halsbury's Laws (4th Edn.), para. 201.

PREMISES
See the note to s. 16, *ante*.

WHOLLY OR MAINLY
The word "mainly" probably means "more than half"; see *Fawcett Properties, Ltd.* v. *Buckingham County Council*, [1961] A.C. 636, at p. 669; [1960] 3 All E.R. 503, H.L., at p. 512, *per* Lord Morton of Henryton. See also on the meaning of "wholly or mainly" (or "exclusively or. mainly"), *Re Hatschek's Patents, Ex parte Zerenner*, [1909] 2 Ch. 68; *Miller* v. *Owners of Ottilie*, [1944] 1 K.B. 188; [1944] 1 All E.R. 277; *Franklin* v. *Gramophone Co., Ltd.*, [1948] 1 K.B. 542, at p. 555; [1948] 1 All E.R. 353, C.A., at p. 358, *per* Simervell, L.J.; and *Berthelemy* v. *Neale*, [1952] 1 All E.R. 437, C.A.

EXTENSION
For the purposes of the Passenger Vehicle (Experimental Areas) Act 1977, s. 2 (7), Schedule, para. 1 (*b*), A.L.S. Vol. 254, no account is to be taken of any advertisement mentioned in this paragraph; see s. 2 (7) of, and the Schedule, para. 14, to, that Act, as amended, in the case of the Schedule, para. 14, by s. 43 (1), *ante*, and Sch. 5, Part II, *post*.

SCHEDULE 2

Section 12

ORDERS DESIGNATING TRIAL AREAS

Applications for designation orders

1. —(1) Not less than 21 days before making an application to the Minister for a designation order in respect of any area the local authority concerned shall publish in one or more relevant newspapers a notice describing the area in question and stating their intention to apply for a designation order in respect of it and the date on which they propose to make the application.

(2) For the purposes of any notice under this paragraph a "relevant newspaper" is any local newspaper which the local authority concerned may consider appropriate.

2. —(1) Before making such an application the local authority concerned shall also notify—

  (*a*) every local authority (if any) whose area adjoins the area specified in the application;

  (*b*) every district council whose area is wholly or partly comprised in, or adjoins, the area so specified;

  (*c*) any person who is already providing a stage carriage service in the area so specified; and

  (*d*) such organisations as appear to the local authority concerned appropriate as representing persons providing or employed in the provision of public passenger transport services in the area so specified.

(2) In this paragraph "public passenger transport services" has the meaning given by section 1 (2) of the Transport Act 1978.

3. Every application for a designation order shall be accompanied by the original or a copy of any representations in writing (by whoever made) which relate to the application and were received by the local authority concerned before the date on which the application is made; and before making a designation order the Minister shall consider any such representations.

Variation or revocation of designation orders

4. Before making an application to the Minister for an order under section 12 (4) varying or revoking a designation order the local authority concerned—

  (*a*) shall notify—

    (i) every local authority (if any) whose area adjoins the trial area in question;

    (ii) every district council whose area adjoins the trial area;

    (iii) any person who is for the time being providing a stage carriage service in the trial area; and

    (iv) such organisations as appear to the local authority concerned appropriate as representing persons providing or employed in the provision of public passenger transport services (within the meaning of paragraph 2) in the trial area; and

  (*b*) shall consult with every district council whose area is wholly or partly comprised in the trial area.

5. Paragraph 3 shall apply in relation to an application for, and the making of, an order under section 12 (4) as it applies in relation to an application for, and the making of, a designation order.

6. —(1) Subject to sub-paragraph (2), an order under section 12 which revokes or varies a designation order may contain such transitional provisions as the Minister thinks fit.

(2) An order under section 12 (4) which revokes a designation order or varies it so as to exclude from the area designated by it any part of that area shall contain such transitional provisions as the Minister thinks fit for securing that any person who has, throughout the relevant period ending with the date of the order, provided a stage carriage service which he will be unable to continue to provide after the time when the revocation or variation takes effect unless granted a road service licence in respect of it, can obtain as of right a road service licence that will enable him to continue to provide that service for as long as the licence remains in force after that time.

(3) In sub-paragraph (2) "the relevant period", in relation to an order under section 12 (4), means such period of not less than three months as may be specified in the order.   **[141]**

COMMENCEMENT
    See s. 70 (5), *ante*, and the note "Orders under this section" thereto.

PARA. 1: NOT LESS THAN 21 DAYS BEFORE, ETC
    The words "not less than" indicate that 21 clear days must intervene between the day on which the notice is published and that on which the application is made; see *R. v. Turner*, [1910] 1 K.B. 346, and *Re Hector Whaling, Ltd*, [1936] Ch. 208; [1935] All E.R. Rep. 302.

CONSIDER APPROPRIATE
    See the note "Satisfied" to s. 5, *ante*.

PARA. 2: ADJOINS
    The primary and exact meaning of the word is "conterminous" or "lying near so as to touch in some part", but it is also used in a looser sense as meaning "near" or "neighbouring" or "in close proximity" though not in strict physical contact; see *Lightbound* v. *Higher Bebington Local Board* (1885), 16 Q.B.D. 577, C.A., at p. 584, *per* Bowen, LJ.; *New Plymouth Borough Council* v. *Taranaki Electric Power Board*, [1933] A.C. 680, P.C., at p. 682; *Re Ecclesiastical Comrs. for England's Conveyance*, [1936] Ch. 430, at p. 440; [1934] All E.R. Rep. 118, at p. 123; and *Buckinghamshire County Council* v. *Trigg*, [1963] 1 All E.R. 403, at p. 407, *per* Lord Parker. It is thought than in para. 2 (1) (a) above "adjoins" means conterminous.

DISTRICT COUNCIL
    See the note "County council; district council" to s. 5, *ante*.

PERSON
    See the note to s. 2, *ante*.

APPEAR
    See the note "Satisfied" to s. 5, *ante*.

PARA. 3: WRITING
    See the note to s. 18, *ante*.

PARA. 4: CONSULT
    See the note "Consulting" to s. 54, *ante*.

PARA. 6: THINKS FIT
    See the note "Satisfied" to s. 5, *ante*.

MONTHS
    See the note to s. 31, *ante*.

DEFINITION
    For "trial area", see s. 12 (1), *ante*; for "designation order", "local authority" and "the local authority concerned", see s. 12 (8), *ante*; for "stage carriage service", see s. 44 (1), *ante*; for "the Minister", see s. 70 (2), *ante*. Note as to "relevant newspaper", para. 1 (2) above; as to "public passenger transport service", para. 2 (2) above; and as to "the relevant period", para. 6 (3) above.

TRANSPORT ACT 1978, S. 1 (2)
    See A.L.S. Vol. 265.

SCHEDULE 3

Sections 21 (2) and 23 (6)
SUPPLEMENTARY PROVISIONS AS TO QUALIFICATIONS
FOR PSV OPERATOR'S LICENCE

Good repute

1. — (1) In determining whether an individual is of good repute, traffic commissioners shall have regard to all the relevant evidence and in particular to —

   (*a*) relevant convictions of the company and its officers, employees and agent;
   (*b*) such other information as the commissioners may have as to his previous conduct, in whatever capacity, in relation to the operation of vehicles of any description in the course of a business.

   (2) In determining whether a company is of good repute, traffic commissioners shall have regard to all the relevant evidence and in particular to —

   (*a*) relevant convictions of the company and its officers, employees and agents;
   (*b*) such other information as the commissioners may have as to the previous conduct of —

       (i) the company's officers, employees and agents in relation to the operation of vehicles of any description in the course of any business carried on by the company; and
       (ii) each of the company's directors, in whatever capacity, in relation to the operation of vehicles of any description in the course of any other business.

Appropriate financial standing

2. Being of appropriate financial standing in relation to an applicant for, or holder of, a PSV operator's licence consists in having available sufficient financial resources to ensure the establishment and proper administration of the business carried on, or proposed to be carried on, under the licence.

Professional competence

3. References in this Part of this Act to professional competence are to the professional competence of an individual; and a company satisfies the requirement as to professional competence if, and so long as, it has a transport manager of its road passenger transport business who is of good repute and professionally competent.

4. Where an individual is not himself professionally competent, the requirement as to professional competence shall be regarded as satisfied in relation to him if, and so long as, he has a transport manager of his road passenger transport business who is of good repute and professionally competent.

5. Where the holder of a PSV operator's licence relies on a transport manager to satisfy the requirement as to professional competence and that manager —

   (*a*) dies or ceases by reason of physical disability or mental disorder to be capable of discharging his duties as transport manager;
   (*b*) ceases to work for the business; or
   (*c*) ceases to be of good repute,

the holder shall nevertheless not be treated as failing to satisfy that requirement until the expiry of such period as in the opinion of the relevant traffic commissioners is reasonably required for the appointment of a new transport manager.

6. Subject to paragraph 10, an individual shall be regarded as professionally competent for the purposes of this Part of this Act if, and only if, —

   (*a*) he is the holder of a certificate issued by an approved body to the effect that he possesses the requisite skills; or
   (*b*) he is the holder of any other certificate of competence, diploma or other qualification recognised for the purposes of this paragraph by the Minister.

7. In paragraph 6 "approved body" means —

   (*a*) a body approved by the Minister for the purposes of that paragraph; or
   (*b*) a body approved by the Department of the Environment for Northern Ireland for

the purposes of section 46A (5) (*c*) of the Transport Act (Northern Ireland) 1967; or

(*c*) a body or authority designated by another member State for the purposes of Article 2 (4) of Council Directive (EEC) 74/562 of 12th November 1974 on admission to the occupation of road passenger transport operator in national and international transport operations;

and "the requisite skills" means skills in the subjects listed in Part A of the Annex to that Directive and, in the case of a licence to cover international operations, also skills in the subjects listed in Part B of that Annex.

Persons engaged in road passenger transport before 1st January 1978

8. — (1) Paragraphs 9 and 10 apply only to persons applying for, and to holders of, standard licences, and accordingly in those paragraphs "a licence" means a standard licence.

(2) For the purposes of those paragraphs, a person was authorised to engage in the occupation of road passenger transport operator at any time if, and only if, at that time —

(*a*) he was the holder, or one of the joint holders, of a public service vehicle licence under section 127 of the Road Traffic Act 1960, or the corresponding provision of the law of Northern Ireland, relating to a vehicle adapted to carry more than eight passengers; or

(*b*) he was by virtue of a permit under Regulation 20 of the Public Service Vehicles (Licences and Certificates) Regulations 1952, or the corresponding provision of the law of Northern Ireland, deemed to be the holder or one of the joint holders of such a licence; or

(*c*) he was so authorised under the law of another member State; or

(*d*) he was the transport manager of a person within paragraph (*a*), (*b*) or (*c*).

9. — (1) An individual or company authorised to engage in the occupation of road passenger transport operator at any time before 1st January 1978 shall be deemed until the contrary is proved to satisfy the requirements to be of good repute and appropriate financial standing and, if so authorised before 1st January 1975, also to satisfy the requirement as to professional competence.

(2) An applicant for a PSV operator's licence, or for the variation of such a licence, shall not be obliged to furnish to the traffic commissioners in support of his application information relating to a requirement which is deemed to be satisfied by virtue of sub-paragraph (1) unless it appears to the commissioners that there are grounds for thinking that the requirement is not in fact satisfied.

10. For the purpose of this Part of this Act, an individual shall be regarded as professionally competent if he was authorised to engage in the occupation of road passenger transport operator before 1st January 1978, and was so authorised —

(*a*) for a period of, or for periods amounting in the aggregate to, two years during the period 1st January 1975 to 31st December 1979; or

(*b*) at any time in the period 1st January 1970 to 31st December 1974. **[142]**

COMMENCEMENT
See s. 70 (5), *ante*, and the note "Orders under this section" thereto.

PARA. 1: INDIVIDUAL
See the note to s. 31, *ante*.

TRAFFIC COMMISSIONERS
See the note to s. 3, *ante*.

IN THE COURSE OF A BUSINESS
See the note "In the course of a business of carrying passengers" to s. 2, *ante*.

PARA. 3: THIS PART OF THIS ACT
I.e., Part I (ss. 1 − 44 and Schs. 1 − 5) of this Act.

PARA. 5: OPINION
See the note "Satisfied" to s. 5, *ante*.

PARA. 7: MEMBER STATE
See the note to s. 27, *ante*.

PARA. 8: PERSON; ADAPTED
See the notes to s. 2, *ante*.

APPEARS
See the note "Satisfied" to s. 5, *ante*.

DEFINITIONS
For "company", "director", "international operation", "national operation", "PSV operator's licence", "relevant conviction", "standard licence" and "transport manager", see s. 44 (1), *ante*; for "the Minister", see s. 70 (2), *ante*; by virtue of s. 1 (3), *ante*, for "the traffic commissioners", see the Road Traffic Act 1960, s. 120 (4), A.L.S. Vol. 124. Note as to "approved body" and "the requisite skills", para. 7 above, and as to "a licence", para. 8 (1) above.

TRANSPORT ACT (NORTHERN IRELAND) 1967
1967 c. 37 (N.I.); not printed in this work.

COUNCIL DIRECTIVE (EEC) 74/562 OF 12TH NOVEMBER 1974
Dir. 74/562/EEC, OJ L308, 19.11.1974, p. 23. Note also s. 44 (4), *ante*.

ROAD TRAFFIC ACT 1960, S. 127
See A.L.S. Vol. 124. That section is repealed by ss. 1 (1), (2), 69, *ante*, and Sch. 9, Part I, *post*.

PUBLIC SERVICE VEHICLES (LICENCES AND CERTIFICATES) REGULATIONS 1952
S.I. 1952 No. 900.

Section 40

SCHEDULE 4

Increase of Penalties in the 1960 Act

Provision creating offence	General nature of offence	Existing maximum punishment	New maximum punishment	Amendment
Section 144 ...	Unlicensed person driving public service vehicle, or employment of such a person.	£100	£500	In section 144 (8) for "£100" substitute "£500".
Section 146 (2) ...	Contravention of regulations as to conduct of persons licensed to act as drivers of public service vehicles.	£20	£50	In section 146 (2) for "£20" substitute "£50".
Section 146 (3) ...	Failure to produce driver's licence for purpose of endorsement.	£100	£200	In section 146 (3) for "£100" substitute "£200".
Section 147 (2) ...	Contravention of regulations as to conduct of passengers in public service vehicles.	£100	£200	In section 147 (2) for "£100" substitute "£200".
Section 157 (2) ...	Failure by person carrying on the business of operating public service vehicles to keep accounts and records and to make financial and statistical returns.	£100	£200	In section 157 (2) for "£100" substitute "£200".
Section 235 ...	Making of false statements.	£200	£500	In section 235 (3) for "£200" substitute "£500".
Section 294 (2) ...	Failure to comply with an order requiring evidence to be given or documents to be produced at an inquiry.	£25	£200	In section 249 (2) for the words from "to a fine" onwards substitute "to a fine not exceeding £200".

[143]

COMMENCEMENT

See s. 70 (5), *ante*, and the note "Orders under this section" thereto.

1960 ACT

I.e., the Road Traffic Act 1960; see s. 44 (1), *ante*. For ss. 144, 146 (2), (3), 147 (2), 157 (2), 235 and 249 (2) of that Act, see A.L.S. Vol. 124.

SCHEDULE 5

MINOR AND CONSEQUENTIAL AMENDMENTS RELATING TO PUBLIC SERVICE VEHICLES

PART I

AMENDMENTS OF ROAD TRAFFIC ACT 1960 (c. 16)

1. — (1) Section 128 (certifying officers and public service examiners) shall be amended as follows.

(2) In subsection (1) (appointment and duties of certifying officers) before "fitness", where last occurring, insert "initial".

(3) In subsection (2) (appointment of public service vehicle examiners), for "shall appoint" substitute "may, with the approval of the Minister for the Civil Service, appoint".

(4) For subsection (3) substitute —

"(3) A certifying officer or public service vehicle examiner shall, in exercising any of the functions of such an officer or examiner, act under the general directions of the Minister."

2. In section 130 (approval of type vehicles), in subsection (3) (withdrawal of approval), for the words from "and" onwards substitute "and thereafter no certificate that any other vehicle conforms to the type vehicle shall be issued; but as regards any such certificate previously issued, the withdrawal of the approval shall not affect the operation of that certificate for the purposes of section 17 of the Transport Act 1980 (certificates of initial fitness or their equivalents).".

3. — (1) Section 131 (certificates of fitness for experimental vehicles) shall be amended as follows.

(2) For subsection (1) (and the side-note), substitute —

"131. Modification of s. 17 of Transport Act 1980 in relation to experimental vehicles

(1) Where it appears to the Minister expedient to do so for the purpose of the making of tests or trials of a vehicle or its equipment, he may by order made in respect of that vehicle for the purposes of section 17 of the Transport Act 1980 dispense with such of the prescribed conditions as to fitness referred to in subsection (1)(a) of that section as are specified in the order.

(1A) While such an order is in force in respect of a vehicle, the said section 17 shall have effect in relation to the vehicle as if the prescribed conditions as to fitness referred to in subsection (1)(a) of that section did not include such of those conditions as are dispensed with by the order.".

(3) For subsections (4) and (5) substitute —

"(4) Where an order under this section in respect of a vehicle is revoked or otherwise ceases to have effect, any certificate of initial fitness issued under section 17 of the Transport Act 1980 in respect of the vehicle while the order was in force shall, for the purpose of that section as regards any use of the vehicle after the order has ceased to have effect, be deemed never to have been issued.".

(4) In section 144 (drivers' licences) —

(a) in subsection (3), for "either such" substitute "such a";

(b) in subsection (6) (duration of licences), for "three years" substitute "five years"; and

(c) after subsection (8) insert —

"(9) Notwithstanding section 2 (1) of the Transport Act 1980, in this section and sections 145 to 148 of this Act "public service vehicle" shall be construed as meaning a stage, express or contract carriage.".

5. — (1) Section 146 (regulation of conduct of drivers and conductors) shall be amended as follows.

(2) For subsection (1) (power to make regulations as to conduct of drivers or conductors of public service vehicles) substitute —

"(1) Regulations may make provision for regulating the conduct, when acting as such, of—

    (*a*) persons licensed to act as drivers of public service vehicles; and
    (*b*) conductors of such vehicles.".

(3) In subsection (2) (penalty for contravention of regulations), after the words "£20, and" insert, "in the case of an offence by a person acting as driver,".

6.—(1) Section 146 (regulation of conduct of drivers and conductors) and section 147 (regulation of conduct of passengers) shall apply in relation to inspectors as they apply in relation to conductors.

(2) In sub-paragraph (1) "inspector", in relation to a public service vehicle, means a person authorised to act as such by the holder of the PSV operator's licence under which the vehicle is being used.

(3) In section 147 (1) (*d*) the words "or other person authorised by the licensee of the vehicle" shall be omitted.

7. Section 149 (power of Minister to modify restrictions on use of roads by public service vehicles) shall cease to have effect.

8. In section 152 (wages and conditions of employment of persons employed in connection with public service vehicles), for any reference to, or to the holder of, a public service vehicle licence or to the holder of a road service licence there shall be substituted a reference to, or to the holder of, a PSV operator's licence.

9.—(1) Section 153 (procedure of traffic commissioners) shall be amended as folllows.

(2) Omit subsection (2) (requirement to hold public sittings for certain purposes).

(3) In subsection (3), for "of an application" substitute "of an opposed application for the grant of a road service licence", and after "where" insert "such".

(4) In subsection (4) (power of commissioners to delegate functions to one of their members), for "requiring to be discharged at a public at a public sitting" substitute "of hearing and determining opposed applications for the grant of road service licences".

(5) After subsection (4) insert—

"(5) So much of subsection (3) above as requires not less than two commissioners to be present at the hearing of an opposed application for the grant of a road service licence shall not apply—

    (*a*) to so much of the hearing of any such application as is devoted to determining whether the commissioners are satisfied as mentioned in section 8 (1) or 9 (1) of the Transport Act 1980 (grant of road service licences for services on routes not otherwise served, or for certain excursions or tours); or
    (*b*) to the remainder of the hearing of any such application in the case of which the commissioners have determined that they are so satisfied.

(6) In this section 'opposed application" means an application with respect to which an objection has been made and not withdrawn, being an objection to which the traffic commissioners are obliged to have regard by virtue of section 5 (3) (*c*) of the Transport Act 1980."

10. In section 158 (power to regulate procedure on applications for licences etc.), in paragraph (*a*)—

    (*a*) for "public service vehicle licences" substitute "PSV operators' licences"; and
    (*b*) after "road service licences", in the second place where it occurs, insert "or PSV operators' licences".

11. In section 160 (1) (regulations for purposes of Part III)—

    (*a*) in paragraphs (*b*) and (*g*), before "fitness" insert "initial";
    (*b*) in paragraph (*cc*) for "section 5 (6)" substitute "section 5 (2)";
    (*c*) for paragraphs (*k*) to (*n*) substitute—

"(*k*) for providing that this Part of this Act, or any provision thereof, shall have effect in relation to—

    (i) public service vehicles registered in Great Britain, while making journeys to or from places outside Great Britain; and
    (ii) public service vehicles registered outside Great Britain, with such additions,

omissions, alterations or other modifications (whether conditional or not) as may be prescribed;"; and

(d) for "and different regulations may be made" substitute "and regulations under this section may make different provision for different circumstances, and may in particular make different provision".

12. The documents to which section 233 (forgery and misuse of documents, etc.) applies shall include—

(a) a certificate of initial fitness under section 17 of this Act;

(b) an operator's disc under section 24 of this Act;

(c) a certificate under section 27 of this Act as to the repute, financial standing or professional competence of any person;

(d) a certificate under section 130 of the 1960 Act that a vehicle conforms to a type vehicle; and

(e) a document evidencing the appointment of a person as a certifying officer or public service vehicle examiner;

and in section 235 (false statements to obtain licence, etc.) the reference to obtaining the grant of a licence shall include a reference to obtaining the issue of such a certificate or disc.

13. In section 248 (power to hold inquiries) after "the London Government Act 1963" insert "or section 23A of the Transport (London) Act 1969".

14. In section 257 (1) (general interpretation), for the words from "and the expressions" onwards substitute "and any expression used in this Part of this Act which is defined for the purposes of Part III of this Act or Part I of the Transport Act 1980 has the same meaning in this Part of this Act as in those Parts.".

15. In section 260 (2) (consultation before regulations are made), for "or they think" substitute "thinks".   **[144]**

COMMENCEMENT
See s. 70 (5), *ante*, and the note "Orders under this section" thereto.

PARA. 1: PUBLIC SERVICE VEHICLE EXAMINER
See the note to s. 16, *ante*.

PARA. 3: APPEARS
See the note "Satisfied" to s. 5, *ante*.

PARA. 9: GRANT OF A ROAD SERVICE LICENCE
See s. 5, *ante*.

PARA. 11: THIS PART OF THIS ACT
I.e., the Road Traffic Act 1960, Part III, A.L.S. Vol. 124.

GREAT BRITAIN
See the note to s. 12, *ante*.

PARA. 14: THIS PART OF THIS ACT
I.e., the Road Traffic Act 1960, Part VII.

PART III OF THIS ACT
I.e., the Road Traffic Act 1960, Part III.

PROSPECTIVE REPEAL
See the note to s. 17, *ante*.

DEFINITIONS
For "certifying officer", see the Road Traffic Act 1960, s. 128 (1), as amended by para. 1 (1), (2) above; for "prescribed" and "regulations", see s. 160 (2) of that Act; by virtue of s. 1 (3), *ante*, for "public service vehicle", see s. 2, *ante*, for "PSV operator's licence" and "road service licence", see s. 44 (1), *ante*; for "the Minister" and "modification", see s. 70 (2), *ante*. Note as to "opposed application", s. 153 (6) of the Act of 1960 as inserted by para. 9 (5) above.

ROAD TRAFFIC ACT 1960

For ss. 128, 130, 131, 144 – 149, 152, 153, 158 (*a*), 160 (1) (*b*), (*g*), (*k*), 233, 235, 248, 257 (1) and 260 (2) of that Act, see A.L.S. Vol. 124; for s. 160 (1) (*cc*) as inserted by the Transport Act 1978, Sch. 2, para. 5, see A.L.S. Vol. 265; and for s. 160 (1) (*l*) – (*n*) as inserted by the European Communities Act 1972, Sch. 4, para. 10, A.L.S. Vol. 205. The provisions mentioned in paras. 6 (3), 7 and 9 (2) above which are to be omitted or cease to have effect are also repealed by s. 69; *ante*, and Sch. 9, Part I, *post*. As to the prospective repeal of s. 130 of the Act of 1960, see the note on the 1960 Act to s. 17, *ante*.

1960 ACT

I.e., the Road Traffic Act 1960; see s. 44 (1), *ante*. For s. 130 of that Act, see A.L.S. Vol. 124, and as to its prospective repeal, see the note on the 1960 Act to s. 17, *ante*.

TRANSPORT (LONDON) ACT 1969, S. 23A

That section is inserted by s. 35, *ante*.

TRANSPORT ACT 1980, PART I

I.e., ss. 1 – 44, *ante*.

PART II

OTHER AMENDMENTS

LOCAL GOVERNMENT (MISCELLANEOUS PROVISIONS) ACT 1953 (c. 26)

In section 4 (power of local authority to provide bus shelters), in subsection (4) (definitions), for the words from "and the references" onwards substitute "and "public service vehicle" has the meaning which it would have in Part I of the Transport Act 1980 if in section 2 (1) of that Act the words "(other than a tramcar)" were omitted.".

TRANSPORT ACT 1962 (c. 46)

In section 4 (5) (by virtue of which the Railways Board are not authorised to carry passengers by road in certain hackney carriages adapted to carry less than eight passengers), for "eight" substitute "nine".

FINANCE ACT 1965 (c. 25)

In section 92 (grants towards duty charged on bus fuel), in the definition of "operator" in subsection (8), after paragraph (*c*) insert —

"(*d*) if and to the extent that the service operates within a trial area (within the meaning of Part I of the Transport Act 1980), the person by whom the service is provided;".

ROAD TRAFFIC REGULATION ACT 1967 (c. 76)

1. So much of subsection (3) of section 1 as prevents a prohibition or restriction on waiting imposed by a traffic regulation order under that section from applying to an express carriage shall cease to have effect.

2. In sections 6 (8) and 9 (8), for the words from "section 135 (8)" to "1960" substitute "section 28 of the Transport Act 1980".

3. In section 104 (1) (interpretation), for the words from "shall be construed" onwards substitute "have the same meaning as in Part I of the Transport Act 1980."

4. — (1) Schedule 5 (speed limits for vehicles of certain classes) shall be amended as follows.

(2) In paragraph 1 —

    (*a*) for "7 passengers", wherever occurring, substitute "8 passengers";

    (*b*) in sub-paragraphs (1) and (5), for the words from "in respect" to "force" substitute "while being used under a PSV operator's licence"; and

    (*c*) in sub-paragraph (2), for the words from "and" onwards substitute "while being used otherwise than under a PSV operator's licence".

(3) In paragraph 26, after the definition of "maximum gross weight" insert —
"PSV operator's licence" means a PSV operator's licence granted under Part I of the Transport Act 1980;".

(4) This paragraph does not affect the power to vary Schedule 5 by regulations under section 78.

TRANSPORT ACT 1968 (c. 73)

In section 159 (1) (interpretation) —

(a) for the definition of "excursion or tour" substitute —
" "excursion or tour" means a stage or express carriage service on which the passengers travel together on a journey, with or without breaks, from one or more places to one or more other places and back;"; and

(b) for the definition of "bus service" substitute —

" "bus service" means a stage carriage service within the meaning of Part I of the Transport Act 1980 which is neither —

(a) an excursion or tour; nor
(b) a service as regards which the condition specified in section 3 (3) (a) of the Transport Act 1980 (long journeys only) is satisfied;".

TRANSPORT (LONDON) ACT 1969 (c. 35)

1. In section 23 (7) (regulation of London bus services: interpretation) after the definition of "road service licence" insert —
" "service of express carriages" means an express carriage service within the meaning of Part I of the Transport Act 1980 or a stage carriage service within the meaning of that Part as to which the condition in section 3 (3) (a) of that Act (long journeys only) is satisfied.".

2. In section 24 (4) (c), for "sections 135 (8) and 163 (1)" substitute "section 163 (1)".

ROAD TRAFFIC ACT 1972 (c. 20)

In section 44 (4) (test certificates: exemption for certain public service vehicles,) for "eight" substitute "nine".

ROAD TRAFFIC (FOREIGN VEHICLES) ACT 1972 (c. 27)

1. In section 4 (2) (b) (circumstances in which drivers of foreign public service vehicles may be required to produce certain documents) —

(a) for "section 127 (1) of the Road Traffic Act 1960" substitute "section 19 (1) of the Transport Act 1980"; and

(b) for "brought into Great Britain to carry persons staying there temporarily" substitute "registered outside Great Britain".

2. In section 7 (interpretation), in the definition of "public service vehicle" for "sections 117 and 118" substitute "Part III".

3. In Schedule 1 (enactments conferring functions on examiners), for "Section 128 (3) of the Road Traffic Act 1960" substitute "Section 16 (1) of the Transport Act 1980".

ROAD TRAFFIC ACT 1974 (c. 50)

An order under section 24 (4) of the Road Traffic Act 1974 appointing a day for the coming into operation of the repeal by that Act of section 130 of the 1960 Act may include provision, to take effect on that day, for the repeal of sections 17 (1) (b) and 28 (6) (b) of, and paragraphs 2 and 12 (d) of Part I of Schedule 5 to, this Act.

LOCAL GOVERNMENT (MISCELLANEOUS PROVISIONS) ACT 1976 (c. 57)

1. In section 63 (3) (b) (hackney carriage stands not to be appointed so as to impede use of authorised stopping places by public service vehicles), for the words from "granted" to "1968" substitute "or PSV operator's licence granted under Part I of the Transport Act 1980".

2. In section 80 (1) (interpretation of Part II) —

   (*a*) in the definition of "private hire vehicle", for "fewer than eight passengers" substitute "fewer than nine passengers"; and

   (*b*) in the definition of "public service vehicle", for "section 117" substitute "Part III".

ENERGY ACT 1976 (c. 76)

In Schedule 1 (permissible relaxations of road traffic and transport law), in paragraph I (I) —

   (*a*) for "use, or cause or permit the use of," substitute "provide any stage carriage service or use";

   (*b*) in paragraph (*a*), for "permit" substitute "certificate";

   (*c*) at the end of paragraph (*b*) insert "; and

      (*c*) notwithstanding that any conditions attached to any licence under Part I of the Transport Act 1980 are not complied with; and

      (*d*) without being obliged to comply with the requirements of section 14 of that Act (duty to publish particulars of stage carriages services in trial areas).".

PASSENGER VEHICLES (EXPERIMENTAL AREAS) ACT
1977 (c. 21)

1. In section 2 (8) (authorised vehicle in experimental area not to be regarded as a public service vehicle) at the beginning insert "Subject to subsection (8A) below," and after that subsection insert —

   "(8A) Nothing in subsection (8) above shall affect the operation of section 14 of the Transport Act 1980 (duty to publish particulars of stage carriage services in trial areas).".

2. In section 2 (9) —

   (*a*) in the definition of "commercial vehicle", for "not more than five passengers" substitute "not more than eight passengers", and

   (*b*) for "section 118 (3) of the Road Traffic Act 1960" substitute "section 2 (5) of the Transport Act 1980".

3. In the Schedule, in paragraph 14 —

   (a) after "notice", in both places where it occurs, insert "or announcement"; and

   (b) for "section 118 (3) of the Road Traffic Act 1960" substitute "paragraph 9 of Schedule 1 to the Transport Act 1980".

MINIBUS ACT 1977 (c. 25)

In section 4 (2) (*c*) for the words from "as if" onwards substitute "in accordance with section 2 (5) of the Transport Act 1980".   **[145]**

The words omitted where indicated by dots apply to Scotland.

COMMENCEMENT
   See s. 7 (5), *ante*, and the note "Orders under this section" thereto.

DEFINITIONS
   For the meaning of "public service vehicle" in Part I of this Act see s. 2, *ante*; for "trial area", see s. 12 (1), *ante*; and for "express carriage service", "PSV operator's licence" and "stage carriage service", see s. 44 (1), *ante*.

LOCAL GOVERNMENT (MISCELLANEOUS PROVISIONS) ACT 1953, S. 4 (4)
   See A.L.S. Vol. 78.

TRANSPORT ACT 1962, S. 4 (5)
   See Halsbury's Statutes (3rd edn.), p. 931.

FINANCE ACT 1965, S. 92 (8) (c)
   For that paragraph as substituted, see the Transport (London) Act 1969, Sch. 3, para. 8, A.L.S. Vol. 185.

ROAD TRAFFIC REGULATION ACT 1967, SS. 1 (3), 6 (8), 9 (8), 78, 104 (1), SCH. 5
See A.L.S. Vol. 165.

TRANSPORT ACT 1968, S. 159 (1)
See A.L.S. Vol. 178.

TRANSPORT (LONDON) ACT 1969, SS. 23 (7)
For s. 23 (7) of that Act, see A.L.S. Vol. 185.

ROAD TRAFFIC ACT 1972, S. 44 (4)
See A.L.S. Vol. 208.

ROAD TRAFFIC (FOREIGN VEHICLES) ACT 1972, SS. 4 (2) (*b*) 7, SCH. 1
See A.L.S. Vol. 208.

ROAD TRAFFIC ACT 1974, S. 24 (4)
See A.L.S. Vol. 226.

1960 ACT
I.e., the Road Traffic Act 1960; sees s. 44 (1), *ante*. For s. 130 of that Act, see A.L.S. Vol. 124, and as to its prospective repeal, see the note on the 1960 Act to s. 17, *ante*.

LOCAL GOVERNMENT (MISCELLANEOUS PROVISIONS) ACT 1976, SS. 63 (3) (*b*), 80 (1)
See A.L.S. Vol. 252.

ENERGY ACT 1976, SCH. 1, PARA. 1 (1)
See 46, Halsbury's Statutes (3rd edn.), p. 2078.

PASSENGER VEHICLES (EXPERIMENTAL AREAS) ACT 1977, S. 2 (8) (9), SCHEDULE, PARA. 14
See A.L.S. Vol. 254.

MINIBUS ACT 1977, S. 4 (2) (*c*) \
See A.L.S. Vol. 254.

TRANSPORT ACT 1978 (c. 55)

1. In section 1 (5) (power of non-metropolitan counties to make grants) for paragraph (*b*) substitute —

"(*b*) to persons providing facilities for sharing motor vehicles not adapted to carry more than eight passengers with a view to meeting the social and welfare needs of one or more communities.".

2. For subsections (1) to (9) of section 5 (community bus services) substitute the following subsections —

"(1) Where on an application in that behalf the traffic commissioners for any traffic area grant a road service licence under Part I of the Transport Act 1980 in respect of a community bus service —

(*a*) the licence shall state that is granted in respect of such a service;
(*b*) the conditions specified in subsection (2) below shall be attached to the licence; and
(*c*) such provision as is mentioned in subsection (3) below may be included in the licence with respect to the use of the community bus otherwise than in the operation of the community bus service.

(2) The conditions to be attached in every case to a road service licence granted in respect of a community bus service are —

(*a*) that any vehicle used in the course of the service is adapted to carry more than eight but not more than sixteen passengers;
(*b*) that the driver of any vehicle being used in the course of the service —

(i) is a volunteer; and
(ii) if not the holder of a public service vehicle driver's licence, fulfils any prescribed conditions for drivers of community buses;

(*c*) that any vehicle used in the course of the service fulfils the prescribed conditions of fitness for use as a community bus; and

(*d*) that there is displayed on any vehicle being used in the course of the service such disc or other document issued by the traffic commissioners as may be prescribed for a vehicle used as a community bus;

and the powers conferred by section 6 (3) and (5) of the Transport Act 1980 to alter, remove or dispense from compliance with conditions attached to a road service licence shall not apply to conditions attached under this subsection.

(3) Traffic commissioners on granting a road service licence in respect of a community bus service may, if they are satisfied that in all the circumstances it is reasonable to do so with a view to providing financial support for that service, include in the licence provision authorising the use of the community bus as a contract carriage or as an express carriage (or both), subject to such restrictions (if any) as the commissioners think fit to impose; and where such provision is included in a licence, the conditions attached under subsection (2) to the licence shall apply to the use of the community bus as a contract carriage or express carriage as they apply to the use of a vehicle in the course of the community bus service.

(4) None of the following provisions, that is to say —

(*a*) section 144 of the Road Traffic Act 1960 (public service vehicle drivers' licences);

(*b*) section 17 of the Transport Act 1980 (certificate of initial fitness, or equivalent, required for use of public service vehicle);

(*c*) section 18 of that Act (power to prohibit driving of unfit public service vehicle); and

(*d*) section 19 (1) of that Act (PSV operator's licence required for use of vehicle as stage, express or contract carriage),

shall apply to the driving or use of a vehicle in the course of a community bus service or in the course of its use as a contract carriage or express carriage in accordance with any such provision as is mentioned in subsection (3) above.

(5) Where a community bus service is provided in whole or in part in Greater London, that service or part shall not be regarded as a London bus service within section 23 of the Transport (London) Act 1969 (under which the agreement or consent of the London Transport Executive is required instead of a road service licence); but where the traffic commissioners for the Metropolitan Traffic Area propose —

(*a*) to grant a road service licence in respect of such a service; or

(*b*) to vary the conditions attached to such a licence,

they shall consult the London Transport Executive about the proposal.

(6) Subsection (7) of section 4 of the Transport Act 1980 (penalty for breach of condition attached to a road service licence) shall apply in relation to a condition so attached under subsection (2) above as it applies in relation to a condition so attached under section 6 of that Act.

(7) Regulations may provide that, in relation to any community bus service provided in whole or in part within a trial area, the preceding provisions of this section shall have effect with such additions, omissions, alterations or other modifications as may be prescribed.

(8) In this section —

"community bus service" means a stage carriage service provided —

(*a*) by a body of persons (whether corporate or unincorporate) concerned for the social and welfare needs of one or more communities; and

(*b*) without a view to profit, either on the part of those persons or of anyone else;

and in relation to such a service "the community bus" means any vehicle used on a regular basis in the course of the service;

"volunteer", in reference to the driver of a vehicle on any journey, means that he is not paid for driving the vehicle on that journey, disregarding —

(*a*) any payment of reasonable expenses incurred by him in making himself available to drive; and (*b*) any payment representing earnings lost as a result of making himself available to drive in exceptional circumstances;

and section 1 (3) and (4) of the Transport Act 1980 (construction as one, etc) shall have effect as if references in those subsections to Part I of that Act included a reference to this section.".

3. Section 6 shall be omitted.

4. In section 7 (3) (vehicles excluded from regulation as private hire vehicles)—

(*a*) for the words "section 118 of the 1960 Act" there shall be substituted the words "section 2 (3) of the Transport Act 1980";

(*b*) for the words "no more than 7 passengers" there shall be substituted the words "no more than 8 passengers"; and

(*c*) for the words "8 to 16 seaters" substitute "9 to 16 seaters".   **[146]**

COMMENCEMENT
See s. 70 (5), *ante*, and the note "Orders under this section" thereto.

PARA. 1: PERSONS
See the note "Person" to s. 2, *ante*.

ADAPTED
See the note to s. 2, *ante*.

PARA. 2: TRAFFIC COMMISSIONERS *
See the note to s. 3, *ante*.

TRAFFIC AREA
See the note to s. 4, *ante*.

GRANT A ROAD SERVICE LICENCE UNDER PART I OF THE TRANSPORT ACT 1980
I.e., under s. 5, *ante*.

PRESCRIBED
I.e., prescribed by regulations made under the Road Traffic Act 1960, s. 160, A.L.S. Vol. 124; see, by virtue of the Transport Act 1978, s. 5 (8), as substituted by para. 2 above and s. 1 (3), *ante*, s. 160 (2) of that Act. The Community Bus Regulations 1978. S.I. 1978 No. 1313, as amended by S.I. 1980 No. 144, if still in force at the commencement of this paragraph, will be the applicable provisions for the purposes of the Transport Act 1978, s. 5 (2) (*b*)−(*d*), as substituted.

SATISFIED; THINKS FIT
See the note "Satisfied" to s. 5, *ante*.

GREATER LONDON
See the note to s. 5, *ante*.

TRAFFIC COMMISSIONERS FOR THE METROPOLITAN TRAFFIC AREA
As to their constitution and functions, see the Road Traffic Act 1960, s. 120, as affected by the Transport (London) Act 1969, s. 24, A.L.S. Vol. 185. For the constitution and boundary of the Metropolitan Traffic Area, see 33 Halsbury's Laws (3rd Edn.), paras. 665, 1162.

CONSULT
See the note "Consulting" to s. 54, *ante*.

LONDON TRANSPORT EXECUTIVE
This body is constituted by the Transport (London) Act 1969, s. 4.

WITHOUT A VIEW TO PROFIT
It seems clear that the activities of a body may be carried on without a view to profit although profits are made; see, in particular, *National Deposit Friendly Society Trustees* v. *Skegness Urban District Council*, [1959] A.C. 293; [1958] 2 All E.R. 601. In fact there is authority for saying that the making of profits is irrelevant if it is only a subsidiary object, *viz.*, only a means whereby the main object of the body in question can be furthered or achieved; see, in particular, *National Deposit Friendly Society Trustees* v. *Skegness Urban District Council*, *supra*, at pp. 319, 320 and p. 612, respectively, *per* Lord Denning.

SCHEDULE 6

Section 45

SUPPLEMENTARY PROVISIONS WITH RESPECT TO TRANSFER UNDER SECTION 45

Legal remedies and pending proceedings

1. — (1) Where any right, liability or obligation is transferred to the successor company by virtue of section 45 that company and all other persons shall, on and after the appointed day, have the same rights, powers and remedies (and, in particular, the same rights as to the taking or resisting of legal proceedings) for ascertaining, perfecting or enforcing that right, liability or obligation as they would have had if it had at all times been a right, liability or obligation of that company.

(2) Any legal proceedings by or against the Corporation which relate to any property, right, liability or obligation transferred to the successor company by virtue of section 45 and are pending on the appointed day, may be continued on and after that day by or against that company.

(3) Any reference to sub-paragraph (1) or (2) to legal proceedings shall be construed as including a reference to any application to an authority, and any reference to the taking or resisting of legal proceedings shall be construed accordingly.

Powers of other bodies

2. The transfer to the successor company by virtue of section 45 of the property, rights, liabilities and obligations of the Corporation shall have effect notwithstanding any statutory or other restriction on the powers of any other body affected by the transfer.

Modification of agreements

3. Where immediately before the appointed day there is in force an agreement which confers or imposes on the Corporation any rights, liabilities or obligations which are transferred to the successor company by virtue of section 45, that agreement shall have effect on and after that date as if—

(*a*) the successor company had been a party to the agreement; and (*b*) for any reference (in whatever terms and whether expressly or by implication) to the Corporation there were substituted, in relation to anything falling to be done on or after that day, a reference to the successor company; and

(*c*) for any reference (in whatever terms and whether expressly or by implication) to an officer or employee of the Corporation, not being a party to the agreement and beneficially interested therein, there were substituted, in relation to anything falling to be done on or after that day, a reference to such person as the successor company may appoint or, in default of appointment, to the officer or employee of that company who corresponds as nearly as may be to the officer or employee of the Corporation.

Loss of office by members of Corporation

4. — (1) Subject to sub-paragraph (2), no right, liability or obligation under any agreement for the rendering by any person of services to the Corporation as a member of the Corporation shall be transferred by virtue of section 45.

(2) Sub-paragraph (1) does not apply to any liability for remuneration or allowances payable in respect of any period before the appointed day.

(3) If it appears to the Minister that a person who was a member of the Corporation immediately before the appointed day should receive compensation for loss of office, he may, subject to sub-paragraph (4), require the successor company to pay that person such sum as the Minister, with the approval of the Minister for Civil Service, may determine.

(4) No such requirement as is mentioned in sub-paragraph (3) shall be made after the expiration of the period of three months beginning with the appointed day.

Compensation payments arising from earlier reorganisations

5. The obligations of the Corporation transferred by virtue of section 45 include any obligations of the Corporation to make payments under regulations made under section 135 of the Transport Act 1968 or section 2 (4) of the Transport Holding Company Act 1972 (compensation for loss of employment, etc. in consequence of reorganisations under those Acts).

Pensions of former members of the Corporation

6. The obligations of the Corporation transferred by virtue of section 45 include any obligation of the Corporation to comply with a determination of the Minister under paragraph 8 (1) of Schedule 1 to the Transport Act 1962 relating to the pension (within the meaning of that Act) payable to or in respect of a former member of the Corporation.

Pension schemes

7. — (1) Subject to sub-paragraph (2), the provisions of section 74 of the Transport Act 1962 (Minister's powers to make provision about pensions in the nationalised transport industry) shall have effect on and after the appointed day as if —

(*a*) the expression "Board" included the successor company; and

(*b*) the references in subsection (1) (*a*) (ii) of that section to the Commission included references to the Corporation; and

(*c*) the reference in subsection (2) (*a*) of that section to a pension scheme in which employees of the Commission, or a subsidiary of the Commission, participated before the date there mentioned included a reference to a pension scheme in which employees of, or of a subsidiary of, the Corporation participated before the appointed day.

(2) Except on the application of the successor company, no order shall be made under the said section 74 on or after the appointed day which has the effect of placing the successor company or a subsidiary of the successor company in any worse position; but for this purpose the successor company or a subsidiary shall not be regarded as being placed in a worse position because an order provides that any changes in a pension scheme are not to be effected without the consent of the Minister.

(3) An order such as is mentioned in sub-paragraph (2) which is made without the application of the successor company shall not be invalid because in fact it does not have the

effect of securing that the successor company and its subsidiaries are not placed in any worse position, but except in so far as the successor company approves the effect of the order the Minister shall as soon as may be make the necessary amending order.

(4) Subject to sub-paragraph (6), any order under the said section 74 and any regulations to which paragraph 17 of Schedule 7 to the Transport Act 1962 applies (which continues in force certain earlier pension provisions) which—

(a) are in force immediately before the appointed day; and

(b) relate to the Corporation, its employees or its pensions schemes,

shall continue in force, subject to any provision made by virtue of sub-paragraph (1), and as respects anything falling to be done on or after the appointed day shall have effect as if for any reference (however worded and whether express or implied) to the Corporation there were substituted a reference to the successor company.

(5) A person who on the appointed day—

(a) ceases to be employed by the Corporation and becomes employed by the successor company; or

(b) is employed by a company which immediately before the appointed day was a subsidiary of the Corporation but on that day becomes a subsidiary of the successor company,

shall not thereby cease to be eligible to participate in any pension scheme in which he was a participant immediately before the appointed day.

(6) Subject to sub-paragraph (5), a person who on or after the appointed day leaves or enters the employment of the group consisting of the successor company and its subsidiaries (in this sub-paragraph referred to as "the NFC group") shall not be eligible by virtue of any provision of an order under the said section 74 made before that day—

(a) to participate in any of the Corporation's pension schemes by reason of any employment outside the NFC group; or

(b) to participate in a pension scheme other than one of the Corporation's pension schemes by reason of his employment within the NFC group.

(7) In this paragraph—

(a) "participant", in relation to a pension scheme, means—

(i) in relation to a scheme under which benefits are or will be receivable as of right, a person who has pension rights under the scheme (whether he has contributed or not); and

(ii) in relation to a scheme under which benefits are not or will not be receivable as of right, a person who (whether he is referred to in the scheme as a member, as a contributor or otherwise) has contributed under the scheme and has pension rights thereunder;

and "participate" and "eligible to participate" shall be construed accordingly;

(b) "pension", "pension rights" and "pension scheme" have the same meaning as in section 74 of the Transport Act 1962; and

(c) references to the Corporation's pension schemes are to schemes established by the Corporation or in relation to which the rights, liabilities and functions of the Transport Holding Company were transferred to the Corporation by the British Transport (Pensions of Employees) (No. 1) Order 1968.

Grants in respect of certain capital expenditure

8.—(1) The obligations of the Corporation transferred by virtue of section 45 include any obligation to comply with terms and conditions attached to a grant made under section 18 of the Transport Act 1978 (grants in respect of capital expenditure by National Carriers Limited or its subsidiaries).

(2) For the reference in that section to the Corporation there shall be substituted, as from the appointed day, a reference to the successor company.

(3) In considering the exercise of his powers under that section in favour of the successor company, the Minister shall take into account any capital expenditure within that section not previously taken into account, including expenditure incurred before the appointed day; and the financial limits set by subsection (2) of that section shall apply in

relation to such an exercise of the Minister's powers as if grants made to the Corporation at any time before the appointed day had been made to the successor company at that time.

Reimbursement for certain travel concessions

9. — (1) The obligations of the Corporation transferred by virtue of section 45 include any obligation to comply with terms attached to a payment made under section 21 of the Transport Act 1978 (reimbursement of amounts paid in connection with travel concessions enjoyed by certain employees and others).

(2) For the references in that section to the Corporation there shall be substituted, as from the appointed day, references to the successor company.

(3) In considering the exercise of his powers under that section in favour of the successor company, the Minister shall take into account any amounts paid as mentioned in that section and not previously taken into account, including amounts paid by the Corporation and amounts paid in respect of concessionary travel enjoyed before the appointed day.

Rating

10. — (1) The obligations of the Corporation transferred by virtue of section 45 include any obligation of the Corporation under subsection (2) of section 162 of the Transport Act 1968 to make a payment to the British Railways Board in respect of any period of occupation before the appointed day by the Corporation or a subsidiary of premises which by virtue of subsection (1) of that section are to be treated for rating purposes as occupied by the Board.

(2) If any dispute between the Board and the Corporation as to the amount so payable stands referred to the Minister immediately before the appointed day, it shall be dealt with thereafter as if the successor company had at all times been a party to the reference.

(3) Any dispute arising on or after the appointed day between the Board and the successor company as to the amount due under the said subsection (2) shall be referred to the Minister for determination, and his determination shall be final.   [147]

COMMENCEMENT
    See the note to s. 45, *ante*.

PARA. 1: PERSONS
    See the note "Person" to s. 2, *ante*.

PARA. 4: APPEARS
    See the note "Satisfied" to s. 5, *ante*.

THREE MONTHS BEGINNING WITH, ETC
    See the note "Five years beginning with, etc." to s. 12, *ante*. As to "months", see the note to s. 31, *ante*.

PARA. 10: BRITISH RAILWAYS BOARD
    See the note to s. 60, *ante*.

PREMISES
    See the note to s. 16, *ante*.

DEFINITIONS
    For "the Corporation" and "the successor company", see s. 45 (1), *ante*; for "the appointed day", see s. 45 (2), *ante*; for "the Minister", see s. 70 (2), *ante*. Note as to "legal proceedings" and "the taking or resisting of legal proceedings", para. 1 (3) above; as to "the N.F.C. Group", para. 7 (6) above, and as to "participant", "participate", "eligible to participate", "pension", "pension rights", "pension scheme" and "the Corporation's pension schemes", para. 7 (7) above.

TRANSPORT ACT 1968, SS. 135, 162 (2)
    See A.L.S. Vol. 178. S. 162 (2) is partly repealed by s. 69, *ante*, and Sch. 9, Part II, *post*, as from the passing of this Act, and it is wholly repealed by s. 69, *ante*, and Sch. 9, Part III, *post*, as from the appointed day as defined by s. 45 (2), *ante*.

TRANSPORT HOLDING COMPANY ACT 1972, S. 2 (4)
    See 42, Halsbury's Statutes (3rd edn.), p. 1564.

TRANSPORT ACT 1962
For s. 74 of, and Sch. 1, para. 8 (1) and Sch. 7, para. 17, to, that Act, see 26, Halsbury Statutes (3rd edn.), pp. 987, 1008, 1033; and for the meaning of "pension" in that Act, see s. 92 (1) thereof.

BRITISH TRANSPORT (PENSIONS OF EMPLOYEES) (NO. 1) ORDER 1968
S.I. 1968 No. 2011. That order was made under the Transport Act 1962, s. 74, as read with the Transport Act 1968, s. 136.

TRANSPORT ACT 1978, SS. 18, 21
See A.L.S. Vol. 265.

SCHEDULE 7

Section 51

AMENDMENTS CONSEQUENTIAL ON PART II

TRANSPORT ACT 1968 (c. 73)

1. In section 7 substitute the words "the Board" —

   (*a*) in subsection (1) (*a*) for the words from "the authority" to the end;
   (*b*) in subsection (3) for the words "the authority or authorities making it"; and
   (*c*) in subsection (4) for the words "the authority or authorities by whom the scheme was prepared".

2. In section 8 (1) (*b*) for "either of those authorities" substitute "the Railways Board".

3. In section 29 (6) for the words from "subsection (2) of the said section" to the end substitute "subsection (1) (*b*) of the said section 7 or, as the case may be, to an order under subsection (1) (*b*) of the said section 8 making any such provision as is mentioned in the said section 7 (1) (*b*), but as if for the reference in subsection (6) (*a*) of the said section 8 to the Railways Board there were substituted a reference to the Scottish Group and the Railways Board".

4. In section 45 (5) for "the authority to whom the directions are given" substitute "the Board".

5. In paragraph 4 of Schedule 16 for the words from "subsection (1)" to "of that section" substitute "subsection (2) of section 67 of the Act of 1962".

6. In paragraph 5 of Schedule 16 —

   (*a*) in sub-paragraph (2), for "either of the authorities to whom this section applies" substitute "the Scottish Group" and for "authority" in both places where it occurs substitute "Group";
   (*b*) in sub-paragraph (3), for "the authority or subsidiary in question" substitute "the Scottish Group or, as the case may be, the subsidiary in question";
   (*c*) in sub-paragraph (4), for "either or both of the authorities to whom this paragraph applies" substitute "the Scottish Group" and for the words from "authority" to "each of those authorities" substitute "Group".   **[148]**

COMMENCEMENT
This Schedule is to come into force on "the appointed day" as defined by s. 45 (2), *ante*; see s. 70 (4), *ante*. At the time of going to press no day had been appointed under s. 45 (2).

DEFINITIONS
For "the Scottish Group", see the Transport Act 1968, s. 24 (1) (*b*), A.L.S. Vol. 178; for "the Railways Board", see s. 159 (1) of that Act.

TRANSPORT ACT 1968, SS. 7, 8, 29 (6), 45 (5), SCH. 16, PARAS. 4, 5
See A.L.S. Vol. 178. Ss. 7 (1), (3), (4), 8 (1) (*b*), (6) (*a*) and 45 (5) and Sch. 16, para. 4 are partly repealed by s. 69, *ante*, and Sch. 9, Parts II, III, *post*.

ACT OF 1962
I.e., the Transport Act 1962; see the Transport Act 1968, s. 159 (1).

SCHEDULE 8

B.R. PENSION SCHEMES

British Railways Superannuation Fund:

New Section
GWR Section
LMSR Section
LNER Section so far as relating to persons admitted to the London and North
    Eastern Railway Superannuation Fund before 1st June 1957
LNER Section so far as not so relating
RCS Section
SR Section

British Railways (Wages Grades) Pension Fund
British Transport Police Force Superannuation Fund
B.R. (1974) Pension Fund
Great Eastern Railway New Pension Fund and New Pension (Supplemental) Fund Trust
    Account
Great Northern Railway Superannuation Fund
Great Western Railway Inspectors and Foremen's Special Pension Fund
Great Western Railway Pension Society
Great Western Railway Salaried Staff Supplemental Pension Fund
Great Western Railway Supplemental Pensions Reserve Fund
Great Western Railway Widows and Orphans' Benevolent Fund
Lancashire and Yorkshire Railway Pension Fund Society
London, Brighton and South Coast Railway Pension Fund
London Midland and Scottish Railway (L.N.W.) Insurance Society
London Midland and Scottish Railway (L.N.W.) Provident and Pensions Society
London Midland and Scottish Railway (L.N.W.) Supplementary Pension Fund and
    Locomotive Foremen's Pension Fund
London Midland and Scottish Railway Midland Friendly Society
London Midland and Scottish Railway (North Staffordshire Section) Friendly Society
North British Railway Insurance Society
North Eastern and Great Eastern Superannuation Societies and Pensions Funds Joint Trust
    Account
Southern Railway (South Eastern & Chatham Section) Enginemen & Motormen's Pension
    Fund Society
Thomas Bantock & Co. Superannuation Fund   **[149]**

COMMENCEMENT
    See the note to s. 52, *ante*.

B.R. (1974) PENSION FUND
    As to its composition, see s. 60 (2) (*a*), *ante*.

SCHEDULE 9

REPEALS

PART I

PUBLIC SERVICE VEHICLES

Chapter	Short title	Extent of repeal
1 & 2 Eliz. 2. c. 33	Education (Miscellaneous Provisions) Act 1953	Section 12.
2 & 3 Eliz. 2. c. 64	Transport Charges &c. (Miscellaneous Provisions) Act 1954	Section 2. Schedule 1.
3 & 4 Eliz. 2. c. 26	Public Service Vehicles (Travel Concessions) Act 1955	In section 1 (7), the words "and two".
6 & 7 Eliz. 2. c. 50	Local Government (Omnibus Shelters and Queue Barriers) (Scotland) Act 1958	In section 7 (1), the words from "and the references" onwards.
8 & 9 Eliz. 2. c. 16	Road Traffic Act 1960	Sections 117 and 118. In section 119 (3) (*a*), the words "or backed". Section 127. In section 128 (2), the words from "In the application" onwards. Section 129. In section 130, in subsection (2), the words from "and such" onwards. Sections 132 to 140. Section 143. In section 144, the words "or act as conductor of", wherever occurring, and, in subsection (3), the words from "and for" to "eighteen". In section 145 (1), the words "or act as conductor of". In section 147 (1) (*d*) the words "or other person authorised by the licensee of the vehicle". Section 149. Section 153 (2). In section 154, the words "or act as conductor of". In section 155, the words "or act as conductor of". In section 156 (1), the words "or backed". In section 158, the words "or act as conductor of". In section 160 — (*a*) in subsection (1), the words "or the Twelfth Schedule thereto"; (*b*) in subsection (1) (*f*), the words "and conductors"; (*c*) in subsection (2), the words "and the Twelfth Schedule thereto".

Chapter	Short title	Extent of repeal
8 & 9 Eliz. 2. c. 16 *(Cont'd)*	Road Traffic Act 1960	In section 163 (1), the words "or act as conductor of." Section 234. Section 240. In section 247 (2), the words from "or (in a case" onwards. In section 257 (1), the definitions of "owner" and "road service licence". Section 258. Schedule 12. In Schedule 17, the entries relating to the Local Government (Miscellaneous Provisions) Act 1953 and the Local Government (Omnibus Shelters and Queue Barriers) (Scotland) Act 1958.
10 & 11 Eliz. 2. c. 46	Transport Act 1962	In Schedule 2, in Part I, the entries relating to section 12 of the Education (Miscellaneous Provisions) Act 1953 and section 135 of the 1960 Act.
1963 c. 33	London Government Act 1963	In section 9 (6) (*b*), the words from "except" to "1960". Section 14 (6) (*d*). In Schedule 5, in Part I, paragraph 25.
1965 c. 25	Finance Act 1965	In section 92 (8), the definition of "road service licence".
1967 c. 76	Road Traffic Regulation Act 1967	In section 1 (3), the words "or express carriage". In Schedule 6, the amendment of section 135 (2) of the 1960 Act.
1968 c. 73	Transport Act 1968	Section 21 (1). Section 30. Section 35 (1), (2) and (3) (*a*). In section 138, in subsection (1) (*a*) the words from "subject" to "granted or backed", and in subsection (3) (*a*) the words "subject as mentioned in sub-section (1) (*a*) of this section". Section 145 (1). In section 159 (1), in the definition of "road service licence" the words from "and except" onwards.
1969 c. 35	Transport (London) Act 1969	In section 23 (6), the words from "except" to "that section". In section 23 (7), in the definition of "road service licence" the words from "and includes" onwards. In section 24 (2), the words "or act as conductor of". Section 24 (3). Section 24 (4) (*b*) and (*d*). In Schedule 3, in paragraph 8, in the subsection substituted in section 92 of the Finance Act 1965, the definition of "road service licence"; and paragraph 11.

Chapter	Short title	Extent of repeal
1971 c. 62	Tribunals and Inquiries Act 1971.	Section 13 (5). In section 13 (6) (*a*) the words from "or to a decision" to "traffic commissioners". In Schedule 1, in paragraph 30 (*a*), the words from "and" onwards.

1972 c. 20	Road Traffic Act 1972	In section 44 (4)—
		  (*a*) the words from "to public service vehicles" to "passengers or";
		  (*b*) the words from "but shall apply" to "1978";
		  (*c*) the words from "if no" to the end.

1972 c. 68	European Communities Act 1972	In Schedule 4, paragraph 10.
1972 c. 70	London Government Act 1972	Section 186 (3).
1973 c. 65	Local Government (Scotland) Act 1973	In Schedule 18, paragraphs 26 and 30 to 35.
1974 c. 50	Road Traffic Act 1974	In Schedule 2, paragraphs 1 and 3 to 5. In Schedule 5, all the entries in Part I except those relating to sections 148 (2) and 239 of the 1960 Act. In Schedule 6, paragraph 1 and, in paragraph 2, the words "or act as conductor of". In Schedule 7, the entry relating to section 131 (1) (*b*) of the 1960 Act.
1976 c. 76	Energy Act 1976	In Schedule 1, in paragraph 2, the words "or act as conductor of" in both places where they occur.
1978 c. 55	Transport Act 1978	Section 5 (10). Section 6. Section 7 (1) and (2). Section 8. Schedule 1. Schedule 2, except paragraph 5.

[150]

COMMENCEMENT
See s. 70 (5), *ante*, and the note "Orders under this section" thereto.

PART II

REPEALS TAKING EFFECT ON PASSING OF THIS ACT

Chapter	Title	Extent of repeal
1960 c. 16	Road Traffic Act 1960	In section 232 (1) (*b*), the words "or 71".
1968 c. 73	Transport Act 1968	Section 6. In section 7 (5), the words "or under section 6 (1) of this Act". In section 8 (6) (*a*), sub-paragraph (iv).

Chapter	Title	Extent of repeal
1968 c. 73 *(Cont'd)*	Transport Act 1968 *(Cont'd)*	In section 45 (6) (*a*), the words "or under section 6 (1) of this Act".

In section 71—
  (*a*) subsections (1) to (5);
  (*b*) in subsection (6), the words "this section and";
  (*c*) subsection (7);
  (*d*) in subsection (8) the definition of "pallet";
  (*e*) subsections (9) and (10).
Sections 72 to 80.
In section 81 (3), the words from "(or, if" to "last vehicle)".
In section 82—
  (*a*) in subsection (1), the words "record or other", "76 or", "record or other" and "record or";
  (*b*) in subsection (2), the words "records or" and "record or".
In section 83, the words "record or other", "76 or" and "record or".
In section 84—
  (*a*) in paragraph (*a*), the words "a special authorisation";
  (*b*) in paragraph (*b*), the words "or authorisation";
  (*c*) in paragraph (*c*), the words "or special authorisation";
  (*d*) in paragraph (*d*), the words "a special authorisation";
  (*e*) in paragraph (*f*), the words "or authorisation".
Section 85 (1) (*b*).
In section 86, the words "and a special authorisation" and "or special authorisation".
In section 87, subsection (2) and in subsection (3) the words "or 79".
In section 89 (1), the words "and special authorisations".
In section 91—
  (*a*) in subsection (1) (*a*), the words "and special authorisations";
  (*b*) in subsection (1) (*b*), the words "and special authorisations", "or authorisations" and "or authorisations";
  (*c*) in subsection (1) (*c*), the words from "or as vehicles" to the end;
  (*d*) in subsection (1) (*d*), the words "and special authorisations", "or authorisations" and "or 79";
  (*e*) in subsection (1) (*e*), the words "or special authorisation";
  (*f*) in subsection (2), the words "or as vehicles used under a special

Chapter	Title	Extent of repeal
1968 c. 73 (*Cont'd*)	Transport Act 1968 (*Cont'd*)	authorisation" and "or special authorisation"; (*g*) subsection (4) (*b*). In section 92 (6), the words "or authorisation" in both places where they occur. In section 94, subsections (4) to (6) and in subsection (8) the words from "but if" to the end. Section 150. In section 162 (2), the words from "who may" to "their recommendations". In Schedule 10, in Part I— (*a*) in the amendment of section 233 (1) (*a*) of the Road Traffic Act 1960, the words "or authorisation"; (*b*) in the amendment of section 233 (1) (*c*) of that Act, the words from "and that paragraph" to the end; (*c*) in the amendment of section 235 (1) of that Act the words "or authorisation"; (*d*) in the amendment of section 263 (1) of that Act, the words from "and the references" to the end. In Schedule 10, in Part II, in the amendment of section 232 (1) (*b*) of the Road Traffic Act 1960, the words "or 71".
1969 c. 48	Post Office Act 1969	In Schedule 4, paragraph 88.
1974 c. 48	Railways Act 1974	Sections 5 to 7.
1975 c. 24	House of Commons Disqualification Act 1975	In Schedule 1, in Part II, the entry relating to the Freight Integration Council.
1975 c. 25	Northern Ireland Assembly Disqualification Act 1975	In Schedule 1, in Part II, the entry relating to the Freight Integration Council.
1978 c. 55	Transport Act 1978	Sections 19 and 20.

[151]

COMMENCEMENT
This Part of this Schedule came into force on the passing of this Act on 30th June 1980; see s. 70 (3), *ante*.

PART III

REPEALS TAKING EFFECT ON APPOINTED DAY UNDER PART II OF THIS ACT

Chapter	Title	Extent of repeal
1938 c. 44	Road Haulage Wales Act 1938	In section 4 (2), the words "the National Freight Corporation,".

Chapter	Title	Extent of repeal
1964 c. 40	Harbours Act 1964	In section 57 (1), in the definition of "the Boards", the words "the National Freight Corporation" and "Corporation or".
1966 c. 27	Building Control Act 1966	In the Schedule, the entry relating to the National Freight Corporation.
1966 c. 34	Industrial Development Act 1966	In Schedule 2, the entry relating to the National Freight Corporation.
1968 c. 73	Transport Act 1968	Sections 1 to 5.

Continued from the Transport Act 1968 row, Extent of repeal:

In section 7 —
(*a*) in subsection (1), the words from "or the Freight Corporation" to "acting jointly" and in paragraph (*b*) the words "the Corporation" and "or Corporation";
(*b*) subsection (2);
(*c*) in subsection (3), the words "subsection (1) or (2) of";
(*d*) in subsection (4), in paragraph (*a*) the words "or the Freight Corporation" and "respective" and paragraph (*b*);
(*e*) in subsection (5) the words "or subsection (2)";
(*f*) in subsection (6), the words "or subsection (2)";
(*g*) in subsection (7), the words from "and in the application" to the end.
In section 8 —
(*a*) in subsection (1), paragraph (*a*) and in paragraph (*b*) the words "or paragraph (*b*) of subsection (4)";
(*b*) subsection (2);
(*c*) in subsection (3), the words "subsection (1) or (2) of";
(*d*) in subsection (4), the words "subsection (1) of" and the words from "and in the case" to "of this section";
(*e*) in subsection (5), the words from "and in the application" to the end;
(*f*) in subsection (6), the words from the beginning to "Corporation; and" and in paragraph (*a*), sub-paragraph (i), in sub-paragraph (ii) the words from "in the case" to "of this section" and sub-paragraph (iii).
In section 44 —
(*a*) in subsection (1) (*a*) (iii), the words "3 (1) or" and the words

Chapter	Title	Extent of repeal
1968 c. 73 *(Cont'd)*	Transport Act 1968 *(Cont'd)*	"the Freight Corporation or"; (*b*) in subsection (1) (*b*) (iii), the words "the Freight Corporation or"; (*c*) in the concluding words of subsection (1) (*b*), the reference to section 3 (1). In section 45 — (*a*) in subsection (1), paragraph (*b*), the word "and" immediately preceding that paragraph and the words "or, as the case may be, the Corporation"; (*b*) in subsection (2), the words "or, as the case may be, the Corporation" in both places where they occur; (*c*) in subsection (3), the words "or the Freight Corporation"; (*d*) in subsection (5), the words "or the Freight Corporation or each of them" and "respective"; (*e*) in subsection (6), the words "or the Freight Corporation". In section 52 (2), the words "and the Freight Corporation", "or the Corporation" and "or Corporation". In section 55 — (*a*) in subsection (1) (*b*), the words "the Freight Corporation and" and the words "of that Corporation or"; (*b*) in subsection (1) (ii), the words "but including a reference to the Freight Corporation"; (*c*) in subsection (1) (iii), the words "or the Freight Corporation"; (*d*) subsection (1) (iv); (*e*) in subsection (4) the words "or with the Freight Corporation" and the words "or Corporation" in both places where they occur. In section 121, in subsection (1) the words from "and sections 116 and 117" to the end and in subsection (2) (*a*) the words "the Freight Corporation or the subsidiaries of that Corporation". In section 125 (4), the words "and to the Freight Corporation". In section 134 (3) (*b*), the reference to section 2 (1) (*g*) (ii) and (*m*). In section 156 (1), the words "the Freight Corporation", "or Corporation", "Corporation or", "the

Chapter	Title	Extent of repeal
1968 c. 73 *(Cont'd)*	Transport Act 1968 *(Cont'd)*	Minister or, in the case of the Scottish Group", and "the Minister or, as the case may be,".
		In section 159 (1), the definition of "the Freight Corporation" and in the definition of "the new authorities" the words "the Freight Corporation".
		In section 160 (3), paragraph (a) and in paragraph (b) the reference to section 4 (1).
		In section 162 —
		(a) in subsection (1), paragraph (b) and the word "or" immediately preceding it, the words "or (b)" and the words from "or, as the case may be", to "that Corporation";
		(b) subsection (2);
		(c) in subsection (3), the words "or the Freight Corporation" and the words "or that Corporation";
		(d) in subsection (4), the words "cr (b)" and the words "of the Freight Corporation or".
		In Schedule 1, paragraph 1 and in paragraph 5 the words from "and, in the case" to the end.
		In Schedule 2, in paragraph 3 (a), the words "5 (3) (a) or"
		Schedule 3.
		In Schedule 4, in paragraph 5 the words from "by or on behalf" to "Freight Corporation, or" and in paragraph 6 the words "the Freight Corporation".
		In Schedule 10, in Part I, in the second amendment to section 4 (2) of the Road Haulage Wages Act 1938, the words "the National Freight Corporation,".
		In Schedule 16 —
		(a) paragraphs 1 and 2;
		(b) in paragraph 4, in sub-paragraph (1) the words "the Corporation and", sub-paragraph (2) and in sub-paragraph (5) the words "the Freight Corporation" and "Corporation";
		(c) in paragraph 5, sub-paragraph (1);
		(d) in paragraph 7 (1), the words "to the Freight Corporation and" and "of the Freight Corporation or";

Chapter	Title	Extent of repeal
1968 c. 73 *(Cont'd)*	Transport Act 1968 *(Cont'd)*	(*e*) in paragraph 8, in sub-paragraph (1) (*d*) (i), the words "the National Freight Corporation" and "Corporation or" and in sub-paragraph (2) the words "the Freight Corporation"; (*f*) in paragraph 9, the words "The National Freight Corporation"; (*g*) in paragraph 10, the words "The National Freight Corporation".
1974 c. 8	Statutory Corporations (Financial Provisions) Act 1974	In Schedule 2, in the first column of the entry amending section 19 (2) of the Transport Act 1962, the reference to the National Freight Corporation.
1975 c. 24	House of Commons Disqualification Act 1975	In Schedule 1, in Part II, the entry relating to the National Freight Corporation.
1975 c. 25	Northern Ireland Assembly Disqualification Act 1975	In Schedule 1, in Part II, the entry relating to the National Freight Corporation.
1977 c. 20	Transport (Financial Provisions) Act 1977	Section 2.
1978 c. 55	Transport Act 1978	Section 17.

[152]

COMMENCEMENT

This Part of this Schedule is to come into force on "the appointed day" as defined by s. 45 (2), *ante*; see s. 70 (4), *ante*. At the time of going to press no day had been appointed under s. 45 (2).

PART IV

OTHER REPEALS

Chapter	Title	Extent of repeal
1967 c. 76	Road Traffic Regulation Act 1967	Section 100.

[153]

COMMENCEMENT

See s. 70 (5), *ante*, and the note "Orders under this section" thereto.

INDEX

187